Patricia Wittberg, S.C.

Pathways to Re-Creating Religious Communities

PAULIST PRESS
New York / Mahwah, N.J.

Used with permission: A portion of the poem "Passover Remembered," from *Womanpriest; A Personal Odyssey*, by Alla Renee Bozarth, from the revised edition, LuraMedia, 1988. "Passover Remembered," was also published in *Stars in Your Bones: Emerging Signposts on Spiritual Journeys* by Alla Bozarth et al, North Star Press: St. Cloud, 1990. All rights reserved by the poet.

Library of Congress Cataloging-in-Publication Data

Wittberg, Patricia, 1947-
    Pathways to re-creating religious communities / by Patricia Wittberg.
      p.   cm.
    Includes bibliographical references (p.)
    ISBN 0-8091-3640-6 (alk. paper)
    1. Monasticism and religious orders.   2. Monastic and religious life.
3. Sociology, Christian (Catholic) I. Title.
BX2432.W476 1996   96-3638
255–dc20   CIP

Published by Paulist Press
997 Macarthur Boulevard
Mahwah, N.J. 07430

Printed and bound in the United States of America

Contents

*This book is dedicated
to all the pathmakers
in new and in long-established
religious communities.*

Preface

I began writing this book in January, 1991, even before *Creating a Future for Religious Life* was released by Paulist Press. I thought of it then (and still think of it) as a follow-up to the last chapter of the first book—as a "How To" manual for persons interested in establishing the kind of "seed communities" I had talked about there.

In April, however, just as I was finishing the first draft of chapter 4, I received a stern phone call from a colleague and mentor who warned me that I would never receive tenure at Indiana University unless I wrote something for an academic audience and published it through a university press. So I laid this manuscript aside—for a very long while. *The Rise and Fall of Catholic Religious Orders* consumed all of my energies (and a significant portion of my bedroom) for the next three years.

It was only last spring that I was able to pick up this manuscript again, but I believe that the delay was a providential one. The historical works I read for *The Rise and Fall*, as well as the sociological research I have been doing on newly-founded religious groups, have enabled me to make this book much stronger than it would have been, had I written it in 1991. The publication of *The Rise and Fall* last November also lent a special urgency to finishing the current work. For *The Rise and Fall* ends, as many reviewers have pointed out, on a very pessimistic note. After analyzing the various social factors that enabled religious life to flourish in previous centuries, I concluded that *all* of these supports had been simultaneously removed in the latter half of the twentieth—and that they do not yet show signs of being reinstated. This conclusion has caused some readers to think that I see no future at all for religious life—that I believe it to be inevitably doomed.

This is not the case. True, the dangers are great, and many, if not most, present-day congregations will die—in their current form. But I am convinced that the hunger which drove people to religious life in previous eras still exists today, perhaps to an even greater extent than it has in the past. If we can just tap into that hunger, there will be an explosive rebirth of religious communities. If we give up and talk about "dying gracefully," or if we spin unfounded theories of what we would like refounded religious life to look like, we will seal our doom. And the religious seekers who would have joined us will go elsewhere. I hope that this book will give some practical advice on the specific issues which any religious congregation must face—and face squarely—in order to refound itself.

This is an ambitious agenda, and one which I am not sure I have fulfilled in any even remotely satisfactory way. But I have received the input of many individuals, without whom this book would have been much worse. Several members of my own congregation, Rose Adelaide Anderson, SC, Marita Ganley, SC, and Rita Hawk, SC, read and commented on all or part of the manuscript. Many other people were helpful in a wide variety of ways: Ann McKean, CSA, Rosemary Jeffries, RSM, Margaret Klotz, OSF, Esther Heffernan, OP, and Joan Marie Massura, OSB. The sisters and associates who comprise Tri-State Conference of Directors and Associates were kind enough to invite me to their meeting and to share their reactions to chapter 7. The participants of the Internet's Sister-List steered me toward valuable sources and helped me track down several obscure references. The founders and members of several new religious communities, most notably the Disciples of the Lord Jesus Christ, the Companions of Christ the Lamb, the Community of Teresian Carmelites, the Monastery of the Holy Cross, the Little Brothers of St. Francis, and the Servants of the Gospel, allowed me to visit them and graciously took the time to answer my questions. To all of these people, I owe a profound debt of gratitude. My thanks also go to the Sisters of Providence with whom I have lived these past five years and who continue to inspire me with their passionate commitment to community presence and prayer. I hope that this book will help all of our communities to grow and flourish in the coming century.

Patricia Wittberg, SC
Indianapolis
May 30, 1995

1

Introduction

Refounding periods. During the past ten or fifteen years, this term has become all too well-known to men and women in religious life as they grapple with the obvious decline in their communities' membership and viability. The historians among them have noted that similar declines occurred quite regularly during previous centuries, but were followed each time by an explosive reflowering of both new and newly-revitalized religious orders.[1] After practically disappearing in the tenth and eleventh centuries, for example, women's monasteries grew exponentially in the twelfth: during that century, one hundred new Benedictine communities were established in Germany, eighty new monasteries in England, and over forty new abbeys (plus a large number of dependent Cluniac priories) in France.[2] So many women attempted to form and join monastic communities in the twelfth century that male groups such as the Cistercians and Premonstratensians imposed strict limits on the number of women's houses which they would be willing to sponsor.[3] James de Vitry is said to have lamented that, in the Liège area alone, over twice as many women wished to enter religious life as there were established monasteries to house them.[4]

And the pattern repeated itself time and again in subsequent centuries. St. Francis attracted his first male followers in 1209; by 1221, there were over 3,000 of them. The Dominican friars, founded in 1215, had provinces in France, Spain, Provence, Lombardy, Rome, England, Germany, Hungary, Poland, Scandinavia, Greece and the Holy Land by 1228.[5] The medieval Beguines comprised 15% of the entire adult female population of

Cologne within one hundred years of their founding, occupying fifty-four separate establishments in that city alone.[6] After a noticeable loss of fervor in the fourteenth and fifteenth centuries, and a catastrophic decline during the Reformation, religious life rebounded again. The Jesuits, founded in 1540, numbered 930 by 1556, 3,500 by 1565, and 15,000 by 1629.[7] In seventeenth-century France, 2,000 cloistered women's monasteries were established, as well as at least eighty-three different apostolic congregations of women. One of these apostolic congregations, the Daughters of Charity, attracted over 800 members during the first twenty-five years of its existence.[8]

Renewed stagnation of religious communities in the eighteenth century, and sharp declines during the French Revolution and its aftermath, were followed by the establishment of the nineteenth-century teaching congregations. In France, 400 new women's communities were founded between 1800 and 1880, and over 200,000 French women entered them.[9] In all Ireland, there had been only eleven convents in 1800, containing a total of 120 sisters. By 1900, there were 8,000 sisters in 368 convents—despite the massive Irish emigration that was occurring at the same time.[10] Quebec counted only 361 men and 673 women religious in 1850; by 1900 there were 2,391 men and 9,601 women.[11] The number of sisters in the U.S. increased from 1,344 to 40,340 between 1850 and 1900.[12]

Can a similar rebirth be expected today? A large number of men and women religious fervently hope so. Several recent writers have called for concerted refounding efforts on the part of present-day congregations, in order to prevent otherwise certain organizational death.[13] Religious communities and their leadership have been urged repeatedly to encourage the rise of refounders in their midst, and to support refounding attempts when and if they do occur.

Surprisingly, however, no study has ever been done of the characteristics of refounding periods. Does refounding *always* follow a decline phase in religious life? If not, what conditions prevent its appearance? What groups of people are most likely to be attracted to orders that are refounded and revitalized around their traditional charism? What groups will prefer the newer, more innovative models of religious life which are being invented at the same time? What competing social movements draw away the individuals who might otherwise have been interested in religious life? What proportion of refounded and new orders succeed, and what are the internal and external circumstances which help to assure their success?

Because the answers to questions such as these have not been widely studied, members of today's religious communities are likely to be unsure of where and how to focus their refounding efforts. Likewise, newly-forming groups are in danger of repeating the costly mistakes that caused the demise of communities in previous eras. In our present pluralistic society, neither newly-founded nor refounding religious communities may be able to afford the luxury of false starts. Many other alternatives, both within and outside of Catholicism, are now available—and attractive—to those persons who would, in former times, have sought to enter religious life.

Recently, I completed a sociological examination of previous refounding periods.[14] This present book is an attempt to apply what I learned in that research to the situation facing religious life today. My focus is not on the reasons which may have contributed to the decline of established communities. This has already been covered by many authors, including myself, in a previous work.[15] Instead, I hope to use what I learned about the conditions in previous refounding periods in order to describe the opportunities and the pitfalls awaiting new forms of religious life today.

Preliminary Assumptions

One important observation regarding the life cycles of religious communities is that each individual congregation passed through its stages of foundation, growth, stabilization and decline in tandem with many others. When one order was undergoing its preliminary expansion phase, it was usually surrounded by many other congregations which were also experiencing (or had only recently completed) a similar spurt of growth.[16] Communities whose life cycles were out of step with the overall pattern—those which had been founded fifty years too soon, for example—usually did not experience the same degree of success as the more cyclically congruent groups did.[17] Other life cycle stages in religious communities have been similarly synchronized: the decline phase of the past thirty years has been experienced by almost all of the established religious orders in the United States, Canada and Western Europe.

It is a fundamental sociological axiom that patterns such as these indicate the presence of large-scale societal forces affecting all religious orders, outside of and in addition to whatever particular problems an individual community may be experiencing. The ability to see the social trends underlying personally-experienced life events has been called the "sociological imagination" by the great American sociologist C. Wright Mills.[18] According to Mills, if a particular married couple divorces, for example, this is a personal problem. But if the divorce rate in a society is such that 50% of all marriages end in divorce, then obviously there are forces beyond the individual level which impact upon the probability of a given marriage's success. Similarly, the growth or decline of one religious congregation may be caused by any number of unique factors. But if the order exists in a larger social milieu wherein dozens or even hundreds of other congregations are likewise growing or declining, then its own fate will be at least partly linked to whatever ecclesial or societal conditions are affecting the other communities. "The sociological imagination enables us to grasp history and biography and the relationship between the two within society.... The first fruit of this imagination...is the idea *that the individual can understand his [sic] own experiences and gauge his own fate only by locating himself within his period, that he can know his own chances in life only by becoming aware of those of all individuals in his circumstances.*"[19]

It is true, of course, that one cannot reduce the working of God's grace in the founding of a particular order, or the heroic personal efforts of that order's founder or foundress, merely to passive reactions in the face of irresistible social forces. Such an assumption would be insulting to the caliber of the women and men involved. But previous accounts of a religious congregation's foundation period, especially when written by the congregation's own members, have often gone to the opposite extreme and have tended to overemphasize the individual and the supernatural at the expense of the societal. Instead of being aware of how a founder's vision and efforts were conditioned by and reacted to forces in the surrounding environment, "the members of religious institutes attributed all the activity of the founders to the direct intervention of God, of Christ, of the Holy Spirit, of the saints, or of the angels."[20] In reality, the founding or refounding of a particular religious order succeeded, not solely because of the efforts or personal gifts of key individuals, but also because these efforts responded to large-scale environmental forces—forces of which the founders may not even have been aware. Developing a successful community was often a haphazard process of trial and error. "The inspired founder, with his perfect blueprint for a new congregation, exists only in hagiography."[21] At times, a religious community might even spring up *in spite of the founder's original intentions*, leaving the putative leader scrambling to catch up: "The founders [of seventeenth-century French congregations] were always led ahead by events, struggling to control and solidify their immensely successful institutes."[22]

In such a time of effortless growth, it may indeed seem as though God has taken over from the efforts of mere mortals. "'Who made your community?' Vincent de Paul once asked his sisters; 'Not Mademoiselle Le Gras; she never thought of it. As for me, alas! I didn't dream of it.'"[23] Despite this appearance of natural—or supernatural—inevitability, however, the Daughters of Charity and other congregations grew because, through the daily problem-solving and the mutual give-and-take of the founders and the first members, a form of religious life was constructed that met the needs and desires of its potential entrants, of ecclesiastical authorities, of wealthy benefactors, and even of the secular state.[24] The members of these various interest groups had their own agendas and their own personal reasons for sponsoring or joining particular types of religious communities. It was through this reciprocal interaction between the founding members and other societal actors, and in the context of larger environmental forces, that the goals and the governance, the ministry and the very charism which defined each new religious order or congregation took its shape.

A basic assumption of this book, therefore, is that God's works are intimately bound to societal events and conditions. No founding or refounding can succeed if it is divorced from its environmental context. And groups which do tap into larger societal trends often develop in ways that are totally unforeseen by the individuals involved, who had thought that they were doing something else entirely. *For today's refounding attempts to succeed, therefore, the leaders and the memberships of religious congregations must know which conditions and trends in the surrounding society are likely to support or hinder their efforts.*

In speaking of studying the conditions and trends in our surrounding society, I do not mean that we should compile another social analysis of the poverty, violence, drug use, or environmental degradation which afflict our country and the world at large. At least, that is not the only type of study which we need to do. Perhaps the following analogy may help to make this clear. Suppose some friends decide to go on a vacation together. They will, of course, study tourist brochures and current conditions to determine where they wish to go. Perhaps their favorite South Florida beach was destroyed by Hurricane Andrew, or maybe ski conditions are bad in Aspen this year. Once they have decided upon a destination, they will obtain maps of the best routes to take: is Route A shorter than Route B? Which is more scenic? Next, they will check their car: with 100,000 miles on the odometer and bald tires, is it up to an Alaskan backwoods trek? Has the oil been changed recently? Then they will inventory their supplies: sleeping bags and insect repellent, beach chairs and suntan lotion, snow skis and down parkas, depending on their needs. They may also note the towns along the way where they can buy gas and replenish their stock of food. Finally, they will set out together. When and if they make a wrong turn or discover that they have forgotten some essential item, they will stop and attempt to remedy the difficulty.

In refounding religious life, our social analyses of current world trends are roughly comparable to travellers studying their brochures and tour guides. Certainly we have to be aware of the changing conditions in our culture, and in other cultures, as we stand at the dawn of the twenty-first century. Are the large hospital complexes and suburban schools which have grown from our founders' original activities *really* needed today? And even if the answer to that question is "yes" (which it may well be), does this mean that *our religious congregations* should be involved in them? Would it be better to turn them over to other lay people while we move on to where we are more needed? And what would this new area of greater need be? Social analysis is obviously necessary to help answer these questions. However—and this is a threatening realization which many congregations avoid—many of our members may disagree about the answers, just as some of the travelling friends may prefer lounging by the ocean while others hold out for hiking the Appalachian Trail. If a religious community is divided over the relative merit of sheltering the inner city homeless or establishing women's spirituality centers, can it choose one over the other without alienating half of its members? Or should it attempt to divide its focus, energies and personnel between both?

Of course, a community may choose to allow each of its members individually to address the social needs he or she sees. This is comparable to our group of friends deciding that they will take separate vacations and send each other post cards. *There is nothing wrong with following individual rather than communal ministries.* In fact, the former tactic is likely to be more flexible and adaptable than the latter. But any community that de-emphasizes its group focus in favor of individual visions will have more difficulty explaining how its members' ministries differ from those of the average lay social worker, health care professional, or church staff member, who may also be living a holy, prayerful life while engaging in a service profession.

In addition to studying our "tour guide" to determine where we wish to go, however, we *also* need to map out our route. If a religious community decides that caring for AIDS patients will be its primary focus,[25] what is the best way to do this? Convert a wing of the order's hospital to AIDS research? Set up hospices? (And, if so, where?) Organize and train a cadre of members to visit and care for dying AIDS victims in their homes? Lobby Washington for more enlightened AIDS legislation? Or simply live and suffer with AIDS victims, in the spirit of Charles de Foucald? A persuasive case could be made for each of these strategies. Which would be best for the targeted AIDS population? Which would be most feasible for the congregation? In addition to disagreeing on a common goal, therefore, community members may also disagree on which "routes" to take to attain it.

We also need to check out our "vehicle" and our supplies: we have to look at the structures and practices of our congregations to see if they are up to addressing the need(s) we have chosen to address. What kind of organization and lifestyle would be best able to meet these needs, now and in the future? Since the needs may last longer than we do as individuals, what type of congregation—what kind of internal organization and leadership structures, what kind of rituals and lifestyle—would be most likely to attract members to take our places when we are gone? Again, an examination of our congregational "vehicles" is just as threatening as examining competing alternatives for group ministry. We look a little dilapidated and precarious, even to ourselves: we have far more than 100,000 miles on our odometers, our carburetors are making funny noises.... And few, if any, newcomers have shown even the slightest inclination to climb in and join us on our journey. Perhaps this is because the mountains are "in" this year and we persist in going to the seashore. Or perhaps it is because we ourselves are not confident in the road-worthiness of our community vehicle, and our hesitation shows.

Or perhaps it is because we really haven't started off yet. Paralyzed by the nagging fear that we don't all agree on where to go, depressed by the evidence that we are getting older and no new members are joining us, worried that, if we do set out, we may take a wrong turn or forget something essential, we stay where we are. We study the maps of the future, the graphs that warn of a widening gap between rich and poor, of the swelling ranks of the homeless and unemployed, of the AIDS crisis or global warming, and we say, "Yes, something should certainly be done about this." We support this or that individual community member who goes off alone to address some pressing issue; we donate money—sometimes quite a lot of money—to help the grass roots lay organizations which are already working on it. But we do not climb in our car, start the motor, and go off *together* to help.[26]

These latter aspects of our refounding journeys are the ones that I hope to begin to address here. The social analyses of other, more capable analysts have already provided us with detailed descriptions of many worthwhile destinations for our journey— of the pressing needs which God is calling Christians to address.[27] We do not need another social analysis. What we *do* need is the communal equivalent of an auto repair manual to help us prepare our congregations to address the problems which social analyses have outlined for us. We need maps to help us choose, if not the best route, at least a route that will not leave us stranded in a ditch miles from our destination or tear the insides out of our congregational "car." We need some idea of where the gas stations, motels and grocery stores (the sources of funds, of political support, of mentoring and expertise, of new temporary and/or permanent members) are located en route. And, once we have started on our congregational refounding journey, we need enough sophistication about the inner workings of our community and how it interfaces with the environment that we know to keep an eye on our gas gauge and to listen for unusual "pings" in the engine. When things go awry in our efforts to achieve our goals—and things *will* go awry in any group that actively responds to its call instead of merely talking about responding—we need to be able to recognize that there is a problem, even if we are not sure exactly how to fix it.

I do not have the knowledge or the experience to fulfill the massive agenda I have just outlined. My aim here is much more modest. Perhaps by looking at previous eras in which religious communities arose and set out on their mission, we can get some hints of the tasks and resources that would be necessary in order to organize a similar group of people today and to mobilize their energies and enthusiasm around a common goal. Perhaps by looking at similar non-Catholic, or even non-Christian, communal groups—the Shakers, the Bruderhof, Theravadan Sangha in Thailand, Nichiren Shoshu communities in Japan—we can learn from their successes and their mistakes. This book is intended merely to provide some organizational concepts and some background data on what has helped other communal religious groups to succeed, both today and in the past. Armed with these concepts and data, perhaps members of religious congregations will be a little better equipped to begin "tuning up" their community (mobilizing member enthusiasm, modifying government and lifestyles, developing new ways to define themselves and attract new members) for the journey. Perhaps they will be able to make a more informed choice of routes to their goal, and become less afraid of mistakes in the process. With the common vocabulary provided by the concepts and data, perhaps they will be encouraged also to network with and learn from other communities in their efforts. The rest is in the hands of the Spirit, and I am more than content to leave it there.

One final comment. This book presupposes that it is both possible and desirable for a group of people to adopt a common goal or focus, and then to sacrifice, at least to some extent, their individual preferences in its service. *If* a group freely chooses to do so, *if* its leaders do not betray its goal by fostering cults of personality around themselves and infantilizing their followers, *if* its chosen goal meets a pressing societal need, *if* its lifestyle and philosophy resonates with that of the surrounding culture, and *if* no serious opposition derails it, then perhaps a new religious community may be born or part of an existing one refounded. Many readers may object and say that this involves too many "ifs" and that failed or runaway communal groups leave their followers dangerously vulnerable. An equally valid form of ministry, they will contend, is contained in looser associations of individuals who support each other while living their own lives and addressing societal needs through their professional occupations or their volunteer activities. Substantial portions of the membership in many religious congregations have already adopted this model, and a wide variety of lay organizations, from the Focolare to Birthright and WomenChurch, are also based upon it. *That this book does not address the associational forms of religious life is not intended as a dismissal of their value or importance.* It is simply because communal religious life is more difficult to establish and nurture within our present culture, that I feel it is necessary for us consciously to mobilize our efforts in order to help it along. If the concepts and information in this book can help such a process, I will be more than satisfied.

Method and Outline of Topics

My study of refounding periods will begin by defining some useful sociological concepts which could aid in the analysis of refounding periods. These concepts, drawn from widely different subfields within sociology, have developed more or less independently of each other. By combining them, I hope to outline a theoretical model for examining how groups of individuals can articulate a new common vision of religious life, enflesh this vision in a unique lifestyle, and arouse both in themselves and in others such a level of commitment to their vision that they are willing to sacrifice all else for it.

After this theoretical model is developed in Part One, it will be used in Part Two to address the five basic choices which the members of any new or refounded community *must* make for their journey. A community must first of all decide where to go and who will take part in the trip. Chapters 5, 6, and 7 will thus address the issues involved in choosing a communal focus and in uniting the membership around it. Once a primary goal has been defined by an order or congregation, moreover, a thousand concrete decisions will have to be made to enflesh this purpose in daily life. A community must choose, in other words, which of many "routes" to take to their destination. The possible variations in these decisions will be the topic of chapter 8. Chapter 9 will consider the resources needed for our communal journey: Where might new recruits be found? How necessary is the support of the church hierarchy? Of lay Catholics? What techniques of networking and mentoring might be helpful? Chapter 10 will address the issue of community "vehicle" maintenance: How can the enthusiasm of the members be kept alive? What leadership problems have bedeviled communities in the past? What size is best for different group purposes? How might decisions best be made? How can mistaken decisions be rectified? Finally, an appendix of "Journeystories" will present some fictional founding and refounding journeys, loosely based on real communities which I have visited and observed. I hope that these accounts will serve as starting points for the brainstorming of the religious congregations interested in refounding themselves, of the church officials interested in fostering and preserving religious life into the twenty-first century (in an environment where its survival is by no means assured), and of all individuals seeking new ways of living out the call which God is speaking in their inmost hearts.

In analyzing these issues, I have relied on a host of recent historical works which have been published on religious communities. A wide variety of excellent studies have been done on specific historical periods, as well as on specific orders, during the past two decades.[28] I have focused primarily on the hermits of the third- and fourth-century Middle East, on the male and female Cistercians, the Beguines and the mendicants of twelfth and thirteenth-century Europe, on the women's congregations of seventeenth-century France, and on the teaching communities of nineteenth-century France, Quebec, Ireland and the United States, since these are the periods most thoroughly covered by historians. The validity of my conclusions thus depends not upon my own original research, but upon the validity of the data compiled by these historians, the honesty and correctness of their judgments and interpretations, and the accuracy of my own interpretations of their conclusions.[29] I have also used the accounts of the workings of past communal experiments, Catholic and otherwise, as well as my own interviews with the members and founders of some twenty newly-established, proto- and quasi-religious congregations.

The primary audience of this analysis are the members of religious communities, both the new and the existing ones, who are attempting to found or refound their congregations. Readers who are interested in a more extensive development of the theoretical issues touched on in Part One, or who would like to learn more about specific historical instances alluded to in subsequent chapters, are referred to the more in-depth sociohistorical analysis I have recently completed.[30] But perhaps a more important response would be to take some of the recommendations in Part Two—which do *not* occur in the other work—and to begin adapting them to our own communities. Thus we can begin to discover which routes lead where, how best to "tune up" our communities to get us where we want to go, and which rest stops, gas stations and supply depots to expect along the way.

PART I:

Useful Sociological Concepts for the Consideration of Refounding Periods

In order to analyze or even to notice the common patterns which occurred in previous refounding periods, it is necessary first to have the conceptual tools for dealing with them. Several useful concepts have been developed in three different branches of sociology: the concept of religious virtuosity from the sociology of religion, the concept of ideology from the sociology of knowledge, and the concepts of frame alignment and resource mobilization from the study of social movements. Chapters 2, 3, and 4 explain these concepts and explore the interrelationships between them, in order to render them useful for a subsequent analysis of refounding periods.

2

The "Religious Virtuoso"

The first concept to be considered is that of religious virtuosity. Despite its somewhat unfortunate connotations,[1] the term "religious virtuoso" simply refers to someone who desires more than the "church on Sunday" level of devotional practice which satisfies others among the faithful.[2] Just as professional artists have organized their entire lives around an activity that may be merely a hobby to the Sunday painter; just as professional tennis or golf players are totally focused on activities that most people consider recreational; just as musicians or philosophers may put their avocations before all else, so religious virtuosi have devoted themselves to a quest for the transcendent spiritual dimension to human existence.[3] Other people may be more innately artistic, athletic, or intelligent (or holier) than the virtuoso, but it is the virtuoso who is driven by an interior hunger to devote his or her entire life to artistic, athletic, intellectual, or religious pursuits. This makes virtuosi seem somewhat "unbalanced" to non-virtuoso observers, as the lives of Van Gogh or Mozart (or Catherine of Siena) can attest.

As the primary basis for their commitment, most religious virtuosi feel that they have experienced some sort of supernatural calling: "If you would be perfect, sell all you have and follow Me" [Mark 10:21]. This spiritual motivation, however, is often supported by several "natural" sources of religious virtuosity. The virtuoso's familial upbringing is the most obvious of these, both in a positive and a negative sense. On the one hand, a religious family background (especially having had a devout mother) has been found to be the most reliable predictor of religious devotion in young adults, and was once a key motivating force for religious and seminary vocations.[4] On the other hand, a dysfunctional family background can result in a "religious addiction" which is superficially similar to true religious virtuosity.[5] The Carmelite vocations of every single daughter of Louis and Zelie Martin (the parents of St. Thérèse of Lisieux) have been cited as examples of both positive and negative familial influence.[6]

In addition to family background, there is also evidence that some predisposition to religious practice may be genetically based. Identical twins raised apart often show strong similarities in their frequency of church attendance and devotional practices.[7] Rather than these genetic and familial roots, however, this chapter will focus on the *societal* contributions to the making of a religious virtuoso. Interior "callings," genetics, and/or parental support, while obviously important, are not sufficient in themselves to induce a particular form of religious virtuosity in an individual. It is the culture in which one lives that determines how (and at times even whether) the calling will be heeded. It is the prevailing cultural values which parents articulate when they either encourage their children to enter religious life or attempt to dissuade them from it.

Societal factors influence religious virtuosity in at least three key ways. The surrounding environment dictates, first of all, the accepted *content* of virtuoso spirituality. In some cultures, the virtuoso is expected to strive for ecstatic mystical union with the divine; in others he/she attempts to master a body of abstract theological literature through arduous and disciplined study. Some religious virtuosi flee the polluting contact of worldly humanity to live alone in deserted places; others join in community with like-minded brothers and/or sisters to model the future eschaton; still others attempt to sanctify their daily work *within* sinful society through "inner-worldly asceticism."[8] The extent to which a religious virtuoso is expected to break with his/her past, to gain wealth or to embrace poverty, to concentrate on serving the poor or to strive for personal sanctification, also varies from culture to culture.

Another way that the surrounding social environment affects religious virtuosity is in specifying the number and types of persons who are expected to practice it. Just as fifteenth-century

Florence witnessed a sudden flowering of artistic virtuosity among a citizenry that had previously seemed no more gifted at painting and sculpture than the inhabitants of a dozen similar Italian towns, so some times and places have been more conducive than others to fostering religious virtuosity in a wide variety of individuals. Third- and fourth-century Egypt, twelfth- and thirteenth-century Italy, France and Belgium, and seventeenth- and nineteenth-century France are all examples of such societies within the Christian tradition.[9] The United States, somewhat surprisingly to many non-historians, is well above average in its cultural encouragement of religious virtuosity. So, for that matter, is contemporary Japan. In other times and places, however, religious virtuosity may be culturally defined as worthless or irrelevant, and the number of persons who bother to devote themselves to its pursuit may be relatively small. Furthermore, in some societies men (or women), peasants (or nobles, or merchants), or particular ethnic minorities may be considered "too carnal," "too sophisticated," or "too primitive" to experience *real* religious virtuosity. It would take an unusual individual in one of these stigmatized groups to pursue a calling to virtuoso spirituality in the face of a prevailing societal assumption that he/she was inherently incapable of doing so.

A third way in which the culture of a particular time and place affects religious virtuosity is in the relationship between the virtuoso and the average religious adherent. In some societies, both the virtuosi and the less-involved are included within the same religious system. In this case, the virtuoso often functions as a teacher or as a model to those whose spirituality and experience are considered to be less developed. The Hindu guru and the Russian staretz are examples of this. At other times, religious virtuosi demand an extremely high level of devotion and practice from *everyone* who would follow the true path. The less devout are considered lost sinners, and the virtuosi refuse to associate with them at all, except perhaps in proselytizing efforts. In such circumstances, groups of religious virtuosi often leave "the world" altogether and attempt to establish a "pure society" of the elect. The Puritans, the Hasidic Jews and the Amish, among others, chose this alternative.

Religious virtuosity, therefore, manifests itself in widely varying aspects, at different times and in different places. *It is by no means certain that it will be channeled into "religious life" as defined by Western Catholicism.* The same hunger that led young Spanish women to emulate the rigorous mysticism of St. Teresa of Avila or young men to follow St. Francis of Assisi around the Italian countryside might, in another instance, inspire those who experience it to practice yoga exercises in isolated mountain cabins, to induce hallucinations by chewing peyote, or to join the Assemblies of God or the Catholic Pentecostal Movement. A major theme of this book is that, in the pluralistic faith environment that exists in the United States and in most Western countries today, Roman Catholic religious congregations are competing with many other outlets for the attention, commitment and dedication of a more or less finite pool of religious virtuosi.[10]

PROBLEMS WITH THE CONCEPT OF RELIGIOUS VIRTUOSITY

Problem I: Elitism

The concept of religious virtuosity implies several problematic definitional aspects. The first and most obvious, for the Christian, is the problem of elitism. As many theologians have argued, the idea of a separate caste of virtuoso disciples was antithetical to the message of Christ.

> Jesus was not a monk or an ascetic who counseled separation from the world, like the Essenes at Qumran. His message was addressed to all people, not just to an elite. He did not proclaim a higher perfection ethic for the disciples, for the chosen few.[11]

The Catholic Church has repeatedly been accused of abrogating this scriptural imperative and considering religious life to be a way of perfection which was superior to the lifestyle of ordinary Christians. As one recent study has pointed out, of the 393 saints canonized between the years 1000 and 1987, only seventy-six were not members of religious orders—and most of these remaining seventy-six owed their sainthood to martyrdom.[12] The Catholic laity, prior to Vatican II, often shared the church's devaluation of their spiritual ability:

I've always treated the word "vocation" as synonymous with religious life.... By not embracing a religious vocation, I had always felt I had chosen something lower.[13]

Even today, a generation after the council's affirmation of the universal call to holiness, there is still evidence that some young people do not consider joining the priesthood or religious life because they do not feel that they are "holy enough."[14]

The extra prestige given to monks and nuns by Roman Catholicism was also the basis for the Protestant reformers' objections to religious life:

First [Luther] argued that monastic vows suggested a superior way of life, different from that of ordinary Christians, and so were contrary to the Word of God. Second, he saw the monastic life itself as an effort to justify oneself before God, and hence, contrary to his doctrine of justification by faith alone. Third, he felt that the vows were contrary to Christian liberty.[15]

For many critics, therefore, the call of Christ to radical discipleship is addressed to *all* Christians and precludes any stratification of believers into a virtuoso and a mass spirituality.

But however *theologically* true it might be that all Christians are equally called to perfection, and however distasteful the very concept of religious virtuosity might be in an egalitarian American society, Christianity is not exempt from the *sociological* axiom that every religion contains followers with varying degrees of enthusiasm and interest. As Max Weber, the sociologist who first discussed the concept of religious virtuosity, put it:

The sacred values that have been most cherished, the ecstatic and visionary capacities of shamans, sorcerers, ascetics and pneumatics of all sorts, could not be attained by everyone....It follows from this that all intensive religiosity has a tendency toward a sort of *status stratification*, in accordance with differences in the charismatic qualifications. "Heroic" or "virtuoso" religiosity is opposed to mass religiosity.[16]

Whatever their ideals of "equality before God," therefore, religions cannot ignore these differences in religious interest among their followers. Attempts to deny the existence of religious virtuosity typically result in two outcomes. First, a "watering down" of the message of the religion to a fairly low common denominator occurs within the church:

> In place of this radical discipleship, what has emerged is a bour-
> geois religion, a cultural Christianity which by carefully distin-
> guishing between public and private life, and thus between
> politics and morality, legitimates a life of comfort and privilege at
> the expense of the radical meaning of the Gospel.[17]

Once this watering down has taken place within a church, its religious virtuosi no longer feel sufficiently challenged by their
membership. The church then experiences a tendency toward
sectarian fission whereby its virtuosi leave to follow a more rigorous call. The Lutherans and Calvinists of the Reformation, for
example, soon found themselves confronted by entire groups of
religious virtuosi—the Hutterites, Mennonites and Spiritualists—
for whom the established Reformation churches did not provide
a sufficiently radical following of Christ.[18]

The phenomenon of religious virtuosity thus poses a dual
problem for all Christian denominations, Roman Catholicism
included. If a separate place is made within the church for virtuoso spirituality—whether this be in the form of religious orders,
"Blue Army" members, or charismatic prayer groups—the danger
will exist that these virtuosi will be considered (and will consider
themselves) to be better than the rank and file of believers.[19] But
if a church *fails* to provide such an outlet for those who feel called
to do more for their faith, it runs the risk that its most committed
and fervent members will desert it for "holier" churches. Recent
studies have shown that this is precisely what is happening to the
various mainline Protestant churches in this country: those who
emigrate to stricter sects were the *most* devout in their former
church; those who immigrate (a smaller number) were the *least*
devout in theirs.[20] The Methodists, Episcopalians and
Presbyterians are progressively shrinking; the Southern Baptists,
Assemblies of God and Jehovah's Witnesses are growing.[21] It
appears that, in every church, the call of virtuoso spirituality
exerts an almost irresistible attraction upon some members. If
the church discovers a way to retain these virtuosi within its own
boundaries, whole religious movements or orders may develop

and grow with startling rapidity. But if no outlet exists for religious enthusiasts within a particular denomination, they will simply go elsewhere, to the great loss of the church they left.

Under the circumstances, then, it seems organizationally (if not theologically) preferable to make some form of virtuoso spirituality accessible within a church to all of the members who desire it, whatever their socioeconomic status, gender, or ethnic group might be. This is often difficult to do. The mere fact that Irish-descended Catholics are overrepresented, and Latino Catholics underrepresented, within American religious orders is evidence that Catholicism's major approved form of religious virtuosity has been less accessible to some ethnic groups than it was to others. The lack of available outlets for their religious leadership and enthusiasm has often been cited as a reason for the conversion of so many Latino Catholics to Protestant Pentecostalism.[22]

In the process of encouraging its religious virtuosi, however, a church may also wish to avoid giving the offensive impression that virtuoso spirituality is somehow superior to the call of gospel discipleship which all of its members have received. Since many sociological theorists have argued that elitism has always been an essential component of religious virtuosity, this may prove to be quite difficult.[23] Any church that wishes to combine *both* a theology of religious virtuosity *and* a belief in the equality of all believers will have to take special steps to reconcile these traditionally antithetical concepts. If religious orders are to continue to exist within Catholicism—and particularly within egalitarian-oriented American Catholicism—then they too must undertake this task. Popularly accessible theological works, sermons, magazine articles, media presentations, and the like will be needed, in order to define the unique call of religious life in a way that does not make it superior to lay spirituality, while at the same time providing sufficient reasons for potential candidates to consider such a lifestyle.

So far, this has not been done, as chapter 5 will argue. A beginning might be the work of Sandra Schneiders and a few other writers, who have started to develop the analogy between religious and other types of virtuosi.[24] A formulation such as Schneiders' *may* someday be sufficient to motivate individuals to enter religious orders, yet still prevent them from pridefully considering themselves superior to the rank and file of Catholic laity. But it has not yet achieved a wide enough circulation to replace the old "way of perfection" rationale for religious life that was discredited after Vatican II. *Roman Catholicism currently lacks ANY commonly accepted articulation for the role of non-ordained religious virtuosi within the church.*[25] Unless and until such an articulation is formulated, the Catholic Church will be in danger of suffering the same problem which afflicts mainline Protestantism: the desertion of its most committed members to sectarian virtuoso groups.

Of course, when religious virtuosi *do* remain within a church, their presence often poses as many problems as their defection would have done. Many religious and church officials seem to harbor the mistaken impression that the current friction between religious communities and the hierarchy is a new phenomenon. Nothing could be further from the truth. The two groups have been in either actual or potential conflict with each other quite often throughout the centuries of their coexistence under one ecclesial roof. The following section outlines some of the reasons for this tension.

Problem II: The Larger Church and the Religious Virtuoso

Religious virtuosi typically pose several difficulties for any church in which they occur. First of all, many churches (and especially Roman Catholicism) teach their members to seek salvation by participating in official rituals, all of which are mediated by the church hierarchy. Religious virtuosi may therefore be suspect "if, instead of relying on the capacity of the institutionalized church to distribute grace, they seek to attain grace by their own unaided power, treading their own pathway to God."[26] For example, some of the early desert fathers claimed to have received the eucharist, and even ordination, miraculously from the hands of Christ, thus bypassing dependence upon the clergy and bishops.[27] Fifth- and sixth-century monasticism began as "a lay protest against the increasing institutionalization of priestly hierarchy."[28] Non-ordained religious virtuosi have often been profoundly critical of priests and bishops, and their suspicion was reciprocated. A recurring theme among the church officials attempting to tame independent movements of lay virtuosi was their "uncontrolled" character. Uncontrollability was especially suspect when it occurred among women virtuosi, such as the female mystics among the thirteenth-century Cistercians and Beguines. These women claimed the ability to discern consecrated from unconsecrated hosts and to tell which priests were in a state of sin. Like the early hermits, they, too, often received the eucharist miraculously.[29] The women's special mystical abilities were intensely upsetting to the clergy, since they threatened to break the clerical monopoly on the channels of spiritual growth.

Another problematic aspect for church leaders is not so much *that* a religious virtuoso attempts to seek some form of spiritual perfection, but rather the particular *type* of religious perfection which the virtuoso emphasizes. It frequently happens that members of a church's hierarchy have approved a single "true" form of religious virtuosity—preferably the one in which they themselves excel—and resist the introduction of all competing types. The hierarchy may emphasize theological expertise, becoming "virtuosi of knowledge," while the pious non-intellectuals may advocate religious asceticism or religious contemplation instead, and may "regard 'dead knowledge' as of negligible value in the quest for salvation."[30] Or church officials may want lay virtuosi, especially lay *female* virtuosi, to confine themselves to praying inside their cloister, and to leave preaching or teaching to the "more qualified" ecclesiastics. The lay virtuosi may not accept this imposed division of labor. Conflict over the non-ordained virtuosi's teaching role, for example, occurred between the hierarchy and the mendicant Dominican and Franciscan preachers in the twelfth century, as well as with religious women in seventeenth-century France.[31]

Finally, the very enthusiasm of religious virtuosi is often disturbing to church officials. If the virtuosi project an air of moral superiority to the average believers, or if they espouse a form of religious expression (speaking in tongues, for example, or ecstatic dancing during their services) which the non-initiated find silly or repellent, they may become a divisive element which weakens the church instead of strengthening it. Some movements of religious virtuosi are also perceived as disruptive by secular forces. Examples would include the pacifism of the Amish and their

refusal to send their children to high school, or the social dislocation caused by thousands of mendicant friars tramping over the
medieval countryside. And of course, the resistance of seven-
teenth- and eighteenth-century rulers to the activities of the
Jesuits ultimately induced Pope Clement XVI to suppress the society. If an established church has built up a valued mutual relationship with a secular regime, it may be sensitive to the objections of
government officials to the activities of its religious virtuosi.

For all of these reasons, therefore, some degree of tension
always exists between official church authorities and religious
virtuosi.[32] Clerical hierarchies typically feel that the virtuosi must
be either tamed or expelled lest they threaten the unity of the
church and its place in society. Established Protestantism, in general, has tended to expel virtuosi rather than accept a dual standard of virtuoso and mass religiosity within the same
denomination.[33] The expelled virtuosi then found or join a sect,
whose more rigorous practices qualify it as a "society of saints."

Catholicism, on the other hand, has permitted the development of several "tamed" levels of religious virtuosity among its
members. The simplest of these is the "collegium pietatis," a
loosely-organized group of individuals within the larger church
who seek to do something extra in their religious practice.[34]
Members of a rosary society, or pilgrims to a particular shrine,
would be examples of this level. A second type is the "fraterni-
tas," individuals who seek some sort of community, however
informal, in their devotional practice. McGuire suggests the
"underground church movement" in American Catholicism during the 1960s as an example. The ultimate expressions of virtuoso religiosity within the larger church are "orders" such as
religious congregations, but the category also includes the
covenant communities among Catholic Pentecostals.[35]

At each level, however, the expression of virtuoso religiosity
had to be subordinated to the hierarchical authority of
Catholicism. Anomalous groups that refused such subordination, as well as those whose mode of organization did not readily
fit into the accepted form which the church had approved for
them, were expelled or suppressed. Or their members simply left
for greener pastures. In certain instances, a church might actually
prefer that its religious virtuosi go elsewhere. The availability of

the "exit option" tends to draw off precisely those who would have been the most likely to push for reform, had they remained within the church.[36] With its disruptive virtuosi gone, the church can remain in its comfortable mediocrity, and the power and perquisites of its elites are not challenged. Of course, if enough members leave, the church hierarchy may ultimately begin to worry. But, even then, they are unlikely to cede to the disaffected virtuosi sufficient authority and independence to tempt them to remain within the fold.

Problem III: Pseudo-Virtuosity

A third difficulty inherent in religious virtuosity is that some individuals may seek virtuoso status for reasons that true virtuosi would consider illegitimate or even harmful. For example, unscrupulous individuals may mimic the "guru" form of religious virtuosity for their own power or personal gain. As studies of various cults have shown, the committed volunteer labor of rank and file members (even if it only involves selling flowers and incense in airports) can create extensive communal wealth to be donated to the guru. Cult leaders may thus enjoy luxurious dwellings, free limousines, and a host of other benefits. Even within the more respectable groups of religious virtuosi, leadership positions may be a form of upward social mobility whereby individuals from working-class backgrounds can find themselves consorting with high church and government officials. Thus, the more a group of religious virtuosi (whether this group is a fundamentalist Protestant sect, a Catholic religious order, or the Shiite clerics in Iran) becomes large, established and powerful, the more likely it will be that its leadership—and perhaps its entire membership—will substitute political or status-seeking motivations for joining it. In some times and places, the established pseudo-virtuosi occupying a group's leadership positions may actively expel any true virtuosi as dangerous, or as psychologically immature.

Psychological deficiencies are, of course, a second "illegitimate" reason why some persons might join the ranks of religious virtuosi. Traumatic personal experiences or dysfunctional family backgrounds may prompt a form of "religious addiction" whereby an individual attempts to alleviate his/her deep-seated feelings of personal worthlessness through some form of obsessive-compulsive religious behavior:

> The classic specifier of Freud's thought, Otto Fenichel, notes that most obsessive-compulsives have a religious problem....The person may feel that she/he is the cause of so much chaos (note the grandiosity in that) and may be continually trying to expiate.[37]

Still another characteristic of religiously addictive behavior is to demand clear-cut, simplistic answers to complex spiritual problems. The common sectarian practice of selectively exaggerating the importance of some particular religious belief or practice to the exclusion of all else may thus attract psychologically immature pseudo-virtuosi.[38]

Those who are psychologically wounded and suffering may also be attracted by the elitist connotations of religious virtuosity. Persons whose self-concepts are precarious may long intensely to become "perfect" and to belong to a community of saints whose salvation is assured. The obverse of this is a need to look down on the "unsaved" as inferior or even demonic. The attraction which the elitist aspect of religious virtuosity has for the psychically fragile (and most human beings are psychically fragile to some extent) may be one reason why it has historically been so difficult to prevent virtuosi from coming to see themselves as a superior class.

"Religion," states O'Meara, "can have a healthy or a neurotic appeal." Unhealthy deformities such as elitism and compulsion "are deeply entrenched in human religion; men and women may enter religion not out of love of God or hope in the future but to calm neuroses."[39] If this is true of religion in general, it is even more true of religious virtuosity.

CONCLUSIONS

"Religious virtuosity" is a concept that may be threatening to the current members of religious orders. Many will feel that they have spent the past thirty years fighting against such an elitist, pre-Vatican II concept, and will strongly resist its reintroduction into any treatment, especially any *prescriptive* treatment, of refounding periods. It is true that the whole idea of a "virtuoso" as compared to a "mass" spirituality appears to be fundamentally at odds with "the basic Gospel call of all followers of Jesus to one and the same holiness."[40] Religious virtuosity also deeply contradicts the fundamental American ideal of equality. As the children and grandchildren of the Catholic immigrants to this country became more thoroughly acculturated to American beliefs and values, they also adopted our culture's dislike of all forms of elitism. This has made American Catholics doubly resistant to the idea of religious virtuosi being a superior caste.

But, as we have seen, the Protestant religious denominations which provide no outlet for religious virtuosity often suffer an exodus of their most committed members to virtuoso sects. Historically, the existence of religious orders has enabled Roman Catholicism to avoid this fate. With the decline of religious orders as a seriously-considered lifestyle option among young Catholics today, however, more and more of the church's youngest and most devout members are leaving it for sectarian or cultic alternatives. Ex-Catholics comprise a disproportionately large percentage of Reverend Moon's Unification Church, as well as a substantial number of converts to Southern Baptist churches.[41] Catholicism cannot afford to continue losing its religious virtuosi in this way. But, if religious life is to continue providing an outlet for virtuoso spirituality within an Americanized Catholic Church, it will be necessary to disentangle and discard its elitist overtones and reformulate it into a more culturally acceptable version. Such an attempt requires the consideration of a second sociological concept: that of ideology.

3

Ideology

The term "ideology" has almost as bad a reputation in popular parlance as the term "religious virtuoso" has in an egalitarian church. Once a neutral term which meant simply a collection of political proposals, "ideology" now commonly refers to a false system of beliefs, whether maliciously constructed or unconsciously adopted, which obscures and ultimately destroys "The Truth."[1] Even among sociologists, ideology retains this connotation of self-interest and bias: "It is one of the minor ironies of modern intellectual history that the term 'ideology' has itself become thoroughly ideologized."[2] Perhaps, Geertz speculates, our distrust and fear of ideology is due to the destructive uses to which several specific ideologies have been put in the twentieth century.[3]

A more neutral definition of the term, however, is simply the "total belief system,"[4] or the "ordered system of cultural symbols,"[5] *without which no human being can think at all*. The phenomena of our daily lives—to say nothing of the inheritance of our personal and national histories—are an unmanageable jumble of events, feelings, interactions and occurrences that must somehow be named and interpreted before we can know how to react to them. The conceptual structure which an individual uses to make sense of his/her world is that individual's "ideological frame."[6] All of us have an ideology; we could not think without one.

32

COMPONENTS OF IDEOLOGIES

Words and Concepts

At their most basic level, ideologies structure our thinking by supplying the terms with which we describe our world. For example, languages such as French, Spanish, or German, which make a distinction between the formal and the informal "you," encourage speakers to focus on equality/subordination and familiarity/distance in a way that English does not.[7] The availability of a word for a concept can actually be said to make that concept real, or at least worthy of notice: "sexual harassment" did exist in American businesses before 1970, but, since a name for it had not yet been coined, it was very difficult to talk about or even (for those not directly involved) to notice. Similarly, English supplies us with words such as "racism," "sexism" and "ageism" to describe discriminatory treatment of African-Americans, women, or the elderly, but not with words to describe discrimination against short people or fat people—injustices which are also present in our society.

The meaning of the terms within an ideology can change over time and place. Prior to 1975 (and even today, in some areas), "rape" did not apply to forced sexual intercourse with one's husband or boy friend. And even when the actual *content* of a word remains the same, the *value* attached to it may change: to call a product or a technique "new" may be a compliment at one time ("new and improved Windex") and an insult at another ("new and outlandish doctrines").

Linkages

Ideologies also supply us with links *between* concepts. Some links are causal: "Blacks are poor because they are lazy" (or "immoral," or "victims of white racism"). Others are links of identity: "Men are naturally aggressive" (or "dishonest," or "creative"). Still others are links of value: "Sexual abstinence is holy" (or "psychologically unhealthy," or "a sin against God"). It is common for the critics of a given ideology to point out that these linkages are unproven. But *many* of our taken-for-granted assumptions about reality have never been proven. Within the memory of most readers of this book, educated Americans have believed that homosexuals could be cured by psychotherapy, or that, if Vietnam "fell" to Communism, all of Southeast Asia would inevitably follow—only to find out later that they were wrong in both cases.

Packages

Causally linked propositions are often amalgamated into ideological "packages," whereby knowing a person's opinion on one issue (e.g., evolution vs. creationism) enables us to predict with fair certainty his/her opinion on another, apparently unrelated, issue (e.g., whether wives should work outside the home).[8] For most people, a logical connection between the two issues is assumed rather than proven: "If you support open occupancy ordinances, you logically should support racial quotas and the Sandinistas."[9] Usually, however, no such logical connection exists. In fact, the positions on the various issues in an ideological package may flatly contradict each other. Cardinal Bernardin, for example, has argued that it makes no sense to oppose abortion and yet support capital punishment. People usually do not question whether the opinions and assumptions which underlie their daily actions form a logical and coherent whole or not; they adopt the package as a set because their friends and family members also believe in it.[10]

Myths

Myths—the stories, characters and events that represent the "really real" to a culture—are also components of that culture's ideology. Mythic characters such as Paul Bunyan, Davy Crockett and "Honest Abe" Lincoln embody qualities which Americans value; the mythic events of our history acquire a sacred aura because they speak to who we really are.[11] Revisionist historians who question these myths risk public wrath. National associations of concerned parents have been formed, for example, to prevent local school boards from adopting texts that paint a less than rosy picture of America's history.[12] Religions also have their mythic figures (Martin Luther, Mohammed, John XXIII, Mother Teresa) and events (the settlement of Salt Lake City, the Exodus), which perform a similar function of defining religious reality. To call Jesus a mythic figure, or the resurrection a mythic event, is not to imply that they were imaginary, but rather that they are, for Christians, fundamental links which tie the Really Real to everyday life.

Ideological Supports

As the vocabulary, the causal connections, the belief packages and the mythic figures which compose a particular ideological frame are built up and elaborated, the resulting mental structure may also be reinforced by a variety of supporting practices. Nathan Hatch's study of the rise of several nineteenth-century Protestant sects shows how the new groups' ideological "roofs" (their belief in religious equality, their insistence on free salvation instead of predestination, their emotionalism, and their millennial expectations) were strengthened and concretized by the "walls" of liturgical forms, governance regulations and theological elaborations which they developed at the same time.[13] Similarly, as contemporary groups of religious virtuosi formulate the vocabularies and belief systems which articulate their identity and purpose, they will also develop ritual expressions to display and symbolize these beliefs, theological and polemical literature to argue their validity, and a plethora of stories, jokes, legends and metaphors, recounted again and again among themselves, to reinforce their convictions and commitment. Some of these rituals and techniques may be invented by the virtuoso group, but most will be adopted or adapted from the surrounding society. It is to this ideological construction and adaptation process that we now turn.

THE SOCIAL BASIS OF IDEOLOGY

The Construction, and Reconstruction, of Ideologies

A fundamental insight of the sociology of knowledge is that all ideologies are *socially* constructed: "Human thought arises and operates, not in a social vacuum but in a definite social milieu."[14] The symbol system of language, the linked hypotheses of cause and identity, the constrained packages of beliefs (whether logical or not), and the myths held by a given individual are all absorbed from his/her surrounding culture. Few persons have the perception or the inclination to construct *de novo* the terms and logical

propositions that would be necessary to reformulate even one
single aspect of their belief systems.[15] Cultural patterns of
thought, diffused across populations as "natural" wholes, function as templates or blueprints for the organization of our social
and psychological processes, in much the same way as the genetic code organizes biological processes.[16] They are rarely questioned or even noticed.

Several conclusions follow from this observation. First of all,
in order truly to understand a belief or a line of thought, one
must study the social situation in which that belief developed.[17] A
reciprocal relationship exists between the ideological frames
that structure the thought processes of individuals and the institutions that shape their surrounding society. On the one hand,
social institutions exist only as long as individuals continue to
believe in and support them; on the other hand, the individual's
beliefs and values are essentially molded by these same social
institutions.[18] The sociology of knowledge attempts to draw out
the reciprocal connections between what human beings hold as
true or good, and the societal milieu which both shapes and is
shaped by these same beliefs and values.

The second conclusion is that, as social environments change,
so do ideologies. First of all, the *name* given to a set of ideological
components may change. Nineteenth-century "Liberalism," for
example, denoted a set of beliefs about governmental non-inter-
ference in the lives of individuals—a political stance that we in
the United States call "conservative" today. The *group of people*
associated with an ideological stance may also change. For example, the mainline Protestant denominations of the nineteenth
century were concerned with elaborating doctrinal creeds, while
the ancestors of the Baptists objected to such formulations as
infringements on individual liberty.[19] Today, on the other hand,
studies have shown that many mainline Protestants do not
believe in the creeds which their ancestors constructed,[20] while
the Southern Baptists have imposed adherence to statements of
faith upon some of their members at virtual heresy trials.[21] This
is a direct reversal of the two groups' previous positions.

Over time, the *specific constellation of separate beliefs* which comprise a given ideological package may also change. Nineteenth-
century feminists were vehemently anti-abortion, for example,

and nineteenth-century Republicans were the champions of the rights of African Americans (at least when compared to nineteenth-century Democrats). As these examples indicate, the content of an ideology—its concepts, its linked assumptions and the composition of its packages—can change radically over time.

A third conclusion is that several competing ideologies may exist at the same time. No one society or culture is totally homogeneous; all are fissured into a multitude of different "social locations" which profoundly influence the ideologies of individuals from different classes, generations, sexes, or parts of the country. To the extent that a person's life experiences are unique because she is a woman, or Chicana, or born after Vatican II, so her belief system—her ideological packages, her myths—will differ from those of 50-year-old Irish-American clerics in Boston, African-American Baptist churchgoers in rural Georgia, and so on. The more pluralistic a society is and the more it is subdivided into these kinds of social locations, the more difficult it will be to provide an integrative ideology for the whole.[22] On the other hand, it is in precisely such pluralistic situations that the most creative ideological systematization is done. In order to validate their political, moral, economic, or theological beliefs to unsympathetic others, competing groups must encourage the rise of political scientists, ethicists, economists and theologians to systematize them into a coherent theory. It is no accident that so many doctors of the church lived in times of active heresy. Heterogeneous or rapidly changing societies often become crucibles for ideological development and systematization.

The reverse is also true: ideological development and systematization *encourages* social change by enabling formerly un-self-conscious groups to develop their own identity and their own definition of their place in the world. Since identity development is an essential precondition before a class, an ethnic group, or any other collection of individuals can organize itself and begin to struggle against oppressive conditions, the leaders of such groups may actively seek out and/or develop an ideology which facilitates this effort.

> Frequently an ideology is taken on by a group because of specific theoretical elements that are conducive to its interests. For exam-

ple, when an impoverished peasant group struggles against an urban merchant group that has financially enslaved it, it may rally around a religious doctrine that upholds the virtues of agrarian life, condemns the money economy and its credit system as immoral, and generally decries the luxuries of urban living.[23]

The prophecies of Amos come to mind here, as do the writings of liberation theologians in Latin America.

When several competing groups each subscribe to a different ideology, conflicts may arise as each struggles to establish its own version as normative over the others. This winning group can then use its ideology to define what the "real" issues are and what should be done about them, thus making it very difficult for its opponents even to articulate their alternative visions. Over time, the ideological perspective of the ruling group becomes codified in the schools, the media, the churches, and the other institutions of a society. Then it is even more difficult to dislodge.[24]

"Truth" and Ideology

A disturbing implication of this treatment of ideology is that it appears to negate the very possibility of objective truth. No one can function without an ideology to structure his/her thoughts, and yet all ideologies, by definition, are *social* constructions that serve the needs of their adherents.[25] Even "objectivity" is an ideology; to claim that one's beliefs/knowledge are "objective" inhibits criticism by stigmatizing opponents as irrational or unscientific.[26]

From the standpoint of the sociology of knowledge, therefore, there would seem to be no *objective* truth or falsity. "False" beliefs, myths and ideological systems are simply those that inhibit people from achieving the optimal functioning of their society. For example, allowing the myth of the family farm to dominate American agricultural policy may blind voters to the fact that a few large corporations' sales overshadow the role of the many smaller farmers. Similarly, the nineteenth century's Horatio Alger stories and its tales of the log-cabin backgrounds of presidential candidates obscured the structural origins of much of that century's wealth and poverty. Such myths are false, not because family farms do not exist or because Lincoln was not born in a log cabin, but because clinging to these beliefs prevents Americans from solving their deep-seated societal problems.

Still, it is disturbing, even to sociologists, to reduce truth merely to whatever is useful for a given group to function.[27] A more epistemologically satisfying stance might be that it is not truth that varies over time and place, but rather the *symbols* which we construct in our unequally effective attempts to grasp the truth.[28] It is these symbol systems—the ideologies—which become more or less "true" from culture to culture and from age to age. "False consciousness...is the result of an inability or a reluctance or a failure to risk the credibility of one's own beliefs (or those one has sympathy for) by passing them through the fire of sociological analysis, which constitutes a critique of their contextual sources and consequences."[29]

The ideological interpretations of what constitutes religious virtuosity have also varied over time and place. The following section will outline some of the dimensions of these variations. *No one version is more "true," more authentic, or holier than another.* The important question is which interpretation best enfleshes the hunger for virtuoso spirituality in a particular environmental context.

IDEOLOGICAL VARIATIONS IN RELIGIOUS VIRTUOSITY

The Worth and Purpose of Virtuoso Spirituality

Religious virtuosity is an ideological concept and, as such, it is subject to all of the many societal influences that shape ideologies. The fact that the *content* of virtuoso spirituality, like the content of other ideological concepts, varies over time and between cultures has already been mentioned (see above, p. 20). But other variations must also be considered. Religions have differed in the *value or purpose* attached to having virtuoso practitioners within the faith. Some religious cultures have held virtuosi in high esteem, considering them to perform valued services for the society and/or church as a whole. Examples of such cultures would include Hinduism, Greek and Russian Orthodoxy, Theravada Buddhism and, of course, Roman Catholicism.

Protestant Christianity, on the other hand, rejected the very idea of a separate virtuoso state. According to the Augsburg Confession of 1530:

> There are many godless opinions associated with monastic vows: that they justify and render men righteous before God, that they constitute Christian perfection, that they are the means of fulfilling both evangelical counsels and precepts, and that they furnish the works of supererogation which we are not obliged to render to God. Inasmuch as all these things are false, useless and invented, monastic vows are null and void.[30]

As we have seen, of course, this official denial of the legitimacy of religious virtuosity did not exempt Protestant churches from having to deal with virtuoso members in their midst.

Christian denominations such as Roman Catholicism and Greek Orthodoxy, which do accept and value the idea of separate communities of religious virtuosi, may do so for widely different *reasons*. The early hermits and consecrated virgins were thought to be valuable to the rest of the church because their prayers secured graces and prosperity for the laity, and because they modeled the coming eschatological age when humankind would live "like the angels in heaven" and the "ache of sexual division would be abolished."[31] Similar intermediary roles were prescribed for cloistered monks and nuns in the Middle Ages and in later periods. For example, religious virtuosi in medieval monasteries provided "a vicarious sacrifice for the whole of Christendom."[32] By their extra prayers and penances, they were thought to store up merit in a celestial treasury which was then dispensed in indulgences to the rest of the faithful, both living and deceased. In contrast, the sixteenth- and seventeenth-century apostolic virtuosi—the Jesuits, Ursulines, and other religious communities of the period—were thought to be soldiers on the front lines of a cosmic battle, striving to win the souls of heretics and heathens from the dominion of the devil.[33]

Some of the legitimating reasons given for religious virtuosity were more successful than others in drawing new members and attracting political and financial support.[34] A study of attempts to establish religious orders in the nineteenth-century Anglican Church illustrates how subtle variations in the way religious virtu-

osity was ideologically legitimated might affect the ultimate success or failure of virtuoso groups.[35] The Anglican hierarchy was
very conscious of the fact that, by failing to provide an outlet for
those who wanted to do more for Christ, they were losing their
most devout members—and especially their most devout *female*
members—either to Methodist sects or to Roman Catholicism. In
addition, the widespread poverty and social dislocation of the
early Industrial Revolution called for a vast expansion in church-
sponsored social service. Anglican religious orders, therefore,
were legitimated by a mixed, but essentially *instrumental*, ideology: their basic purpose was to keep female religious virtuosi within Anglicanism and to provide committed and inexpensive
laborers to staff the church's social programs.[36] This ideological
justification for religious life was essentially different from that
advanced by nineteenth-century Roman Catholicism; namely,
that religious orders were primarily a way to achieve spiritual
perfection for oneself and graces for the church, and only secon-
darily as a way to serve the needs of the poor. As an alternative
ideological rationale for religious life, mere instrumental service
was less successful in attracting potential entrants. Furthermore,
many among the Anglican hierarchy remained deeply suspicious
of the "Romish" idea of spiritual perfection, and were reluctant
to support these communities.[37] As a result of their less persuasive ideology of virtuoso spirituality, Anglican religious orders
remained much more peripheral to the larger church than
Roman Catholic orders did.

Ideological Packages and Religious Virtuosity

It is important to remember also that religious virtuosity is
only one aspect of Christianity's, and the broader society's, larger
ideological systems. In different times and cultures, therefore,
the desirability of joining a community of religious virtuosi
might be bound with other religious and secular beliefs into widely different "packages." For example, the traditional Catholic
belief that celibacy was superior to sexual activity helped support
both the existence and the exalted status of communities of celibate religious virtuosi within the church.[38] Judaism, Islam and
Protestantism, which did not value celibacy, did not include it as
a component in their versions of virtuoso spirituality. Similarly,

the Catholic belief that obedience to designated authorities was superior to an autonomous working out of one's own salvation encouraged communal rather than individualistic forms of virtuosity.[39] As these traditional Catholic beliefs fell out of favor and were discarded in post-Vatican II Catholicism, some key ideological underpinnings of Catholic religious life were also weakened.

Religious virtuosity could also be packaged with secular political beliefs. The nineteenth-century French assumed that religious life was utterly incompatible with liberal political views; in contemporary El Salvador, on the other hand, the majority of young recruits come to seminaries or novitiates because of the witness which priests and religious have given against that country's conservative regime.[40] In some times and places, a religion has become linked in the public mind with national identity. When this happens, religious virtuosi may become the vanguards in the struggle for cultural autonomy. The Tibetan Buddhist monks in exile at Dharmsala, India, would appear to be one example of this.[41] So would the Iranian ayatollas during the regime of the Shah, as well as Irish and Polish religious orders during periods when those countries were dominated by outside oppressors. More recently, Orthodox Christianity has been reported on the rise in Greece and in the Balkans, as a sign of national identity there.[42]

The changing beliefs which are packaged with religious virtuosity may make it more or less attractive to various groups of potential adherents. The virtuoso spirituality of contemporary Protestant fundamentalist sects, for example, assumes the divinely-ordained character of women's subordination.[43] This is a change from the sectarian virtuoso movements in eighteenth- and nineteenth-century Protestantism, which gave women much *greater* equality than the mainline churches did.[44] The amalgamation of religious virtuosity into a package of beliefs that includes acceptance of a repressive class system, the natural inferiority of women, the aesthetic superiority of the Latin mass, or the necessity of obedience to the Roman curia, means that persons who might have been attracted by the idea of a more intense or demanding spiritual life will be repelled by its seemingly inextricable links to these other issues.

Competing Ideologies of Religious Virtuosity

Societies may also differ in the *number* of competing ideologies of religious virtuosity which are available to the seeker. In eleventh-century France and Italy, for example, the only religion was Catholicism, and the only officially accepted form of religious virtuosity within Catholicism was the monastic model. Few women's monasteries existed at all, and the men's houses accepted only the wealthier classes. Religious virtuosi in whole segments of the medieval population were thus denied *any* acceptable form of expression for their calling. The pent-up force of thwarted religious virtuosity among women and the lower middle classes helps to explain the explosive growth of the Franciscans and Dominicans, and also of various "heretical" virtuoso groups such as the Waldensians and the Humiliati.

The United States today, in contrast, provides a plethora of *competing* outlets for religious virtuosity. Subgroups that feel excluded from one religious tradition's form of spiritual perfection can switch to another; individuals who are put off by an element in one denomination's ideological package can search for a church in which religious virtuosity keeps better company. Recent research, however, indicates that religious diversity within a society has contradictory effects on spiritual practice. On the one hand, more forms of religious virtuosity may be available to potential virtuosi. On the other hand, religious diversity and ethnic diversity appear to depress the total amount of virtuoso spirituality in the society, so that fewer persons are attracted to any of the forms.[45] Historians have noted that most previous religious orders arose within the "crucible" of the solidly Catholic societies of southern Europe, and that comparatively few developed in the more pluralistic environments of England, Germany or the Netherlands.[46] The availability of competing alternatives may thus mean not only that there will be fewer American Catholic virtuosi, but also that these few individuals may feel less compelled to devise new forms of religious life within Catholicism to substitute for declining and no longer viable ones, and may find it easier to join one of the more attractive cultic or sectarian groups.

Implications

Exactly how religious virtuosity fits into the larger ideological schema of a church thus has profound implications for whether its virtuosi will leave their parent body or remain within it, for how religious virtuosity will manifest itself, and for whether and to what extent its virtuoso movements will succeed. The cyclic character of Catholic religious life, for example, is probably peculiar to the way religious virtuosity has been shaped by the Catholic ideological structure: the solitary forms of Eastern virtuoso spirituality, such as wandering holy men, hermits and the like, do not exhibit these cycles.[47] If the post-Vatican II belief systems of Catholics are successfully reworked to provide a new set of ideological underpinnings for religious life, it is quite possible that the form of its life cycles will also change.

Another important implication of ideologies of virtuoso spirituality is that these ideologies will be differently attractive to the occupants of different social locations. Depending on societal circumstances and the particular virtuoso ideology, men may be more attracted to religious life than women (or vice versa); one particular ethnic group more than another; or the working class more than the middle class. Certain geographic areas may produce an abundance of vocations; others will produce few or none. Since ideologies are usually adopted in part, at least, because they benefit the group which adopts them, it is probable that a given expression of religious virtuosity will flourish only among those subgroups for whom it provides concrete personal advantages. These advantages will certainly include the opportunity to participate in a spiritual quest (a quite powerful motivation, especially to those who were denied this opportunity in the past). But religious virtuosity may also provide the additional inducements of social mobility, power, or education. The interplay between the attraction of the extra material benefits which a particular form of religious virtuosity offers, and its ideological need to emphasize the pre-eminently *spiritual* basis of virtuoso religion, may lead to tensions within a group of religious virtuosi. An important focus of sociological study would be to determine exactly who is attracted to what form of religious virtuosity in a society, and why.

CONCLUSIONS

In western Christianity, religious virtuosity is primarily a *group* phenomenon, and is expressed in sectarian churches, communal lifestyles, and charismatic prayer groups more often than by solitary hermits or wandering "holy men." The organization of these group manifestations of virtuoso spirituality implies the more or less simultaneous adoption and/or adaptation, often by quite large groups of people, of some justifying ideology which makes this particular form of religious virtuosity appear desirable and feasible. At certain times and places, (for example, in the "Burned-Over District" of upstate New York during the early nineteenth century), a large number of people may be stirred up by a new virtuoso belief system. Dozens or even hundreds of competing groups of virtuosi, modeled on this ideological system, may spring up within a short time and in close proximity. Such group phenomena require the consideration of concepts from the third of our sociological disciplines: the study of social movements.

4

Social Movements

Sociologists use the term "social movement" to refer to phenomena as diverse as the Civil Rights Movement, the "Great Awakenings" of eighteenth- and nineteenth-century American Protestantism, and anti-alcohol crusades such as the early temperance rallies and current efforts to curb drunk driving. All of these are "conscious, collective, organized attempt[s] to bring about or resist large-scale change in the social order by non-institutionalized means."[1] Social movements differ from more transitory collective behavior such as vandalism after rock concerts, or the sudden mass popularity of Hula Hoops or Ninja turtles, in that the latter types of behavior are not consciously oriented toward social change. Institutionalized organizations such as the National Association of Manufacturers or the American Medical Association are also not social movements, because their members are considered to be part of the established governing elite and, as such, are committed to the status quo.

Social movements often contain organized subgroups—very many such groups, if the movement is large and widespread. These subgroups are called Social Movement Organizations (SMO's for short). Thus, the feminist movement includes SMO's such as NOW (the National Organization for Women), WEAL (Women's Equity Action League) and NWPC (National Women's Political Caucus), which focus on general women's issues, as well as a host of other groups with more specialized foci—abortion rights, battered women, child care, and so on. Anti-movement SMO's may also arise (Phyllis Schlafly's STOP-ERA, for example). The relationship of these social movement

46

organizations to each other and to societal elites, why social movement organizations form, succeed or fail, and what induces people to join them, are all topics for sociological investigation.

THEORIES OF SOCIAL MOVEMENTS

Resource Mobilization Theory

Resource Mobilization theorists assume that the potential for social movements exists in *all* societies. Whether or not a particular movement actually develops, however, depends on the *access of some initial group of individuals to the resources* which can be used to spread their message and to attract new members. Resources for spreading the message include material advantages such as money, meeting places, and (today) access to a copier, fax machine, or personal computer. Social resources are also important: networks of friends who can be persuaded to help or to join the movement, sympathetic allies in high places, key media contacts, and the like. Still another social resource is the type of internal organization which exists within the movement organization. Tightly organized and bureaucratized groups are more effective for achieving specific political goals. Loose, decentralized groups more readily mobilize a large number of individuals for widespread societal change.[2]

Other resources are important because they help a social movement organization attract new members. Proffered incentives, such as the opportunity for an education, social status, or power, may be valuable resources for this reason. Also, it often helps if a social movement organization's leaders are drawn from higher economic or educational strata than are the rank and file participants. Such leaders may have greater skill and experience in administration or public speaking, or they may have valuable connections with government officials. Ruling elites may also be less likely to repress a dissident movement if it is led by one of their friends or former schoolmates.[3] On the other hand, drawing its leadership from the elite class may "co-opt" the group, toning down its more radical demands so that it does not really provide the benefits desired by its rank and file members.[4]

Social movements also have ideological resources. These

include emotionally powerful slogans or symbols, readily explainable goals, and "repertoires of collective action," whereby the goals can be achieved. For example, tactics such as the sit-ins of the early Civil Rights Movement did not develop spontaneously. Activists had first to discover which kinds of stores would be the best targets. Next, they had to learn how to assemble a sufficient number of protestors, school them in appropriate non-violent behavior, and arrange for logistical support, media coverage and bail money.[5] Once the sit-in technique was refined and shown to be effective, its use spread rapidly from state to state, as other Civil Rights activists learned about it from friends, at church conferences, or in the African-American press. The sit-in became such a valuable resource that it was later adopted by the student, peace, and right-to-life movements.

Both ideological and more practical motivations can induce prospective members to join a social movement organization. New recruits may be attracted because they truly believe in the movement's collective goal or because they desire the personal benefits which participation will provide. "Since the motives combine in an additive way, they can compensate for one another. If the collective motive is weak, zero, or negative, other motives can be so strong that a person is willing to participate. If the collective motive is strong, the social motives and/or the reward motives can be negative without making a person unwilling to participate."[6]

In addition to the material, social and ideological resources possessed by an aspiring social movement organization, the presence and strength of opposition forces is also important to its success. Sometimes competing social movements, or competing SMO's within the *same* social movement, may oppose the new group. For example, the male leaders of the 1960's Civil Rights and student movements objected to the rise of the feminist movement, because they believed that it diverted attention from the *real* struggle against racism or the Vietnam War. Alternatively, an established movement group such as NOW, the Sierra Club or the Union of Concerned Scientists may resent a new group which "poaches" their membership, or which threatens long-lasting and carefully-nurtured ties to the establishment by "irresponsible" radical demands. The presence of existing

SMO's can thus be detrimental to the rise of newer groups, and new organizations tend to avoid competition by organizing in different areas or among different populations than their predecessors did.[7]

The opposition of competing social movements or SMO's is not the only obstacle which a new social movement organization must face. The governing elites—whether state, or church, or economic—may also be so strong that an incipient social movement is doomed to failure. It is helpful, therefore, if the elite is preoccupied or weakened in some way: if, for example, it is divided into subelites which are competing with each other. In such a case, a social movement organization may find itself courted by one of the competing elite factions and may be able to extract valuable concessions from it. Or the attention of the elite may be focused on other, "more important" issues, and they may be comparatively open to granting the demands of the movement organization.

Summary and Application

For the resource mobilization theory of social movements, therefore, whether a concerted movement develops out of the generalized discontent in a society depends upon how much power is possessed by the rising SMO's to counter the competing movements, movement organizations, or societal elites who wish to stop them. Power comes from a variety of resources—material resources such as money, property, or printing presses; social resources such as efficient internal organization, leadership skills, or networks of friends and political associates; personnel resources such as a large number of enthusiastic recruits; and ideological resources such as catchy slogans, useful repertories of action, or persuasive doctrines. To the extent that religious communities are discrete social movement organizations within a larger wave of congregational founding/refounding, their success will also depend upon the extent of the resources which they can tap. In subsequent chapters, we will examine how new and refounded communities have mobilized the resources available to them. First, however, we must consider another, equally valuable way of studying social movements, that of Frame Alignment.

IDEOLOGY AND SOCIAL MOVEMENTS:
FRAME ALIGNMENT THEORY

Whereas resource mobilization theorists view ideological elements simply as useful tools to win over skeptical authorities or recruit new members, Frame Alignment Theory focuses on the indispensable role which ideology plays in defining the entire worth and purpose of the movement. Both individuals and organizations have ideological frameworks which they use to interpret and to give meaning to occurrences in their own lives and in the world at large.[8] One of the tasks which a successful social movement organization must therefore accomplish is to make clear how its explanation of some societal event or condition is superior to the often unconscious ideologies of the potential recruits. First of all, people must be encouraged to rediagnose their situation: Is our poverty the result of God's inscrutable plan or the whims of fate—or is it because we are oppressed by rapacious and evil landlords? Are the king and his nobles wise and benevolent— or are they weak and corrupt? Recruits must next be persuaded to accept the movement's interpretations of the correct solution to their problems, and of the strategies and tactics necessary to achieve it: Given that so many of our menfolk drink their wages away in saloons, should we lobby the city council for restricted hours in these establishments, or should we march out with axes and torches to demolish them ourselves? Finally, people must be made to feel sufficiently confident of the indispensability of their contribution to the movement's success. Why should *I* bother donating my time and money—and perhaps risking my life—in the service of a Quixotic gamble that is going to fail anyway? No social movement can succeed unless at least some people find its vision and objectives persuasive. The process by which the separate ideological frameworks of individuals are modified and/or linked to that promulgated by a particular social movement is called "Frame Alignment."

Techniques of Frame Alignment

The alignment process is a result of active, and very serious, ideological work by everyone involved. In our daily lives, we are constantly updating the ideological underpinnings which

inform our view of the world. We compare and discuss significant events with our friends and families, we share jokes and stories with them, we recommend a movie, book, or newspaper
column to their attention.[9] In this manner, groups of friends,
members of a church, residents in an ethnic neighborhood, or
employees in a business firm come to share common and mutu-
ally-reinforced interpretations of their daily world. A social
movement organization must attempt to intervene in this
process of ideological formation. If it does so successfully, it
may vastly improve its chances of enlisting entire groups of individuals to its cause. The task of frame alignment is complicated,
however, by the competing efforts both of other social movement organizations and of the established elite to win adherents
for *their* ideological frames.[10] If the elite win in this competition
(and they have the powerful resources of the media and the educational system to promote their perspective), no outside social
movement will be able to succeed. If a competing social movement organization is more successful at frame alignment, then
its interpretation will become the accepted one, and subsequent
organizations will be constrained to adopt its ideological packages and recommendations instead of their own. Since frame
alignment is so vitally necessary, social movement organizations
have developed several techniques for accomplishing it more
effectively.

The most common technique of frame alignment is *Frame
Bridging.*[11] This occurs when a social movement organization
contacts a group of individuals who are already likely to hold the
same ideological interpretation of some situation as the organization does. The organization is thus assured of a sympathetic
audience for its recruitment efforts. Computerized address lists
and mass mailing technologies make frame bridging especially
easy. Groups as diverse as the Moral Majority, Common Cause,
and the Committee for a Sane Nuclear Policy purchase subscrip-
tion lists from periodicals with a given editorial slant in order to
cull them for potential new recruits. Bread for the World and
Saul Alinsky's Industrial Areas Foundation enlist the efforts of
churches to reach sympathetic congregants. Through frame
bridging, a small social movement organization can increase its
influence quite rapidly.

A second technique is *Frame Amplification*. In using this technique, an organization isolates a specific value or belief which individuals in the targeted recruitment group already hold and then attempts to increase its salience or centrality. For example, people may already believe that the family is a good thing or that finding God in one's life is important, but they may not have felt it was necessary to worry much about these issues. It is the task of the social movement organization to convince them that the family or the spiritual life is so important or so threatened that people must devote more of their time and efforts to preserving it—preferably by joining the organization. Beliefs about how serious the threat to the family is, or about who is to blame for its decline, or about how powerful the antifamily forces are, may also have to be addressed. Social movement organizations can attempt to amplify desired beliefs and values among their targeted groups by mailings, talks, ads, etc. They may also encourage their current members to raise the issue at dinner tables, in church socials and around the water cooler with their families, friends and co-workers. Even among movement members, periodic frame reamplification is necessary in order to maintain the group's original fervor. "...[T]he various movement participants we observed spend a good deal of time together accounting and recounting for their participation; they jointly develop rationales for what they are or are not doing."[12]

A third technique of frame alignment is *Frame Extension*. Whole groups of potential members may be more interested in other issues, rather than in the one the social movement organization is trying to promote. The social movement organization must then convince them that its own agenda must be addressed before these other goals can be achieved. For example, the largely white and middle-class members of the Peace Movement attempted to enlist working class and minority support by arguing that, if arms spending was reduced, more money would be available for social welfare programs. A danger in extending a social movement's ideological framework in this way is that its focus may become diluted and "fuzzy." If this happens, the movement may ultimately end up so vague as to appeal to no one.

The most difficult frame alignment task is *Frame Transformation*. At times some key aspect of a social movement's ideology is actually antithetical to the culture of the larger society. A movement may be promoting peaceful disarmament in a militarized and xenophobic society, for example, or sexual abstinence and asceticism in a hedonistic one. In this case, the social movement organization must attempt to discredit some of the central beliefs or values in the dominant culture and to substitute its own. While obviously difficult, frame transformation is not impossible. In the past decade, for example, Mothers Against Drunk Driving has achieved notable success in transforming the cultural image of drinking and driving from a macho activity to that of a public menace. Changing a single belief or value of the larger culture is called "domain specific" frame transformation. "Global" frame transformation, on the other hand, changes a culture's entire "sense of ultimate grounding."[13] Mass religious conversion movements, of which the United States has witnessed several throughout its history, are the most obvious examples of global frame transformations. In each of these, a formerly irreligious population experienced widespread conversion rates. On the early nineteenth-century American frontier, for example, the Methodists alone grew from 14,000 members to over a million, and the number of preachers per capita in all Protestant denominations tripled even as the total population was doubling in size.[14] This occurred in a population that had formerly been almost completely unchurched. Paradoxically, it is often the most thoroughly irreligious cultures which are the most vulnerable to waves of religious enthusiasm.[15] Thus global frame transformation is not as unlikely as it may appear.

IMPLICATIONS OF FRAME ALIGNMENT PROCESSES FOR RELIGIOUS VIRTUOSITY

Recruitment through Preexisting Networks

Social movements spread most efficiently when they are able to alter the ideological frameworks of whole groups rather than convert adherents on an individual-by-individual basis. Groups which already possess strong interpersonal networks and a common set of cultural beliefs are the most easily mobilized, especially if organizations can appeal to some aspect of the beliefs

which the group's members already hold.[16] This means that the
spread of a social movement will usually be along preexisting
lines of communication among family members, friends, neighbors, or fellow ethnics. "Collective activity does not spread like
ripples in a lake when a rock is thrown into the water, but like the
channels of other types of diffusion—through natural and social
channels of communication."[17]

Similarly, movements of religious virtuosi will spread, initially
at least, through kin and friendship ties. For example, the first
converts to the Church of the Latter-Day Saints were Joseph
Smith's own family. Recent studies have found that between 57%
and 82% of the converts to religious virtuoso groups as disparate
as Protestant Pentecostals and Nichiren Shoshu Buddhists were
attracted and recruited by means of social networks.[18] A similar
pattern of network recruitment has occurred in the foundation
periods of Catholic religious communities. One study of women
entering two nineteenth-century convents in Limerick, Ireland,
found that between 17% and 23% of them had one or two biological sisters already in the same community.[19] If the network
pool is extended to include aunts, cousins, and friends, these per-
centages would undoubtedly be higher. One might expect, therefore, that the "waves" of previous religious foundations, as well
as any future founding/refounding attempts, were and will be
the most successful among populations with extensive internal
ties, rather than among isolated individuals.

The Mass Media and Religious Virtuoso Movements

In contrast to previous eras, the potential recruits to today's
movements of religious virtuosi are likely to have received much
of their prior information about it from television, newspapers
and other sources in the mass media. *This means that the ideological frameworks of the media personnel are important determinants of
the growth of the movement.*[20] If the followers of a particular form of
religious virtuosity are depicted by newspaper reporters or TV
anchors as uneducated, bigoted, or silly, this public image may
do irreparable harm to the virtuoso group's chances for survival.
Overemphasis by the media of a religious organization's weaknesses may also be harmful. For example, the attention given by
reporters to the Vatican's heavy-handed treatment of the sisters

who signed the *New York Times* abortion ad, as well as the more recent coverage of the underpayment and consequent dire financial straits of Catholic religious communities, have helped establish a public image of nuns as powerless, oppressed and incompetent to handle their own affairs. This has undoubtedly deterred some young women from entering.[21]

Media personnel may also be influenced by the larger, secular ideological packages prevalent within American culture. Reporters, TV screenwriters and other media workers are among the *least* religiously sophisticated in our society.[22] Their depictions of religious virtuosi, from charismatic faith healers to the Amish, are often combined with their taken-for-granted assumptions about the intellectual rigidity, psychological immaturity and/or sexual repressiveness which these "religious fanatics" must "naturally" have, assumptions which anyone familiar with the targeted group would immediately dismiss as ridiculous. But those whose knowledge is limited to what they see on TV or read in the newspapers will assume that the beliefs and values depicted there accurately represent the true beliefs and values held by these religious virtuosi.

Groups of religious virtuosi today, therefore, often do not have control over the way they will be seen by society at large. This makes their recruitment efforts even more problematic than they would otherwise be. Frame bridging efforts may fail if the targeted groups, who in reality would have been quite amenable to joining the virtuoso movement, are laboring under the false assumption that it really stands for something other than it does. The other frame alignment techniques may be equally difficult. Picking out and amplifying a group's true vision or purpose from among all the other beliefs with which it has been lumped together in the media—even if this is not an accurate representation of the group's entire ideological package—may be difficult, if not impossible. A still further complication may occur if an already established group of religious virtuosi has established its particular ideological framework so firmly in the popular mind that all variant formulations by newer groups are either dismissed as illogical or else are forced to conform to the dominant model. If everyone knows that "real" sisters teach or do parish work, then a group of mime actresses who perform passion plays—or a collection of solitary anchoresses living in church basements—may have trouble getting anyone to take their version of religious life seriously. ("But what *good* does it do to sit in St. Monica's undercroft all day?" "Surely it's undignified to tell the sacred story of Christ's passion dressed like *that!*")

Before a truly innovative religious virtuoso group can survive in such an inhospitable environment, a global frame transformation may be necessary. While such total ideological transformation is certainly possible in a culture, either intense social strain or powerful movement resources—or both—are usually needed to achieve it. A complex and delicate combination of persuasive ideology, competent and charismatic leadership, societal needs and sympathetic allies may have to coincide before any large-scale religious virtuoso movement can transform the ideology of the larger society to its own vision. In the interim, perhaps as many as 99% of all incipient religious virtuoso movements may die at birth. But when environmental conditions are more favorable and a global frame transformation does occur, successful movements may suddenly spawn so many virtuoso groups that an observer would have trouble keeping track of them all.

Cycles of Religious Virtuosity

Like all social movements in Western society, movements of religious virtuosi are cyclic in nature.[23] These cycles, of course, are not identically repeated in each historical epoch. In one period, religious virtuosity may be part of a different ideological package than it is at another, or the movements may involve participants from different social classes or from different parts of the country at each of their subsequent incarnations.[24] But whenever a religious movement's framing efforts do resonate with some underlying societal strain or need, they precipitate a global transformation in the cultural worldview which makes the movement's way of life attractive to an ever-larger pool of potential members.[25] At the apex of the spiral of mobilization, a threshhold effect may even be achieved whereby individuals who are outside the ethnic group or social class in which the movement was initially confined are impelled to join it by the sheer numbers of the others in the society who have already done so. Subgroups of virtuosi from each of these social locations—each ethnic group or social class—coalesce within the larger movement, as individual apostolic orders did in seventeenth-century France or as separate evangelical sects did in early nineteenth-century America. The competition among these groups often leads to the invention of new elements within the larger movement's ideological framework, which, in turn, appeals to still more people.[26] It is a time of creativity and growth.

Ultimately, however, the movement collapses. According to those who study them, all social movements alternate between "phases of high public involvement and phases of privatization."[27] To account for the decline and demise of individual religious orders, or of whole social movements of religious foundations, is not within the scope of this book. As the ideological frame of an order crystallizes into a set pattern and as changes in the surrounding environment render its worldview less and less relevant, as its ministerial activities become obsolete or unwanted and as new recruits enter for reasons of pseudo- rather than true religious virtuosity, the reasons for its decline may be obvious. What will concern us in subsequent chapters is, rather, the analysis of the specific conditions—internal and external, material, social and ideological—under which such a period of decline ends and a new movement of growth and expansion begins. We will also consider the conditions which may short-circuit refounding periods at their inception.

CONCLUSIONS

Religious life is poised upon a decision nexus at the present time. Over the past thirty years, we have experienced a profound, and total, ideological transformation of our most fundamental assumptions about what it means to be religious virtuosi within the Catholic Church. For that matter, many, if not most, of us are extremely doubtful whether *any* version of a concept as "elitist" as religious virtuosity can have a legitimate place in true Christian spirituality. But even if we have rejected our former status as religious virtuosi, we have not successfully substituted a *new* definition of our role within the church. However well grounded we may be as individuals, we don't know who we are *as a group*. Until we can articulate *who* we are and *why* we are, and until we can do so in a way that is attractive to twenty-first century Christians (and I strongly suspect that merely resuscitating the traditional pre-Vatican II concept of religious virtuosity as a superior, holier way of life would not be attractive in this context), we will not be able to refound our communities.

Not only have our ideological frames become seriously misaligned and possibly defunct, many of our other resources have also dwindled. In former times, networks of supportive parents, bishops and priests used to encourage the idea of religious vocations, and channeled many interested young men and women to our communities. By and large, we have lost this important recruitment resource. Furthermore, many of our congregations currently possess neither the financial ability nor the public relations expertise to counteract such pervasive and damaging media stereotypes as the flighty and idiotic nun or the sexually predatory priest or brother. We are losing our financial and reputational resources. As our communities' membership ages, fewer and fewer of our members may have the stamina to fulfill even the most necessary leadership roles. We are losing our leadership resources. Since fewer of our members staff our institutions (which may not seem all that different from other school and hospital systems, anyway), widespread popular recognition of our ministerial efforts has decreased. We are losing the political resource of our formerly appreciative supporters. Without a coherent ideological frame, without necessary survival resources, how can we hope to refound our communities?

So is it worthwhile even to bother beginning a refounding "journey"? Is there a destination/goal that could redefine our purpose and attract new companions on the way? The growth of fundamentalist churches, cults and various new age movements shows that there *is* a profound spiritual hunger in our society, a pent-up potential for religious virtuosity that is quite strong. Religious communities must develop and articulate ways to meet this hunger, to address, however hesitantly and imperfectly, the deepest needs and discontinuities in our society. *Only if we do this successfully will we initiate the refounding of Roman Catholic religious life in the twenty-first century.* Part Two will explore how we might begin.

PART II:

The Refounding Journey

5

Where Have We Gone Before?

Just as a group of travelling vacationers would have to decide, before they ever left home, what kind of vacation they wished to take together and where they wished to take it, so religious communities need a common definition of what it is that they have dedicated themselves to—and why. This is the same as saying, in the language of the previous section, that they need a new and compelling ideological frame to define and legitimize their religious virtuosity. There is ample evidence that many sisters, brothers and priests in religious communities currently lack any such definition.[1] And communities whose members are unclear about their role and purpose are correspondingly less likely either to attract new members or to retain the ones they already have.[2]

So where should religious begin to look in order to discover their goal and purpose for the twenty-first century? If, as I will argue, they are virtuosi of a sort—virtuosi shorn of their elitist past, but virtuosi nonetheless—then it would be a good idea to learn what role(s) artistic, intellectual, and/or religious virtuosi have adopted in the past. I believe that the life calling of all types of virtuosi is to formulate a response to "the sharpest anguish" or the "sustained dissatisfaction" of their society and culture.[3] No sociocultural system is ever perfect. There is always some internal contradiction in its deepest values and/or some new technological, political, or economic development which has not been adequately integrated into the beliefs and behaviors of its people. The longer this cultural misalignment continues, the more galling it becomes—like an ill-fitting shoe which grows more uncomfortable as the day passes. The virtuosi of a society are those who are the most driven to find a solution to the increasingly insistent questions of their age. Artists and musicians strive to embody this answer in their art and music; intellectuals and philosophers construct new paradigms for it in their writings. In like manner, religious virtuosi seek to develop a *spiritual* solution and to enflesh it in their very lives. Insofar as today's religious congregations are communal groups of religious virtuosi, therefore, their success will depend on whether or not they can uncover the "sharpest anguish" of the twenty-first century and on how effectively they can formulate a spiritual answer to it.[4]

It should be emphasized at the outset that determining the grounding purpose of religious life (i.e., the way it will seek to answer the fundamental concerns of our age) may *not* necessarily be the same as choosing a societal group to target for service. To assume that the primary focus of new religious orders will be their apostolic ministries, is to assume that the sharpest anguish of the twenty-first century will be the same as that of the seventeenth—the century when the apostolic model was first developed. As I will attempt to show in this and the following chapter, such an assumption may be mistaken.

THE RISE OF MINISTERIAL FOCI IN RELIGIOUS LIFE: A BRIEF OVERVIEW

The insertion of ministerial works as a primary (or even a secondary) purpose for religious life is a relatively new phenomenon in history, and one that has been confined, by and large, to religious virtuosi within Western Christianity. Wandering Hindu sadhus, Theravada Buddhist monks and Sufi mystics traditionally have not performed apostolic service. Neither have most varieties of Christian virtuosi. The main reason for the lifestyle of the third and fourth century hermits and the early medieval monastics was their own personal sanctification through asceticism and prayer. Whatever work the monk, nun, or hermit did—basketmaking for the hermits, agricultural work, manuscript copying, or needlecraft for the monks and nuns—was *not* a ministry. Such activities were either a grudgingly-accepted necessity for material sustenance or an ascetic discipline for the perfection of one's own soul. Religious rarely came into contact with outsiders in the performance of these tasks, and they often attempted to locate their hermitages or monasteries in extremely remote areas so that they would not be distracted by the importunings of needy petitioners. While some medieval monasteries did provide valuable social services such as sheltering the poor and aged or educating the children of the nobility, these were accidental by-products of other monastic functions. Monastic schools, for example, were established primarily to develop the literacy of the monastery's own novices.[5]

Beginning in the twelfth and thirteenth centuries, some versions of religious life did begin to add individual ministerial service as an optional activity. The regular canons and the Beguines are two examples. Many canons and Beguines, however, did *not* perform such service. They preferred instead to concentrate their efforts on the traditional virtuoso activities of prayer and asceticism.[6] In like manner, while some individual mendicant friars may have served the poor, the primary purpose of their orders was preaching and evangelizing. It was rare for a medieval community to be expressly established for service, and such groups were not particularly well-respected:

> Confusion persisted in canon law and church practice regarding the precise status of the hospitaller orders. It seems—although existing studies are quite inadequate—that medieval authorities simply did not give much thought to the question of whether or not the hospitallers were true religious. The work of the hospitaller was arduous and menial, and hospitallers were undoubtedly recruited from the lower social ranks....Thus, while the services performed by the hospitallers were recognized to be valuable to society, their actual work was disesteemed as vile and degrading; the hospitallers themselves seem to have existed without setting significant precedents or stimulating thoughtful discussion.[7]

Throughout the first 1500 years of its existence, therefore, the primary purpose of *real* religious life in Western Christianity was the perfection of the virtuoso's own soul and (especially for the mendicant friars) the salvation of the souls of others. Whatever other ministerial services these groups happened to render (teaching, sheltering the homeless) were peripheral to their main goals.

Only with the rise of the apostolic religious communities in the seventeenth century did ministerial service begin to be advanced as a reason, in and of itself, for religious life. The Jesuits' main goal was to "minister where no one else will."[8] Women in the new, non-cloistered French communities spoke of doing "all the good that [was] possible" for their fellow Christians.[9] Even so, the traditional view that ministry was less holy than prayer and asceticism persisted, and competed with the new ideology. Teaching children, for example, was originally justified, not as valuable in itself, but as a penitential discipline:

> The documents repeat insistently that teaching is *penible*, a word which carries connotations simultaneously of painfulness and dif-ficulty. The teaching sisters seem to have taken up their vocation as a new form of mortification, comparable to but less venerable than washing the feet of beggars.[10]

Founders such as Vincent de Paul and Jean-Pierre Medaille fought long and vigorous ideological battles to establish ministry as a valid activity for their followers. Even so, such service remained a secondary purpose at best. Canon Law continued to hold that the primary goal of religious life was the sanctification of individual religious.

It has rarely been accurate, therefore, to identify—even partial-ly—the basic purpose of religious life with performing a work or service in the church. I would argue instead that the primary rationale for the existence of any form of religious virtuosity—in Western or Eastern Christianity, in Buddhism, Hinduism or Sufism—is to enact a spiritual response to the basic dilemmas of its surrounding culture. Catholic religious orders have at times developed ministerial foci in the process of addressing the sharpest anguish of their age, but this was not always the case. The presence of a needy group is *the symptom or result of a sus-tained cultural discontinuity*, not the discontinuity itself. During most of the centuries in which religious communities have exist-ed in the church, few groups have identified their purpose pri-marily as caring for a particular need. Furthermore, the religious communities that did narrow their self-definition to a single min-isterial focus were the most vulnerable to extinction once that need changed.[11]

THE PURPOSE(S) OF RELIGIOUS VIRTUOSITY

What, then, were some of these basic cultural dilemmas that previous religious orders were established to address? Today's religious may not be accustomed to thinking in this way, and so may have difficulty envisioning exactly what "sharpest anguish" or "cultural discontinuity" means. Several recent historical studies, however, have documented how previous models of religious life addressed the dilemmas of their own eras. Perhaps a summary of these studies might help to illustrate the process.

The Medieval Mendicants and the Rise of a Monetary Economy

According to Lester Little,[12] the first five hundred years of the medieval period were characterized by a primitive "gift economy." Money was rare, and people lived on self-sufficient rural estates. There was little differentiation in social roles: one was either a noble landowner/warrior or else a peasant farmer. For over half a millennium, therefore, the church's theology and spirituality had no need to deal with the vexing issues of urban and commercial life.

When towns and commerce began to revive in the middle of the twelfth century, however, an acute crisis of spiritual ideology occurred. No readily accessible answers were available from church authorities regarding a wide variety of pressing questions on money and the new economic system. Was owning private property legitimate at all? (The early church fathers had said, after all, that property-holding held no place in the ideal, divine society.) Was private property merely a necessary evil in this imperfect world? Or could it be an absolute good? Was it permissible for doctors, teachers and lawyers to charge professional fees, since they were simply dispensing the knowledge that God had given to them without charge? How could one determine a fair price for goods, now that money was commonly used in place of gifts and barter? Was making a profit permissible, or did merchants, as the popular belief went, inevitably sin every time they sold something at a higher price than what they had paid for it? Thirteenth-century Christians had intense, and very mixed, feelings about the whole idea of money, which was often depicted in popular art as feces or vomit. Other aspects of the new economic situation, notably the

proliferating social divisions, the widening gulf between the rich
and the poor, and the increased sophistication of the middle-class
laity, also posed challenges to the spiritual ideology which the
church had traditionally used to interpret its world.

"The unique achievement of the friars was their creation of new
forms of religious expression specifically for the urban sector of
society and those people dominant within it."[13] The mendicants
had moved quickly to staff the new universities, where they developed techniques of oral disputation unknown in the earlier
monastic schools. Lively theological debates were encouraged as
the friars hammered out a theology and praxis for their new urban
and commercial world. Franciscan and Dominican moral theologians developed justifications for private property, profit and
trade, and began work on a distinction between interest and usury.
The newly-rediscovered works of Aristotle and the other Greek
philosophers were assimilated into scholastic thought. With
greater psychological sophistication, confessors began to emphasize intention and contrition in their treatment of sin, whereas
their predecessors had focused less on the motive than on the actual act committed. The friars also invented new techniques of pastoral communication to reach the urban masses. Preaching had
formerly been restricted to bishops; for the wandering Dominican
and Franciscan *priests* to give sermons was an extremely popular
novelty. The friars developed special training programs for
prospective preachers, and even published "how-to" books on the
subject. Many of these books contained lists of new similes,
metaphors and examples drawn from the language of the urban
marketplace, which would be readily understood by their audience.

But it was not only by their intellectual efforts that the friars'
new model of religious life addressed the challenges and
unsolved dilemmas of the new age. The mendicants' own personal poverty was a lived witness to the negative aspects of a
money economy, directing their listeners' attention to heavenly
treasures which neither rust nor moth consumed. Through their
teaching and their very lives, therefore,

> the friars confronted the chief problem of the new society, namely
> money-making. In the first place, they rejected money-making for
> themselves, turning instead to the recently matured ideal of volun-

tary poverty. Secondly, however, they persisted in the linguistic and formal mode of the money makers, while avoiding the spiritually harmful aspects of such people's work. And thirdly, having themselves demonstrated part of the way, they provided for the leaders of urban society a revised moral theology that approved of money-making in certain, carefully defined circumstances. *The friars' spirituality was both determined by, and a determining factor within, the new urban society.*"[14]

By modeling an answer to the most basic sociocultural questions of their era, the mendicants provided both the intellectual concepts and the pastoral techniques which the church needed to remain vital and relevant in its new environment.

Cultural Strains in Other Refounding Periods

In a similar manner, the other versions of religious life answered the discontinuities and strains within their own eras. During the late Roman Empire, for example, "Christians shared with their contemporaries...a haunting sense of the distance between God and humanity, between the heavenly and the earthly, between God's invisible creation—the angelic society—and God's visible creatures—the material world and the human race."[15] Such a cultural preoccupation explains the popularity of Origen's doctrine that Christians could, through virginity and asceticism, achieve "the pre-existing purity of soul" of Eden and of the angels in heaven.[16] Through celibacy, young Christian men and women proclaimed that they had renounced citizenship in a decayed and corrupt secular state in exchange for membership in the kingdom of heaven. This "radical youth culture" of virginity attracted large numbers of fourth-century men and women to the eremitic version of religious life. Women, especially, found that the life of a consecrated virgin gave them social prestige, freedom from familial constrictions, and spiritual equality with men.[17] Celibate ascetics, male and female, were "spiritual athletes," honored by the rest of Christian society as quasi-angelic mediators with an otherwise inaccessible divine realm.[18]

In like manner, the monastic movement of the fifth and sixth centuries spoke primarily to the stresses and preoccupations of the early post-Roman period and the barbarian invasions. Like the hermit, the monk was a spiritual athlete or soldier, a "recruit

trained and equipped" to fight against evil under his comman-
der, the abbot.[19] And monastic life itself became a model of an
ideal social order. Both of these images were intensely attractive
in the widespread chaos of the period.

In the sixteenth and seventeenth centuries, new challenges
again arose to threaten the established societal worldview. Prior
to the Reformation, all Europeans were Catholic by definition—
in much the same way that, until recently, all Mexicans or
Brazilians were Catholic—even if they never attended church services and were ignorant of basic Catholic doctrine.[20] The
Protestant reformers, on the other hand, emphasized the necessity of a *personal and informed assent* by each individual to his or her
faith—a sharp contrast to the traditional Catholic assumption. In
addition, the Protestants proclaimed a "world affirming" and
activist ethic of attaining personal salvation through attention to
one's secular occupation. This contradicted the "world rejecting"
ethos of Catholic virtuoso spirituality.[21] Encounters with non-
Christian peoples in Asia and North America also challenged
Catholics, who believed that these "pagans" would be consigned
to hell if missionaries did not bring them the faith. The sixteenth
century was a new and wider world, a world in which each imper-
iled soul—at home and abroad—would have to be reached and
persuaded to make an individual assent to Catholicism before
they were lured to error by the Protestant heretics.

The apostolic orders were founded to answer these challenges.
The spiritual innovations of the Jesuits and the teaching ministry
of orders such as the Ursulines and the Congregation de Notre
Dame, were part of a new model of religious life, one both influenced by and responding to the challenge of Protestant evangelization. The Spiritual Exercises of St. Ignatius were an attempt to
arouse in Catholics the same personal commitment to the cross of
Christ that was being advocated by Reform theologians. The apostolic model of religious life was also the first to advance ministerial
work as a key component of Catholic religious virtuosity—an adaptation to the "world-affirming activism" of Protestant spirituality.

The Charism(s) of Religious Life

Up to and including the apostolic orders of the sixteenth and
seventeenth centuries, therefore, each version of religious life

responded either to some basic challenge which new societal developments—new inventions, new ways of thinking, new economic systems—posed for the Catholic/Christian worldview, or else to the profoundly felt cultural strains and dissatisfactions arising from these new developments. In the language and concepts of the last chapter, religious orders in each of these refounding periods responded to the strains and discontinuities of their era with a "global frame transformation," in which the entire definition of what Catholic virtuoso spirituality entailed was radically changed. The members of these religious communities were engaged in intensely creative ideological work on the cutting edge of social thought, as they constructed with their very lives a spirituality for the new era.[22] The answers which they devised were of greatest interest to the people in the cultural centers of their societies, for it was the educated and the members of the ruling classes who were the primary participants in whatever new social or economic order was being developed.[23] Most of the recruits for the new models, therefore, were drawn from this center—from university students and intellectuals, from the merchant class, and from the nobility.[24]

In the light of the theory that I have sketched here, one might draw a distinction between the *Charism* of religious life in a given era and the *charisms* of individual religious orders. The former term refers to the new ideological frame which religious communities devised for addressing the fundamental cultural discontinuities of their age. It includes their definition of what the basic purpose of religious life in the church actually was, as well as what were the primary activities—prayer styles, fasting, ministry, and the vows—which marked a religious. *Only insofar as its Charism speaks to the basic questions and issues which trouble people in the larger culture, will religious life in a particular period flourish or decay.* If the Charism speaks only to the concerns of one sociocultural group, it will attract recruits primarily from that group.[25]

The "charisms" of individual religious orders refer to the particular practices which each community uses to develop and enflesh its own version of the larger Charism. These would include specific prayers, ministerial institutions, or ascetic practices, as well as whatever "flavor" a group retained because of the ethnic, geographic, or class origins of its members. It is important not to confuse "charism" with "Charism." Members of religious communities that failed to distinguish between the two often attributed an exaggerated importance to some peripheral aspect of their lives—staffing a particular institution, for example, or reciting a specific prayer in a specific way. Not only were such individual practices more vulnerable to the winds of change and fashion, but focusing on them often distracted religious from the more important task of updating and transforming their larger ideological frame when it was needed.[26]

NINETEENTH-CENTURY TEACHING CONGREGATIONS: THE FAILURE OF IDEOLOGICAL ADAPTATION

The Modernist Crisis

As had been the case in previous time periods, the nineteenth and early twentieth centuries witnessed profound social, intellectual, political and technological changes. Such changes resulted in a world that exhibited severe internal stresses and dilemmas— the injustices of industrial and monopoly capitalism, rampant nationalisms that culminated in two world wars, racism, internal and external colonialism, and the like. The prevailing ideologies of the period also posed profound questions for the traditional Catholic worldview. Nineteenth-century liberal democrats initiated the separation of church and state, and stripped both the bishops and the pope himself of the lands they had formerly ruled. The prevailing emphasis on science and reason among nineteenth-century intellectuals "eliminated from experience all that [was] not susceptible to verification and measurement; everything, that is, which belonged traditionally to the dimension of the sacred."[27] Even the Bible was subjected to scientific scrutiny. Marxists labeled religion the opiate of the people; new secular disciplines such as sociology and Freudian psychoanalysis considered religion to be an outdated refuge for the immature and the misfits of society.

Such attacks awoke in church leaders a sense of seige and a "belligerent antimodernism" that was intensely suspicious of new ideas or lifestyles.[28] As early as 1832, Pope Gregory XVI had publicly condemned such basic teachings of liberal democracy as the separation of church and state, freedom of the press and freedom of religion.[29] As the century progressed, the Vatican exerted greater and greater pressure on priests, bishops and theologians not to deviate from the neo-Thomistic scholasticism that had been anointed as the only acceptable basis for theological speculation:

> Seminaries did not encourage research or debate or even much curiosity. Students learned their philosophical and theological lessons mostly by rote, the way law students memorized precedents. Seminary professors seldom pressed their students, nor indeed were they much pressed themselves, to go beyond what the manuals contained.[30]

Unlike previous periods, therefore, the nineteenth- and early twentieth-century church did not respond to its new sociocultural milieu by devising a new spirituality and a theology to address its challenges, but retreated instead to the formulae of the past.[31] As the decades progressed, the disjuncture between the largely static concepts and categories prevalent in Catholic thinking and the preoccupations of mainstream Western culture widened. Without a more congruent set of ideological concepts to express them, the underlying truths of Catholic spirituality—which might have had much to say to an increasingly inequitable and warlike age—were misunderstood and discounted by a largely secularized cultural center.[32]

Models of Religious Life in the Nineteenth Century

In previous refounding periods, it was Catholicism's religious virtuosi who had been the most sensitive to strains such as these and who had devised new types of religious life to address them. *But the nineteenth century refounding of religious orders was based almost entirely on a resuscitation of the seventeenth-century apostolic model.* The basic Charism—the underlying ideological frame—of the two models was the same; only a few peripheral differences, such as government by a central motherhouse as compared to separately independent local convents, distinguished them. Even revitalized mendicant and monastic communities such as the Dominicans or the Benedictines were conformed to the apostolic model, and lost much of their earlier distinctiveness. At the same time, the neo-apostolic communities were forced to adopt some monastic practices that were antithetical to their original spirit.[33] The result was an often poorly-articulated amalgam of ideological elements drawn from previous centuries, which utterly failed to address the roots of the current era's most pressing new issues.[34] The liberal democracy that was the foundation of the new European and North American states found no echo in the prevailing interpretation of religious obedience, which remained supremely indifferent to such concepts as due process or the consent of the governed. The systemic injustices which seemed endemic to capitalism were met by a religious ministry that addressed (albeit heroically) the effects of these injustices rather than their causes, as well as by a vow that interpreted "poverty" as asking permission to use a piece of stationery.[35] The rising spirit of egalitarianism so evident, especially in America, was antithetical to the traditional assumption that members of religious orders were a spiritual and hierarchically-organized elite, superior to ordinary Catholics.

The failure to develop a new and distinct model for religious life affected the nineteenth-century women's congregations even more than it did the men's. *Many nineteenth century women's congregations were originally founded without reference to any specific Charism at all.* In some cases, for example, groups of pious women first organized informally to do a particular ministerial work and only adopted a Franciscan, Dominican, or Vincentian Rule later, when they applied for official status.[36] The work came first, then the "Charism." Many other congregations owed their origins to ethnic divisions in some parent community. In still other instances, a community might be begun by a bishop or priest, who was interested primarily in the services the women would perform. "Priests and bishops seemed to see no difference between the different types of rules provided that the sisters were useful."[37] The founding cleric thus borrowed an already-written constitution for "his" sisters, making only minor adaptations. Langlois argues that even the names of many congregations often reflected prevailing fashion rather than any concrete spirituality.[38] Communities founded in one decade were more likely to be named after spiritual attributes (Wisdom, Providence), whereas groups begun at another time would be named after the saints, or, at still other times, after incidents in the lives of Jesus and Mary.

As a result, the underlying Charism of many nineteenth-century women's congregations was especially ill-defined and vague. Based as it frequently was on incompatible borrowings from earlier centuries, and imposed from the outside, it often was not a central focus in the sisters' daily lives. The *charisms* of the communities were more salient: a particular ethnic flavor, a few unique customs and, above all, a ministerial focus on a specific set of institutions. It is not surprising, therefore, that communities often concentrated more on these peripheral distinctions, rather than on the underlying assumptions of the Charism they had inherited from previous centuries. There was little incentive, or time, for them to do the ideological work that would have articulated a new model of religious life—even if church authorities had allowed such innovation.

The Effects of Charism Misalignment on Recruitment to Religious Orders

Because a resuscitated seventeenth-century apostolic model for religious life did not take into account some of the most central beliefs and values of mainstream nineteenth-century culture, religious communities tended increasingly to recruit members from the peripheries of their societies—from Brittany and southern France rather than from Paris, from rural Ireland, Bavaria, and Quebec, or from immigrant communities in the United States. Subcultures such as these had been less touched by the new philosophies and questions of the nineteenth century, and recruits from these backgrounds were, therefore, less perturbed by the disjunctures between the ethos of religious life and the prevailing beliefs and values of mainstream culture. Furthermore, remaining strongly Catholic was often a way for oppressed peripheral subcultures to assert their identity in the face of oppression by a non-Catholic cultural center. Religious life in Quebec, Poland and Ireland, therefore, was often attractive as a statement of peoplehood.[39] Finally, religious communities—especially *women's* religious communities—offered their members an education and an opportunity to use their talents;

opportunities that were scarce to persons of their gender, class, or ethnicity in the larger society.

As was pointed out in the preceding chapter, it is possible that individual, personal motives can be sufficient to attract recruits to a social movement organization, even when the ideological motives are less compelling.[40] This seems to have been the case for the nineteenth-century religious congregations. One must be careful, however, not to leave the impression that the men and women who entered religious life at this time did so merely for selfish reasons of personal gain or social prestige. The opportunity to develop one's talents to the full and devote them to a challenging, worthwhile and holy project is a personal motive to some extent, but it is not less admirable for being so. Often, it was only by entering a religious order that Catholics—especially female Catholics—of the working or peasant classes could find an outlet for their religious enthusiasm and energy. In addition, the ideological assumptions of religious life were not yet offensive to these groups. Coming as they did from encapsulated Catholic subpopulations, the entrants to nineteenth- and early twentieth-century congregations still believed in the superiority of religious over lay life, in the divine authority of superiors, and in all of the other ideological elements religious life had inherited from the seventeenth century and earlier periods, elements which more acculturated populations would have found objectionable. However, as the middle of the twentieth century approached and Catholicism's formerly marginalized subpopulations became assimilated into the mainstream culture—*a culture whose chief preoccupations and assumptions had never been adequately incorporated into an ideological frame for religious life*—the model's lack of congruence became more and more evident. Beginning in Europe after World War II, country after country saw a drop in religious vocations.

Pius XII responded to this decline as early as 1950, when he called upon communities to adapt or eliminate the outdated practices that were deterring modern youth from considering religious life. Initially, however, the pontiff's urgings met with little concrete response on the part of the rank and file members of religious congregations.[41] Only after the Second Vatican Council did communities actually begin to address the ways in which their

Charism, and their charisms, were out of step with the needs and major issues of the larger society. By this time, however, secular society had had over one hundred years to develop without any significant input from religious life, and most of its basic assumptions had already formed a strong and internally coherent ideological frame of its own. When religious attempted to incorporate some of the beliefs and values of this frame into a new version of religious life, other elements of the "package"—elements far less salutary for the growth or even the continued existence of their communities—were often adopted as well. Commendable progress was made in reworking the idea of vowed poverty to include systemic social change and standing with the oppressed. But the corporate dimensions of obedience and community life were never successfully reconciled with the assumptions of liberal individualism.[42] The inherent ideological weaknesses of the nineteenth-century model for religious life became more evident as communities began to look at it more closely:

> Many religious orders have, to a large extent, lost their distinctiveness....Monks want to know, for instance, who they are in relation to the apostolic tradition. Conversely, members of apostolic religious orders want to know how their spirituality is distinct from that of the monastic tradition.[43]

The ideological efforts of the post-Vatican II period, while intensely creative in many respects, did not fully succeed in constructing a new legitimizing framework for religious life.

As a result, *neither the liberal nor the traditional model of religious life offers an appealing form of religious virtuosity that resonates with the needs and concerns of late twentieth-century Western culture.* The continued movement of formerly encapsulated Catholic subpopulations into the cultural mainstream (the rise of third generation American Catholics to the middle class, for example, or the development of a secular French society in Quebec after the Quiet Revolution) has meant that fewer and fewer young people today find the traditional model of religious life either attractive or meaningful. Traditional religious congregations, therefore, have experienced sharply declining numbers of prospective entrants, compared to those of a generation ago. On the other hand, the members of most "liberal model" congregations have become so thoroughly assimilated into the individualism of mainstream culture that they are often unable to explain to prospective entrants exactly how their model differs from other forms of lay service in the church.[44] The assimilation of religious orders also prevents them from fulfilling their prophetic role: the new *raison d'etre* which post-Vatican II theologians have articulated for them. It is difficult for chapter delegates or congregational leadership to come up with a statement of corporate mission that is in any way challenging or specific, for fear that the rank and file members, who are now thoroughly committed to their own (often very worthwhile) individual ministries, will refuse to follow it.[45] As Joan Chittister has stated, religious congregations "have done a great deal to foster the prophetic individuals in their midst, [but] they have done very little to function as prophetic groups."[46] In other words, religious communities have not addressed the basic strains and discontinuities of their society in a corporate or collective way. And, unless they do, they will not survive.

CONCLUSIONS

It is not enough that individual sisters, priests or brothers within religious communities may be living prophetic lives of heroic sanctity and service. Every lay person is called to do the same—and many are heeding this call. Such individualized religious virtuosity, however, except in very exceptional cases, cannot articulate a definitive answer to the prevailing strains and cultural discontinuities of an entire age. A corporate group, drawn together and organized around a specific, *lived* virtuoso spirituality, can have a far larger impact than its members could as individuals.

But what should the focus of this new model be? How should a religious community set about choosing a new self-definition, a goal for its refounding journey? The remaining chapters in this section will consider the choices such a community must make. I do not presume to recommend what the outcome of each choice should be. But I do believe that every community must find its own answer, *as a community and not as separate individuals*, to four basic questions: *where* to go, *who* will make the journey, *how* to get there, and what *resources* they will need along the way.

6

Decision #1:
Where Do We Want To Go?

If there is to be a religious life within the Catholic Church in the twenty-first century, then its basic Charism—the fundamental definition of what it is and why it exists—must resonate with the deepest anguish, discontinuity, or strain of at least one twenty-first century culture. This may be middle-class European-American culture, or it may be that of some other North American group: Chicanos, Asian-Americans, or African-Americans; the elderly, the working class, or the inner city poor; artists, migrant farm workers, or battered women. Cultures in Asia, Africa and Latin America will also need unique models of religious virtuosity to meet their own internal strains. These are likely to be very different from those of Western Europe or the United States.

In some parts of the world, the traditional seventeenth/nineteenth century model of religious life may still attract new members. In eastern Africa, for example, the number of sisters has increased from under 3,000 to over 10,000 during the past three decades, matching the almost fivefold increase in the Catholic population there. Almost one-third of the 184 novices entering the Christian Brothers in 1992 were from Africa. There were only sixty-six U.S. Jesuit novices in 1992; there were 340 in Indonesia that same year. Some analysts predict that India will soon produce more Jesuits than any other country.[1] Moreover, the number of novices reported for religious congregations in Europe and North America have often been inflated by including their Third World entrants: an Italian newspaper recently reported that

"Only Filipino Nuns Are Left in Italy's Convents." Of 1,026 current novices in Italy, the paper stated, 643 are from abroad.[2]

There have been several reactions to these figures. The leaders of some religious communities believe that their Third World members are the vehicle which God has chosen to carry their spirit and mission into the future—and, in the process, to bring about a salutary de-Europeanization of religious life. Church officials see Asian and African religious as uninfected by the materialism, feminism, and sexual freedom that has seduced the European and American young. "Pornography has become a mass phenomenon and has extended its enormous seductive power over an incredible number of people," declared one Italian bishop. "It has become almost impossible to give a sound moral education to the young, who are increasingly unable to exercise self-control and unprepared to make a mature and responsible gift of their lives."[3] For these observers, it is pointless to expect that significant numbers of middle-class Western European or American young people will ever choose religious life again. In the future, they feel, Asian and African members will be the salvation of religious communities.

But other observers are not quite as sanguine. Filipino bishops have criticized the recruiting tactics of various European orders, charging that they are trying to reverse their membership declines by enticing destitute Third World women to enter them. Others wonder whether Christian religious virtuosi in non-Western cultures might be better served by communities that were not so thoroughly based on European models.

Most importantly for our argument here, *to write off middle-class Euro-American culture as unable to produce a form of religious life that will address its own strains and discontinuities—as previous models had addressed the strains of their respective centuries—is to defect from our responsibility as religious to take part in the formation of one of the most influential "center" cultures of the world.* Nineteenth- and twentieth-century liberal culture developed largely without input from Catholic religious orders. This lack of input is perhaps one reason for some of the destructive tendencies which our society has exhibited during the last century. It is certainly the reason why so many of our culture's spiritual seekers have looked for the answers to their personal quests in Zen Buddhism, crystals or Christian fundamentalism, rather than in Roman Catholic religious life.

We cannot afford to let this happen with twenty-first century culture. We need to found, or refound, religious communities that will be a formative influence in American and European society, which means that we need to develop a new model of religious life that will significantly touch thousands—or tens of thousands—of both the current and the next generation of Europeans and Euro-Americans. If, in the process, we also manage to create a religious community that attracts African-Americans or Latinos, or an international one with a strong Asian or African contingent, so much the better. The pros and cons of intercultural membership will be discussed in chapter 7. Every social class, every subculture of our society and every culture of the world should have access to a liberating and psychologically healthy virtuoso spirituality that resonates with the primary concerns and preoccupations of its members. This is true of migrant Latino farmworkers and seamstresses in Haitian garment factories. It is also true of middle-class American college students and office workers. Any group whose spiritual thirst is unaddressed by Catholicism will seek to satisfy it elsewhere. And Catholic Christianity will be the poorer if they do. The thirst is there. What kinds of religious virtuosity—what kinds of religious communities—will quench it?

TACTICS FOR DISCOVERING A NEW
FOCUS FOR RELIGIOUS LIFE

How shall we discover a new goal, a new meaning for religious life? If the theoretical and historical analysis of chapter 5 is correct, religious communities will flourish most whenever they address the deepest strains of their society. How do we determine what these strains are?

One unproductive method of inquiry would be to look at the defects of the familiar models—whether of the "fossilized" apostolic/monastic religious life of pre-Vatican II years or the "amorphous and disintegrating" liberal model that replaced it—and to try to construct a new version by reacting to the mistakes of the old:

> It would be easy to think about a future model of religious life as the reverse image of the present liberal model, but would it be

worthwhile? We could think, for example, that if the liberal model
is pluralistic, then a newer model would be more unified; if the
present model of religious life is still quite patriarchal, then a
future model must be more feminist. Maybe and maybe not....The
future is always more original than our thinking of it.[4]

In a sense, the liberal model of religious life and the traditional or
neo-traditional versions are mirror images of each other: the one
emphasizing and celebrating what the other has denigrated or
discarded. *But both are focused on the same set of issues, whether to
affirm or condemn.* The basic cultural questions of the twenty-first
century may be entirely different. The burning issues of previous
decades may have become completely irrelevant, while the new
"deepest anguish" may not be adequately addressed by *either*
model. If this is so, then neither liberal nor traditional religious
communities will attract a sufficient number of members to serve
as the model for refounding religious life.

Another possibly deceptive exercise is to look at specific current problems that need fixing. There are any number of these
problems, and several extremely competent social analyses are
available to outline them for religious communities.[5] But if we
assume that the goal of religious life in the twenty-first century
will be to work on one of these problems, we are making the subconscious assumption that the *underlying meaning* of twenty-first
century religious life will be the same as it was in the ministerial-
ly-focused seventeenth- and nineteenth-century versions.[6] This
may not be the case. The presence of needy groups or economic
inequities may be merely a symptom of a deeper and more basic
strain. Addressing a particular symptom may be a worthy goal for
associations such as Oxfam, Amnesty International, or Bread for
the World. Religious virtuosi, however, need a deeper and more
basic focus.[7]

How then, does a religious community discover what the
"deepest anguish" of our age is? To start, they should look at the
religious groups—both within and outside of Catholicism—that
are experiencing sustained and successful growth. This should
be done even (especially!) if they find the philosophy or theology of the growing group to be antithetical to their own. It is crucial that religious communities not be so blinded by the ideology

of a successful virtuoso organization that they refuse to utilize the ideologically-neutral recruitment, public relations, or mobilization tactics that have contributed to the former group's success. The Congress for Racial Equality, the Right to Life Movement, and the anti-Vietnam War protesters have all engaged in sit-ins to achieve their goals, even though they may have profoundly disagreed with each other on almost every other issue. Just as a successful mobilization tactic invented by the Civil Rights Movement was later adopted by other, completely different struggles, so the established religious communities may be able to learn useful practices from even the most ideologically antithetical groups.

On a more threatening level, however, we may discover that certain elements of a new group's ideology, while deeply disturbing or even contrary to our own beliefs and values, are nevertheless more congruent with contemporary preoccupations than our own version is. Or we may find praiseworthy ideological elements "packaged" together with beliefs or practices that are extremely objectionable to us. In this case, the challenge will be to create a new ideological frame for religious life that includes the best elements of both the old and the new, which may mean deemphasizing elements of our own ideological frames that we still hold dear. This is, admittedly, quite difficult. On the other hand, nothing will be accomplished by avoiding the issue or condemning the growing groups without examining them.

A second way to discover the deepest anguish of a society would be to search its TV dramas, sitcoms and talk shows, its scholarly studies, newspapers and magazines, its novels, movies and popular music, for recurring themes or issues. Is there some basic hunger that keeps surfacing over and over again? What are the topics of the most popular nonfiction books? Of the most well-attended weekend seminars? These market-driven cultural artifacts may show us what the seekers of our society—religious and quasi-religious—are looking for. Are they searching for more and better ways to reduce social inequality? Or for something else?

A Focus for Twenty-First Century Religious Life

I would like to suggest that the most keenly-felt cultural strain of our post-modern, Western society is not education, health care, or even the presence of some needy group—as pressing as these other issues may be. Rather, it is *a desire for community and spiritual depth*. This conclusion has been reached by a large number of social critics, who increasingly express reservations about the cultural individualism that leaves each American "suspended in glorious, but terrifying, isolation."[8] Such writers worry that "there is no longer a truly 'local' community, a place where people carry on all or most of their activities together."[9] This lack is most acutely felt among the youngest age cohort of adults, but Americans of all ages experience it. As TV producer Norman Lear noted:

> To put our problem another way, and in one word, we are lonely. Lonely for feelings of connection. Lonely for institutions that believe we matter and will reach out to help us.[10]

The hunger that Lear was describing surfaces in a variety of ways. According to a review essay in one sociology journal, a plethora of books has been published on the subject of "community" within the past few years, and "citation indexes show an astronomical increase in references to the term in the popular press since 1990."[11] A communitarian quarterly, *Responsive Community*, is now in its third year. Popular new "How To" manuals describe how to create communities, and entire organizations have been established to promote them.[12] Articles in newspapers and magazines bewail the loss of community and discuss how to recapture it.[13] Movies, books, and TV shows depict modern American life as isolating, atomized and sterile, lacking in even the most basic connections between individuals. Architects and builders advertise "planned communities" for young singles and the elderly, who are presumably the most disconnected members of our society. Cities schedule an increasing number of communal functions—St. Patrick's Day parades and Oktoberfests, food festivals and mini-marathons—to draw their populations together. Some social analysts even feel that a significant reason for the rising number of massive sports events is that they create quasi-communities among their fans.[14]

Since we no longer inhabit the kinds of long-lasting communities that nourish "a sense of depth over time," our culture's founding myths are attenuated and diminished.[15] One woman pastor in New England feels that it is this desire for community and spiritual depth that draws people back to her church:

> I think people are lonely. I think people's lives feel empty and dead for a lot of people, no matter how much money they have. I mean we haven't developed a middle class theology to address our emptiness...and we are not inspired. I think there is just this pervasive emptiness...[Once people return to church] it's empowering, a real deep sense of coming home again...of something that was missing and then reaching some real deep places that people weren't even aware of.[16]

Many psychological problems stem, DiIanni writes, "from meaninglessness, the sense that life in a consumer society is hollow, that all is banal and trivial."[17] Another author notes that "the idea of God no longer governs the way we organize our lives." The resulting emptiness, trend watchers inform us, drives many persons to seek spiritual answers on their own.

The emergence of spirituality is "a grass-roots movement."[18] Books with spiritual themes are becoming increasingly popular.[19] *Newsweek* devoted the cover article of its November 28, 1994, issue to the "Search for the Sacred." Prayer is becoming more overtly popular.[20] Films and even rock music albums are much more likely to emphasize spiritual themes than they were in previous decades.[21] Most of these spiritual images, however, are quite eclectic; few are anchored in traditional Catholic (or even Christian) spirituality. And, as Baby Boomer seekers are discovering, engaging in their individualistic mystical quests involves a major drawback: the Boomers lack the communal structures to pass on to their children what they have learned.[22]

As a result, there are abundant indications that those now entering virtuoso religious groups—whether these groups be Catholic religious communities, Zen ashrams, or fundamentalist sects—do so because they seek community and prayer. One writer has noted a shift to spiritual disciplines such as weekend retreats and prayer hours among the Southern Baptists. There has been a shift in focus from social justice concerns to spirituality among United Methodists, who have even attempted to develop a Methodist form of monasticism.[23] Eastern Orthodoxy is gaining converts in the U.S. because it is perceived as "more rooted in mystery and paradox."[24] Over 150 Protestant congregations have converted en masse to Orthodoxy. Observers believe that the same hunger is behind the movement of Latinos into evangelical and Pentecostal sects—a development which many consider to be far more significant and widespread even than the growth of base ecclesial communities.[25] A best-selling French book, *The Revenge of God*, chronicles the resurgence of Islam, Christianity, and Judaism as a direct reaction to "a deep malaise in society" that can no longer be interpreted in the terms of Enlightenment secularism.[26] "The prominent reality which faces us now is the growing hunger for spiritual nourishment among lay Christians."[27]

The many new religious communities which are forming in Catholicism (and ecumenically) also illustrate this hunger for spirituality and prayer. Of the twenty-five such communities I have visited, all have contemplation and prayer as their primary focus. Any ministerial activities which these groups perform are on a part-time basis only. There are very few exceptions to this trend—primarily the few new communities founded by bishops rather than arising from the grassroots.

Membership figures for established religious orders reflect a similar search. Nygren and Ukeritis report that contemplative communities have the highest percentage of new members (11.7%), while apostolic religious have the lowest (5.6%).[28] Several recent studies find that those currently seeking to enter religious life "express their purpose not so much in terms of service but in terms of community; that is, they seek to fulfill personal needs of belonging to a meaningful group that shares similar values, especially those of Christian living. Unlike the outward focus of earlier eras, today's recruits seem more focused upon personal spiritual development."[29] Even the Associate Programs recently established by so many congregations are valued by their participants primarily because of the opportunities they provide for spiritual sharing and community, and *not* as a means for participating in the orders' apostolates.[30]

Related to the communities' focus on spirituality is engaging in certain types of evangelization. Several new religious groups in the United States have this as their secondary raison d'être (after contemplation and prayer). The Little Brothers of St. Francis spend several afternoons each week in "street evangelization"—praying with and befriending the homeless of Boston. The Companions of Christ the Lamb, the Verbum Dei Community, the Handmaids of the Sacred Heart of Jesus, Mary, and Joseph, and the Franciscan Sisters of St. Clare, among others, hold workshops and retreats to teach Christian contemplative prayer forms. Still other groups engage in youth evangelization and parish missions. One new monastic community attempts to provide the most beautiful and prayerful liturgies possible for urban office workers. Established congregations in this country are also adopting ministries of prayer evangelization, as the increasing number of retreat centers in motherhouses indicates.

The emphasis on community, evangelization, and spirituality is also evident in the new European religious congregations, all of which share an explicit spiritual emphasis as well as an intense community life.[31] Of the thirty-four new French communities listed in one 1989 directory, at least twenty gave prayer and contemplation as their primary focus. Only three were primarily involved in a specific apostolic work.[32] It is ironic, several writers observe, that "many of the white, middle-class members of religious communities, especially women religious, have rejected and moved out of older forms of community life. At the same time, however, newer members, especially those from minority groups, come looking for the very forms of local community life that current members reject."[33]

POSSIBLE OBJECTIONS

Objection #1: What About Ministry?

But isn't this an extremely selfish focus? How can anyone in good conscience ignore the cries of the poor, the injustices of world capitalist imperialism, the arms race, crack babies, and the homeless in order to pursue his/her own spiritual gratification through membership in an exclusive clique of the "saved"?

Such a criticism is indeed valid for some of the new virtuoso groups—both inside and outside Catholicism. Many do exhibit a disturbing indifference to the injustices of our society or, worse still, a chauvinistic glorification of American culture that refuses to admit any injustice exists at all. But in focusing exclusively on spirituality, evangelization, and communal belonging, these groups have reacted to what they perceive as an excessively secular focus on the part of apostolic Catholic orders (or, in the case of fundamentalist Protestant sects, to the "excessive" emphasis on the social gospel by the mainline denominations). Such a lopsided emphasis on mission over the spiritual life, they feel, has made liberal religious orders and mainline Protestant churches indistinguishable from social work agencies.[34] The liberals retort that the new groups, in their self-centered preoccupation with their own spirituality, are ignoring the basic Christian commandment to stand with and care for the poor. Each of these two camps appears more attuned to the deficiencies of the other's mode of religiosity than they are to their own. There seems to be a lack, on both sides, of a "unifying perspective" that links personal spiritual growth to social justice.[35]

Many of the new religious groups, however, do minister to the poor and downtrodden, and do so with an enthusiasm that puts more established congregations to shame. The Community of San Egidio, now twenty-five years old and some 15,000 members strong, *requires* each of its members to be engaged in some direct work for the poor—over and above whatever secular occupation they may have. "They seem to know every gypsy and beggar in Rome, the truly needy and the sham. They run a dining hall that provides a sit-down meal to 1200 people four days a week—sit-down rather than a bagged meal in order to preserve the dignity of the poor."[36] Other groups live with the poor, as the poor live, in a ministry of presence.[37] For all of these new communities, however, their service flows from their spiritual life, which remains primary. The San Egidio Community may engage in an impressive number of ministerial activities several times a week, but they meet *daily* for prayer and scripture-sharing.

The members of the new groups might therefore respond that the most basic social defect of our time, the fundamental discontinuity which religious life is called to address, is not simply that poor people, drug addicts or the homeless exist, *but rather that the rest of us feel so little obligation to help them.* The lack of community or spiritual groundedness and the rampant individualism of late twentieth-century liberal culture have caused us to disconnect

from the needs of those around us. The most successful classes
in our society are "seceding" from the rest—withdrawing into
exclusive suburbs and private schools, sheltering their income
from taxes, and donating only to the "charities" (art museums,
for example, or the Ivy League schools) that they themselves
use.[38] Even among established religious orders, only a bare
majority of the members express a commitment actually to work
with the poor, whatever their official mission statements may
proclaim.[39]

Many of the new religious communities have therefore concentrated on witnessing to the spirituality and communal bond-
ing our culture so sorely lacks, both by their own lives of prayer
and by their active evangelization efforts. They appear to assume
that, once these needs are met and once our own hearts are converted to fellowship and prayer, our society's callousness toward
the poor will resolve itself.[40] Still, it cannot be denied that this
requires a leap of faith. The evangelization which most of the
new groups engage in with their largely middle-class clientele
involves primarily teaching them how to pray—*not* awakening
their hearts to the plight of the oppressed. The unifying perspective that would link our culture's intense communal and spiritual
longings with an outward orientation toward the poor has yet to
be articulated. Until and unless it is, the new groups will be in
danger of descending to a narcissistic self preoccupation that
will, in time, breed its own downfall.

Just because the new and growing religious communities are
more congruent with the hungers of the larger society, therefore,
does *not* mean they are perfect. *All* models of religious life—like
all other human endeavors—have blind spots and weaknesses. It
is here that a fruitful collaboration between the new and the
established communities would be most desirable. By working
together, both groups could begin to create a successful integration of the apostolic charism with the new spiritual/communi-
tarian focus. This could result in several different styles of
religious life. One group might engage in a *communal* apostolic
ministry (*not* a collection of individual ministries), based on
some carefully articulated and frequently reinforced spiritual
reasoning. As an example of this, the grounding spiritual belief
of Mother Teresa's Missionaries of Charity is that each and every

poor person they serve is Christ himself. This belief is continually reiterated in Mother Teresa's own conferences and writings for her sisters, and is repeated and enacted by the members themselves in their daily apostolate. Their spiritual focus outlines the distinction—both for the sisters themselves and for outside observers—between their ministry and social work. A second path might be to concentrate on a purely spiritual and communitarian focus while living with the poor in a ministry of presence—but not specifically engaging in any particular social service to them. Both of these paths are currently being explored by new communities that appear to be growing. Other, even more successful, ways of integrating a spiritual/communitarian focus with an apostolic one—of addressing both our culture's spiritual hunger *and* its systemic inequities—might be devised.

Objection #2: Overemphasizing Community Is DANGEROUS!

Another serious objection is that communal groups have the nasty habit of adopting deindividualizing practices that are positively harmful to their members' psychic health. In addition to lurid media accounts of Jonestown, MOVE, or Waco, most religious can cite incidents from their own early years in stultifying and soul-destroying "communities"—stories of God-given talents quashed and denied, of life-giving friendships poisoned and thwarted, of self-esteem wrecked and hopes ruined. At least since the Sister Formation Movement of the 1950's, religious have struggled to redress this inbalance by affirming and celebrating the worth of the individual and each member's personal responsibility for his/her own spiritual development. These religious have an excruciatingly clear vision of the dangers of reestablishing "community" as a primary goal for religious life.

Younger generations, however, may have a keener sensitivity to the defects of the liberal, individualistic model than they do to the defects of a traditional, communal version which they do not even remember. They may argue that today's liberal religious are overly professionalized, with little real commitment to the mission and ministry of their congregation.[41] With youthful idealism, they may be more attracted to the image of a team enthusiastically cooperating in the quest of a common goal:

The image that comes to mind is that of a spiritual factory, or perhaps a spiritual project of enormous importance conducted by teams of sacred technicians working together with a feverish energy. With this image in mind, the monastery is a sort of special laboratory, a Los Alamos of spiritual technology, capable of attracting the best and the brightest of personal spiritual practitioners in any society. No wonder that the camaraderie that is established is so intimate and intense.[42]

Young seekers may also question whether any religious group can make a real impact on the world unless its members permit the group to monitor their personal fidelity to the values and goals they have chosen as essential.[43]

In their enthusiasm for community, of course, the new groups may unwisely dismiss or discount the very real psychic and physical harm which communal demands can inflict upon individual members, and the ways in which communal decision-making can detract from an individual's personal responsibility for his/her own growth. Such naivete is a real danger. Many idealistic experiments have already self-destructed in a welter of power abuses, recriminations and broken dreams. Others have hardened into extremely unhealthy quasi-cults, betraying both their original vision and the faith of their members. It is for this very reason that the input of established religious congregations is so necessary for new communities. The members of the older groups have had a century and a half of experience to teach them which practices work to build community and which are destructive and dangerous. Without their input, the new groups are likely to repeat disastrous mistakes, mistakes which, at best, may seriously distort their original vision, and which, at worst, may prove fatal. But the new groups have much to offer established communities as well, especially with their youthful enthusiasm.

A PASSIONATE, COMMUNAL RESPONSE

It may well be that the preceding analysis will turn out to be wrong. The fundamental organizing principle of the next model of religious life may not be spirituality and evangelization, but rather something as yet unforeseen. In addition, many religious virtuosi may prefer to address social strains individually rather than in a collective group. If our society's basic hunger is for spirituality, this *could* be met by retreating to isolated hermitages or building up a private library of "New Age" books. If the deepest anguish is homelessness or substance abuse, this could be addressed by the efforts of dedicated individuals (Mother Hale's work with crack babies in Harlem comes to mind here). Individualistic responses to societal strains are the norm in American society. As they have become acculturated, American religious communities reflect this tendency.

Currently, most religious congregations have evolved into associations composed either of individuals or of small (two or three-member) groups, each addressing somewhat different goals in a variety of ways. Many communities have become "lifestyle enclaves," collections of people who share only the one or two features of their private lives that they have decided to share. "The group is a place where one pursues a private lifestyle, not a shared life."[44] Even the spiritualities of the congregations have become individualized, as some members discover that the charismatic renewal best meets their personal needs while others prefer centering prayer or creation spirituality.[45] "Patterns of practice—such as ritual, aesthetic, and ethical ways of living together—which define the community as a way of life, are absent."[46]

There is nothing wrong with pursuing one's personal spiritual quest, or with responding to a ministerial call that one alone can hear. Such spiritual self-determination is a necessary counterweight to the deindividualizing conformity so often imposed by the previous model of religious life, which never truly came to grips with the personal freedom valued by nineteenth- and twentieth-century liberal culture. In many times and places, religious virtuosity has been lived individually rather than in groups.[47] But, if one of the basic hungers in our present culture is for community and connectedness, then it is probable that some new collective dimension will have to be invented for religious life to replace the communal practices discarded after Vatican II. A congregation without a clearly-articulated, visible, and *collective* goal will not survive as a group, although its members may continue to perform valuable services as individuals.[48]

Communities must resist a definition of their mission that is broad enough to please the great majority of the members but lacks the specificity to provide a clear identity for the community....If the membership lacks this clear understanding of the mission and identity of the community, then the individuals cannot relate their particular contributions in ministry, lifestyle and spirituality to some larger goal. *This disjuncture between individual experience and the identity and mission of the whole institute leads to a loss of a sense of significance for the individual members and makes it difficult to attract new members, who need to know clearly what they are being asked to join.*[49]

And the collective goal will have to be a demanding one. Whether it is responding to the love of God in one's own life, witnessing the Good News to others or meeting the needs of the poor, the goal must engage all the members collectively, personally and *passionately*. One of the most striking characteristics I observed during my interviews with the founders and members of new religious orders is their ability to articulate specifically what makes their community unique, and their enthusiastic willingness to expound on their charism at great length. In contrast, it is precisely this compelling sense of communal mission that liberal religious orders have found so hard to develop. The liberal model of religious life has downplayed the importance of an integrated vision. Stressing a common purpose is seen as limiting individual freedom, which is, after all, the primary value of liberal Western culture.[50] As a result of this mindset, the community leaders studied by Nygren and Ukeritis were unable to articulate a specific, collective mission for their congregations, or even to prioritize what the components of such a mission might be.[51] And, without such a "compelling sense of mission," a congregation "can neither appeal to nor develop the tremendous sense of generosity" of its own members or potential entrants.[52] "By their own admission, members of religious orders see indifference and a lack of passion to be a major threat to themselves as persons and to the broader scheme of religious life in relation to other social systems in the society."[53]

Of course, if some of the members of a community do develop a common vision to which they can become passionately committed—so passionately committed that they are willing to devote their entire lives to it—further difficulties will develop. Most of the other members will not share this vision. *Developing a vision of sufficient strength and specificity to refound a community will inevitably split a congregation.* "Every serious effort at congregational renewal arrives at the point beyond which one cannot go without accepting the possibility, indeed the likelihood, of a divided community. This is the Rubicon of communal renewal."[54] The members and the leadership of most religious congregations instinctively shrink from doing anything that would divide them in this manner. Most have strong ties of affection and affiliation with each other, which militate against any subgroup embarking on a new or challenging course that might leave the others behind.[55] Rather than alienate the members who wish to open prayer ashrams in the inner city, engage in full-time evangelization on college campuses, or reclaim strip-mined land in an organic forestry/creation spirituality project, the community devises a "mission statement" that is vague enough to encompass all of these visions. And thus it becomes progressively less clear what the congregation stands for or why it exists at all.

CONCLUSION: MAKING THE CHOICE

In the times when it was most alive, religious life was a profoundly creative and daring effort to enact and enflesh the underlying spiritual dimension of the gospel in a new cultural milieu. It was a joyous and exciting quest of such sweep and power that it attracted the best and the brightest of a society into its ranks. In defining to their culture *what that culture was in its deepest essence*, religious communities sparked a global frame transformation that truly inculturated the church in the new world order, while at the same time sacralizing the world order with its presence. To work for a new refounding period in the twenty-first century means to work to effect precisely this sort of transformation again.

How to begin? Religious communities must first choose where they wish to go *as a group*. The destination has to be specific enough to distinguish the community both from other communities and from non-vowed lay life. Vague mission statements that their members "live the gospel of Jesus Christ by proclaiming God's love among all people and serving them generously," or "commit [themselves] to improving the conditions of those who suffer from injustice, oppression and deprivation of dignity," or "share in Jesus' redemptive mission to proclaim the Good News of God's universal love and to recreate the face of the earth,"[56] are not sufficient. *All Christians are called by their baptism to do these things.* What specific lifestyle, spiritual focus or ministry—of the many worthwhile and beautiful lifestyles, spiritual foci and ministries—will a community choose as its distinctive purpose?

Since it is inevitable that not all of the current members of a religious congregation will agree on a single destination, the subgroups that do wish to commit themselves to a specific goal, lifestyle or focus may need to be partially separated from the rest of the community—incubated, in fact—while they develop their vision. Some communities are already doing this. DiIanni reports that the Marist provinces in France and Italy (as well as the Dutch Blessed Sacrament Fathers) have each established separate houses for young entrants. Many of these men come to religious life from the Focolare, the charismatic renewal, or the Neocatechumenate Movement, and their spiritualities "give some of the 1960's-style French Marists the heebie-jeebies."[57] Rather than expecting the new members to adapt their spiritual outlook to that of the older majority, they are being allowed to develop their own version of the community's charism. Because of the interaction between the *intimiste* spirituality of the young and the post-Vatican II spirituality of the old, "the seminarians have been reflecting on the meaning of their Marist vocation with an intensity I have not seen elsewhere."[58] If a subgroup within a community feels passionately about a new version of the order's traditional charism, if they wish to articulate and enact it in a new and intense lifestyle, can the rest of the community trust and support them?

Another promising development is the willingness of several federations of established communities—the Benedictine, Franciscan and Carmelite federations most particularly—to support and mentor new groups.[59] Sociologists who have studied organizations have noted a "liability of newness."[60] A new business venture, a new social club, a new private school, or a new church is most vulnerable to failure during the first year of its existence. It has not yet carved out a niche for itself or a market for its product; there are a multitude of key decisions to be made and no precedents to guide their making; and there may even be hostile competitors deliberately creating obstacles for it. Similarly, most of the new, experimental religious communities are small and in a precarious position, with enthusiastic but inexperienced young members, sparse finances, and often skeptical diocesan supervisors. Communication links with the federations of established orders can help the new groups avoid many mistakes. Some federations, however, have been less hospitable than others to new groups. Several founders I interviewed were told to "find the support of a bishop and grow and then come back to us and we'll see about admitting you." Isolated from the input of established orders, the new groups often flounder and die.

Whether the experimental communities are composed of a subgroup from an established congregation or a collection of idealistic twenty-year-olds with a vision, they are the fragile seeds of the future of religious life. Many of these attempts will self-destruct, and the members will need to be picked up, cherished, and encouraged to try again. Somewhere, somehow, one of these attempts will articulate the new goal, the new destination, for religious life.

There are other choices to make, however, in addition to where to go. The second pressing issue is who will take part in the journey. Those who are willing to experiment with some new and intense focus for religious life, as well as many of the new recruits who may be attracted to join them, may desire several different levels of involvement. Some may choose to commit themselves for life while others stay only for a few years; some may tithe a number of hours a week while others devote all of their time to the effort. Moreover, if a group's goal is sufficiently specific and engaging to serve as a refounding base, it will appeal primarily to those subcultures whose deepest preoccupations it addresses. This may mean that a particular model will attract most of its members from a single social class or a single ethnicity. The next chapter will discuss some of the implications of various types and degrees of membership for refounding a religious community.

A CHECKLIST FOR THE JOURNEY

- Why do we wish to exist as a community?
  - What purpose/goal energizes and enthuses us?
  - What purpose/goal energizes others in our congregation?
  - How many different energizing goals are there?

- If we had to explain to a young person how being a member of our community differs from being a member of any other religious congregation, what would we say?

- Is it important that our community continue to exist in the future? Why?

7

Decision #2:
Who's Going?

Most of the writers and theologians who have attempted to describe the religious life of the future have made three assumptions about its membership: 1) that communities will be far smaller, but that they will somehow act as a "leaven" in society; 2) that communities will be more "inclusive," open to persons of the opposite sex, married couples, or even non-Catholics; and 3) that communities will be culturally diverse instead of being over 95% Euro-American as they are now.[1] The leaders of many congregations appear to share these assumptions: many are preparing for a future membership of drastically reduced size, and over two-thirds of them are also "adapting their definition of membership to include full or partial membership by the laity."[2] Most men and women religious orders appear to agree with these views. For example, only 16% of the sisters, brothers and religious order priests surveyed by Nygren and Ukeritis believed that inclusiveness was undesirable.[3]

As this chapter will attempt to show, however, the reality is somewhat more complicated. It is highly unlikely that a small group of religious, no matter how vibrant and dedicated, can act as a leaven in society, *unless* certain specific preconditions are met. Inclusivity, if improperly defined, can blur the boundaries of a religious congregation to such an extent that it ceases to exist in any meaningful form. And recent social commentators have wondered whether mono-ethnic schools, businesses and churches might sometimes be preferable to culturally diverse ones. It is possible—and perhaps desirable—for a religious community to be a leaven, to be inclusive and to be culturally diverse, but determining whether and how to achieve these goals requires both preparation and forethought.

RELIGIOUS COMMUNITIES AS LEAVEN IN SOCIETY

If religious are to be the virtuosi whose lives articulate a spiritual response to our culture's most basic strains and discontinuities, then there will have to be a fairly large number of them. A small group is simply not visible enough to make the kind of societal impact that would need to be made, nor does such a group usually have access to the funds that would enable it to make up for its lack of numerical strength by purchasing media exposure or establishing highly visible institutions. It is true that sometimes a single virtuoso—a Michelangelo, a Kant, or a Francis of Assisi—can, by virtue of their sheer genius, have a transforming impact on their culture, *but the very existence of these men[4] was contingent on the background milieu provided by a large population of lesser virtuosi.* Renaissance Florence, for example, had dozens of painters' and sculptors' studios, each employing scores of master artisans and their apprentices, at the time Michelangelo studied there. Venice, Rome and Milan were similarly rich in opportunities. Otherwise, the sculptor of the David and the Pietà might have remained a quarryman all his life. In a similar manner, there may be a Catholic teenager somewhere in the U.S. today with the *potential* for writing mystical lyric poetry that definitively voices Americans' spiritual hungers—or for catalyzing a shelter network that links suburbanites and inner city drug addicts together in love and mutual help (and cures them of their addictions to crack and consumerism in the process). But, if religious communities are too small, this teenager may never learn of their existence. Without the support of a like-minded community to encourage and channel her gifts, she may end up a bored reader of romantic paperback novels or a burned-out social worker in an underfunded municipal agency. Such eventualities are especially likely if the potential virtuoso is a young woman, since women virtuosi—artistic, intellectual and literary as well as spiritual—often lack the supportive networks to nurture and promote their gifts.

Many writers today maintain that communities should not be preoccupied with "mere numbers" as an indication of their success or failure: that it is possible for even a very small group to transform the larger society. This has rarely, if ever, been true, and it certainly is not true today. In the religiously pluralistic environment of the United States, there are many models for spiritual seekers to choose from. Holiness and the God-quest will be defined by the choice of the majority—who are just as likely to pick membership in fundamentalist sects or the use of crystals as they are to consider Catholic religious life. If American religious virtuosity becomes identified with one of these other models, then friars, monks and sisters may occasionally turn up in silly photocopying and computer ads or in movies like "Sister Act," but they will be seen as comic figures scarcely to be emulated.

Other writers criticize the preoccupation with numbers as resulting from suspect motivations, such as the necessity to staff existing institutions or the desire for increased congregational prestige. But the desire to grow may also spring from joy and enthusiastic commitment to one's way of life—a happiness that one wants others to share. In any event, religious who wish to be a leaven in society—to enflesh in their lives a solution to its most basic hungers—*cannot* resign themselves to a diminishing membership.

Conversely, if religious communities truly become a leaven, large numbers of people will desire to join them. Joan Chittister notes that religious communities in the nineteenth-century United States typically began with only three or four individuals.[5] This is true, but *they did not stay at that level very long*. The first recruits usually joined the infant congregation within a few months of its founding (or were actually waiting for the foundress when she arrived from Europe), and most groups could expect a steady inflow of five or ten new entrants per year after that. Any religious congregation, new or refounded, that successfully provides an answer to some basic societal strain can expect a similar growth pattern today. Yeast *grows* in bread, or else it is dead and useless.

Implications for Today's Religious Communities

To truly be a leaven in society, therefore, religious must be numerous enough to affect, significantly, some major sector of it.

A numerically large membership can be achieved in several different ways. There may be a large number of small communities (under 50 members each)—who may or may not network with each other. A threshhold level for influence would be at least twenty such groups in every diocese with 500,000 Catholics (approximately the size of the dioceses of Baltimore, Miami, Milwaukee, New Orleans, or Oakland).[6] Some of these new, small communities might be descended from the experimental subgroups of present day religious congregations that were described at the end of the last chapter. Others could be entirely new communities. Currently, however, very few established congregations have spun off any experimental refounding communities at all. Also, while there are some new, small religious communities being founded in the U.S. today (a total of approximately 100 nationwide), there have not been nearly enough to reach this threshhold level. Most dioceses do not have a single new religious community within their boundaries. As it currently stands, therefore, it does not seem likely that a sufficient number of small communities—new or refounded—will develop to serve as a leaven in twenty-first century American society.

Alternatively, there may be a few communities that grow quite large. Using the same proportions as the preceding paragraph, this would imply one community of 1,000 members (or two communities of 500 members each) in the dioceses mentioned above. Currently, of course, some of these dioceses *do* have 1,000 or more religious within their bounds. But most of these men and women are over the age of seventy. By the year 2010—little more than a decade away—few of them will remain active. And there is no evidence as yet of any new or refounded religious congregation growing to a sufficient size to replace them. The second alternative, therefore, also seems unlikely.

A third alternative is for religious communities to have a small core of full members together with a large number of extended members. This is the solution that appears to have been adopted most frequently, both by the new religious communities and by established congregations in their associate programs.[7] The core/extended membership model has shown sufficient promise to make it the best candidate for attracting the quantity of members which any future form of religious life will *have* to attract in order to be truly a leaven in our world. In such a model, a diocese might have only two or three small "core" groups of twenty or thirty religious, but each of these would be connected to a larger pool of some 200 or 300 "extended" members. Restructuring religious communities along this model, however, will not be easy. The extended members would have to be intensively involved in the specific goal or purpose of the order, and, of necessity, would expect some degree of rights and access corresponding to their higher level of investment. The existence of several types of members within the same community thus requires careful consideration of the second assumption about future membership: inclusivity.

INCLUSIVITY

At their joint meeting in 1989, the members of LCWR and CMSM predicted that, in the future, inclusivity would be an essential component of religious life:

> In 2010, religious communities will be characterized by inclusivity and intentionality. These communities may include persons of different ages, genders, cultures, races and sexual orientation. They may include persons who are lay or cleric, married or single, as well as vowed and/or unvowed members. They will have a core group and persons with temporary and permanent commitments.
>
> These communities will be ecumenical, possibly interfaith; faith-sharing will be constitutive of the quality of life in this context of expanded membership. Such inclusivity will necessitate a new understanding of membership and a language to accompany it.[8]

The prospect of expanding their boundaries in such a fashion, however, has aroused a good deal of apprehension among many of the present members in religious communities. "Fears of loss of identity and unwillingness to allow others, who are not vowed members, to share our way of life are still very much evident."[9] Many members express ambivalence about inclusivity: should our associates be present at chapter and perhaps learn things about us that should be private? But isn't it elitist not to include them? What should the difference be, in practice, between full and extended membership? Many religious sense instinctively that there are pitfalls on the way to establishing an inclusive community with several different types of membership, but they are not sure how to avoid these difficulties. Others, looking at the associate programs already operating in their communities, wonder what all the fuss is about.

Types and Modes of Membership

If a core/extended membership model is to enable future religious communities to be a leaven in their society and culture, such a model would probably have to look something like the following: members would choose to commit themselves to the group for a specified period of time or for life. Some might devote themselves full-time to the goal of the group, renouncing all other occupations and possibly living together in an intentional, core community. Others would live in their own houses or apartments, with their own spouses and families, following their own professions or occupations, and connect with the core group on a weekly or monthly basis. The members might circulate between levels—devoting a few years of their young adulthood to "core" participation, for example, then moving to the extended community while raising their children, and finally returning to the core in their later years. There could even be several types of associate membership—one new and experimental Carmelite community has both "vowed" and "promised" lay associates. The former meet weekly with the core community, follow a more rigorous daily prayer schedule, and have a voice in community affairs; the latter meet monthly and do not participate as intensively in the activities of the group.

Many members of present day religious communities, upon reading the above paragraph, may object, "But we already do this! We *have* an associate program. We have our Third Orders, our Oblates—we've had them for years. This is nothing new." I would argue, however, that any new types of core/expanded membership, if they are to be the leavening, prophetic religious life of the future, will differ profoundly from most associate and Third Order programs as they exist today. First of all, as John Lozano points out, the oblates of the past were not really considered to be members of the community:

In the past, there was a trend toward separation. At best, secular Christians were supposed to belong to a religious family, in a clear situation of dependence, as members of a "Third Order" or of an association orbiting around a male order.[10]

This is also true of today's associate programs. The most recent writing on such programs emphasizes that, canonically, associates are *not* members of the religious communities with which they are connected.[11] The preferred terminology is that associates are in a *relationship* with the congregation. The tendency is to discontinue use of terms like "associate members" and "co-members"; one director estimated that only one community in her entire region of over twenty congregations continues to use this vocabulary.

In contrast, the extended members envisioned in the new model *would* be true members, as necessary and essential to the community as the core members. Several experimental Carmelite communities whose members I interviewed saw their core/extended membership distinction through the analogy of a wheel: without the hub, which remains still, the wheel is useless. Without the rim, which comes into contact with the road, the wheel is similarly useless. The members saw the core community as the hub, the extended community as the rim: "And the spokes which connect the rim and the hub are the spirituality and practices of Carmel."[12] Both types of members were essential to the group. Both underwent a rigorous novitiate and celebrated their vows at the end of this period with a formal incorporation ritual. In at least one of these communities, moreover, members rotated from the "rim" to the "hub," as their lives changed and called them to different levels of involvement.

In contrast, as several recent surveys have shown, associate programs are often considered by the vowed members as peripheral and of little concern to them. Almost half of the vowed religious participating in one 1989 survey agreed with the statement that "The Associate Membership Program has little to do with the future life of the congregation."[13] The majority of the associates interviewed in the same survey did not believe that they were an integral part of the congregation either. This led the researchers to conclude that many of the respondents—vowed and associate—

considered associate programs as "only an appendage" to *real* religious life. Except for a small minority of the vowed members who were actively involved, most religious were indifferent to the existence of their associate programs and paid little attention to them. Such attitudes will need to change if the core/extended model is to be adopted by a refounding community.

Another absolutely essential feature of the core/extended model, and contrary to the practice in most current associate programs, is that *there would be a perceptible lifestyle difference between the core community and the extended members.* Many religious who are full members of their present congregations live in apartments, follow a professional career, pray daily, and interact with the rest of their congregation on a weekly or monthly basis— if that often. With the exception of their vow of celibacy and consequent lack of a spouse or children, their daily lifestyle may be almost indistinguishable from that of the congregation's associate members. This does not mean that these religious have chosen an "inferior" lifestyle—such an assumption is insulting to the associates. But it does mean that the definitional boundaries between associates and members have become vague in many instances. When asked how the associates' commitment differed from vowed commitment, "none of the sisters interviewed had clear answers."[14] The associates, too, "were less clear...in defining how their associate commitment was similar to or different from the permanent commitment of the vowed members."[15] Even persons active in promoting the associate movement nationwide were vague about this distinction. One widely-circulated description of the coming "generation" of associate programs envisioned the actual merging of associate and vowed lifestyles in a way that several critics consider questionable: "Why are the two being so closely mixed together and still claiming two levels of commitment and two different rules of life?"[16]

In such a situation of ambiguity, the vowed members may actually appear to be getting the worse deal of the two—they are committed to celibacy and have little control over the money they earn, while the associates receive all the benefits of friendship, spiritual sharing and even, sometimes, electoral voice without any of the onerous personal restrictions imposed by the vows:

In these instances, aside from the belief about a vocation as a unique call, there is little to be gained by the enormous sacrifice to the vowed life as compared to the affiliate requirements for membership.[17]

Most communities' descriptions of the associate form of belonging also contain "very little material that delineates concrete expectations for the persons associating."[18] Thus, not only is the distinction between associate and vowed membership blurred, the distinction between associate membership and the life of the average Christian who is *not* an associate is also unclear. As a result, the 1989 survey found that "most religious and associates currently involved in the associate programs are ambiguous about the purposes and future direction of these programs."[19]

To adapt themselves to the core/extended model described in the preceding section, therefore, religious communities would have to clarify their boundaries so that a real and valued difference, flowing from the fundamental communal goal of the congregation, would exist between the lifestyles and the responsibilities of its core and its extended members. Sufficient membership demands would also have to be established for the associates—again based on the fundamental charism of the congregation—to distinguish extended membership from non-membership. This clarification process will differ depending on the focus of the refounding community. In a monastic community that chooses a common spiritual focus as its goal, for example, the core members might be the ones who devote themselves full-time to fostering the development and spread of this focus—staffing the house of prayer, developing different types of liturgies, teaching meditation styles, composing sacred music or art, doing spiritual direction, planning prayer days, writing and/or publishing books on their particular spirituality, etc. The extended members would practice the spirituality in their daily lives, regularly attend the liturgies or prayer days, and perhaps aid the core members in their other activities. In apostolic communities that choose ministry to the homeless or evangelization of the unchurched as their defining focus, the core might engage in this work full-time while the extended community would regularly volunteer their services, either performing the same tasks as the core on a weekly or monthly basis or else providing some other type of support. Again, members could rotate from the core to the extended community and back, depending on the movement of the Spirit in their own lives. *But it would be immediately evident which membership category an individual had chosen, as well as the difference between membership in the community and non-membership.* Whatever the goal or purpose is that gives a community its basic definition and its reason for existing, it must be enfleshed in such a way as to clearly define both the internal and the external boundaries of the group.

A final aspect that would distinguish the new model from current associate programs is that truly meaningful forms of participation in the life and government of the congregation would exist for each type of membership. Currently, most religious communities provide their associates with only limited opportunities for such involvement:

> The survey data show that associate programs are loosely structured and not overly demanding. They do not encourage commitment of the associates through well-defined expectations, i.e. time requirements, personal investment, etc....The activities of associate programs are limited and communication with associates is generally sparse....Associates are often not sufficiently challenged by the level of commitment their programs demand.[20]

Most associates receive only a monthly newsletter, and fewer than half meet even as often as once a month with either the vowed religious or the other associates.[21] The programs themselves are usually run by a vowed member (or members), rather than by the associates.[22]

This lack of involvement inhibits the associates from taking ownership of the program, and keeps them overly dependent on the core community. According to studies of other voluntary groups, the three main factors which foster strong connections among the members of such groups are involvement in decision making, frequency of communication, and the amount of influence the organization exerts upon the life of the individual member.[23] If associates meet only once a month or less, if their connection with the community is only a segmentalized part of their lives, and if (as is the case with most programs) they have no formal involvement in community affairs, then their relationship with the community is a tenuous one.

Adapting associate programs to the core/extended model requires, first of all, a clear and accepted definition of all its types of membership:

> Even if religious life is considered a system with varied types of belonging, each type of belonging needs some particular parameters for existence....
>
> First, there is a need for a clearer definition of associate membership....Determining what this new type of membership means in contemporary religious life raises questions about what vowed membership means....
>
> Second, there is need for clarity about appropriate types of congregational involvement....Greater involvement of associates increases their level of commitment to the associate program and to the congregation.
>
> Third, there is a need for greater attention to total congregational involvement in the associate program....Encouraging religious who are indifferent or resistant to associate membership to become more involved is a major issue affecting the future of these programs.[24]

One promising tactic is to give the associates full control over their program, while the core members govern their own affairs. The Maryknoll Lay Associates Program seems recently to have adopted this model.[25] Other distinctive tasks, responsibilities, privileges, and benefits will have to be developed and tested so that both the associate and the vowed members can clearly and enthusiastically articulate both *who* they are and *why* they are.

The Importance of Boundaries

Isn't this all terribly elitist? Doesn't focusing so much on lifestyle and governmental boundaries erect more walls of separation to divide a world and a church that is already far too fractured? In the years since the Second Vatican Council's document on the Church in the Modern World, the idea of boundaries has been discredited among many religious. In part, this is the result of a confusion between *having* a boundary (being able to tell who is and who is not a member), and arbitrarily preventing willing and qualified applicants from *crossing* the boundary. Just because communities may have unjustly excluded certain social classes or ethnic groups from membership in the past, it does not follow that the boundaries themselves should be eliminated. To attempt to do so would, in fact, be to write a community's death warrant.

Why are boundaries so important? The basic sociological definition of any "group" is

> a collection of people interacting together in an orderly way on the basis of shared expectations about one another's behavior. As a result of this interaction, *members feel a common sense of "belonging." They are able to distinguish members from non-members and expect certain kinds of behavior from one another that they would not necessarily expect from outsiders.*[26]

Boundaries are the way a group's members define who they are and why they exist as a group; they "provide a frame of reference for individuals who are members."[27] Without clear boundaries marking the difference between belonging and not belonging to a religious community, there are few reasons—other than inertia and friendship ties—to remain a member of it:

> For me, it's a matter of convenience. It gives me a freedom, a base of operations, an identity, friendship with certain other women who make up *the* congregation for me. If they were not here, I would leave....I never wanted to marry and have children, so why leave now? There is not a good reason not to be here.[28]

The lack of a group identity, of which diminished boundaries are a key symptom, is also the major reason why few people join religious communities:

> The diminishment (perhaps in some cases, a loss) of corporate identity by religious communities seems to me to be the first and most important reason for the lack of vocations. There is little reason for a person to make and keep a lifelong, total commitment to a community if the community cannot make clear to itself and its members what it is, where it is going, and why.[29]

Many researchers have found that young people are interested in the support of a group strongly and openly committed to a transcendent value, and that they no longer see this in religious life.[30]

Establishing clear and appropriate boundaries, so that the difference between being and not being a member is readily apparent, is an essential step in any group's construction of its identity. Unless a group has boundaries, it cannot long exist.

Techniques of Boundary Maintenance

There are several effective techniques for demarcating—and celebrating—where a group's boundaries are. One of the most common of these is to ritualize entrances and departures. Nygren and Ukeritis found that the orders which appeared the strongest had "high commitment rituals and practices to differentiate this group from any other."[31] Reception and vow ceremonies are obviously examples of this. Orders that adopt temporary membership as an option might also want to develop "departure ceremonies" to celebrate the completion of a member's time within the community.

But such rites of passage, however meaningful, usually occur only once. Other important boundary markers are the ongoing lifestyle differences that distinguish members from non-members, extended members from core members. Ideally, these lifestyle differences should touch a member's life daily, as a continuing reminder of his/her belongingness in the group. Past lifestyle changes practiced by religious communities have included styles of dress (the habit), common living, and specific customs such as the saying of particular daily prayers. A community may wish to readopt some version of these practices. Other possible lifestyle changes include dietary restrictions (e.g., vegetarianism), common ascetic practices (fasting, giving up television, makeup, or jewelry) or involvement in a specific ministerial or spiritual activity. Paradoxically, Nygren and Ukeritis found, the orders which expected the highest cost from their members in the terms of these lifestyle changes were the ones that appeared to be the strongest.[32]

A final technique for boundary maintenance is to specify levels of responsibility, access, or privileges which are available to members but not to non-members. Who may have a voice in establishing community policy on how funds will be disbursed, leaders elected, or ministries conducted? Who may participate in the community's prayer meetings or spirituality workshops? Who will be permitted to mentor a novice, serve on a board, celebrate a liturgy? In spelling out the answers to such questions, religious communities determine key features of where their boundaries are.

I would like to reiterate here that establishing such boundary markers does *not* mean that they have to be exclusive. People may be able to cross them freely—in either direction—whether they are male or female, black or white, Spanish- or English-speaking, high school or college graduates, even Catholic or non-Catholic, *as long as they are willing to adopt the lifestyle or responsibilities that define membership*. A young man may join the core community of a group that cares for abandoned crack babies, serve for a few years after college, and then move on. A wife and mother may participate as an extended member of a contemplative community while her children are young and her husband is alive, and join the core as an older widow after her children are grown. Several commentators have noticed the reluctance of Americans today to make permanent commitments.[33] Creating easy movement between the degrees and types of membership could address this difficulty. Membership in a community can be inclusive: all ages, genders, races and classes may be welcome to cross the boundary. *But the boundary must remain.*

Implications for Today's Religious Communities

Recreating such membership distinctions will necessitate difficult—even excruciating—decisions. I want to be very clear here that a successful refounding attempt *must* redefine a community's boundaries in such a way as to totally obliterate old status categories and create new ones. Former associates who were not considered "real" members would be given a certain degree of actual voice in community affairs—but would also be expected to adhere to a more rigorous participation standard than was previously demanded of them. Formerly full members who were unwilling to commit themselves to total, "core-level" participation would join the former associates in the extended member category. Obviously, attempting such membership reshuffling would quickly get very messy. For example, many congregations have members who received their graduate degrees, only to find that satisfying and professionally fulfilling positions were unavailable except in distant states. These brothers and sisters now have tenure, friendship networks, or established client bases apart from the main community. What would happen to such individuals if their community redrew its boundaries to conform to the core/extended model described above? Those among them who wished to remain core members would have to abandon their life's work and join in a new group effort that might utilize none of their training or talents. Furthermore, if a community picks one focus to define its core, it will exclude whole segments of the congregation who are unwilling or unable to participate in that focus. Suppose an order of brothers decides that middle-class suburban high schools really do not need their presence any more, and that the community should refocus its ministry on troubled inner city youth. This may leave a sizable proportion of their vowed membership, recruits from these same high schools thirty or forty years ago and trained to teach middle-class students, threatened and angry.

Any attempt to redefine a congregation's identity, and then to draw its membership boundaries so as to make this identity clear, will utterly destroy the old community. And there is no clear certainty that a new one will be born from the ashes. A good many religious will refuse to participate in such a rash endeavor, and understandably so. If the boundaries were redrawn and core membership delimited, these men and women would be left outside. What financial and legal arrangements would be made for them? What social networks could be established to cushion the transition? Could membership transfers be arranged, so that the dissidents in a community newly refocused on monastic contemplation could move to an apostolic one in their area of interest, while more contemplative-minded members of the latter community switched to the former? And what about all the friends left behind? Rather than precipitate such chaos and disruption, a community could scarcely be blamed if it chose to remain with its inclusive, ambiguous, *safe* membership categories—and thereby abandoned refounding before they started.

Establishing several distinct types of membership would cause still other difficulties. The relative proportion of core to extended members will vary from community to community, and a group with a small core and a large extended sector will have very different internal dynamics than one with reversed proportions. There are also practical decisions concerning the amount of involvement and voice to allocate to the core and the extended members, and compelling arguments could be made for each of a wide variety of arrangements.[34] The current associates in many apostolic communities report that they joined the associate program primarily for reasons of communal sharing and prayer.[35] What are the implications of having a core membership defined by apostolic service and an extended one defined by shared spirituality—or vice versa? Initially, a congregation with different types of membership will be drawing its boundaries and defining its membership requirements largely by trial and error. It will also have to do this boundary redefinition in the context of suspicion and interference on the part of church officials. Canon law, after all, explicitly states that there can only be *one* type of membership in a religious congregation. Diocesan and Vatican authorities have thus been quite reluctant to approve communities with more than one type of membership. Several newly-established communities, for example, have had to incorporate themselves as three separate entities—one for men, one for women and one for married couples—rather than as the single community its founder had envisioned.[36]

Since any true boundary redefinition will disrupt people's lives so intimately and so extensively, it will always be bitterly contested. For this reason, although sociologists are emphatic that social groups absolutely *must* have boundaries which clearly demarcate their membership, they are equally unanimous in stating that it is difficult, if not impossible, for already-established groups to redraw their boundaries as radically as they need to be drawn. Too many people have vested interests in the present arrangements: in a religious community, they have given their very lives to them. *An entire congregation, therefore, should not even try to redraw its boundaries in the manner I have described in this section.* Too many people would be hurt. Instead, a parent community should spin off experimental subgroups, each of which could draw its boundaries and establish its membership categories when it begins its existence. For the first few years, the group should feel free to modify its membership criteria if it becomes evident that their initial decisions were flawed. It is dangerous to clarify a model too soon, while it is still in flux. The

parent congregation can, and should, mentor and support its off-
shoots as they gradually work their way to new definitions of
membership and belonging.

The issue of inclusivity thus involves a set of profoundly disruptive decisions, a fact which is dimly sensed by most religious.
Blurring the distinction between members and non-members in
the name of inclusivity will destroy the reason for having a community at all. Defining membership by friendship networks will
exclude newcomers, and may also divide a congregation into
cliques.[37] Yet creating membership categories that are truly
meaningful may be more divisive yet. The most charitable
course is probably to provide several options: membership in
the current congregation, with its somewhat indistinct boundaries (and correspondingly dubious prospects for survival
beyond the lives of its current members), or participation in one
or more offshoot groups, each with a specific focus and with
membership types corresponding to these foci. The participating subcommunities could network with each other, sharing
findings of what does and does not work, challenging groups
that appear to have strayed from their vision, and providing a
safety net for the members of groups that fail. The original community would mentor and support these small experimental
groups, much as the larger Franciscan, Carmelite and
Benedictine federations are currently doing with the new communities in their respective traditions (see above, pp. 93–94).
Only thus can sufficient communal creativity be fostered, and a
sufficient number of core and extended members be recruited,
to rearticulate the charism of a religious community as a leaven
in the twenty-first century.

But who will these new members be? We have already touched
on the possibility of including both men and women, both married couples and single persons, and even both Catholics and
non-Catholics in at least some of a community's membership levels. There is another dimension in membership variety, however:
that of race, ethnicity and social class. Will the religious communities of the future contain persons from these different social
groups, or will they continue to attract recruits primarily from a
single cultural background? Which is preferable, and for whom?

Answering such questions requires consideration of the third concept in this chapter: cultural diversity.

THE PROS AND CONS OF CULTURAL DIVERSITY

In the spring of 1993, *Sixty Minutes* aired an explosive segment entitled "Equal But Separate." Lesley Stahl interviewed African-American students at a major university, students who were choosing to live in all-black dorms, study in the African-American cultural center rather than in the (white) library, eat at all-black cafeteria tables, and even sit on all-black park benches around the campus. The few African-American students who attempted to mingle with whites were ostracized by their peers for being "incog-negroes" and "forgetting where they came from." As one young woman stated: "I already know *all* about whites, believe me. I want to celebrate who *I* am, who African-Americans are."

Traditionally, most nineteenth-century religious congregations in Canada and the United States drew their members from a single class and/or ethnic group.[38] Persons from different socioeconomic or cultural backgrounds often felt isolated and uncomfortable. At times, the alienation experienced by ethnic minorities became so severe that they broke away to form new congregations. This happened most frequently among the Polish sisters in predominantly German congregations and among the French-Canadian sisters in predominantly Irish communities.[39] Such splits left the resulting orders even more ethnically homogeneous.

Society's class divisions were also replicated in the nineteenth-century religious communities. In addition to the lay/choir distinctions established in some orders, whole congregations often acquired a reputation for drawing their members from a particular class:

> To put it bluntly, certain congregations traditionally have been regarded as more "prestigious" or "important" than others.... Teaching sisters who concentrated their efforts in private academies rather than parochial schools were more likely to attract [members] from families capable of paying the higher tuition.[40]

Communities vied to open academies in order to attract a better social class of entrant.

Many present-day congregations, therefore, began a century ago as ethnically and socioeconomically homogeneous groups, and remain such even today.[41] Most of the foundation periods prior to the nineteenth century also produced largely homogeneous communities. The mendicants recruited primarily from the merchant bourgeoisie and university students; the early medieval monasteries contained, almost exclusively, noble members. Most seventeenth-century apostolic orders drew their members from the upper and upper-middle middle classes.[42] Rarely, if ever, did a religious community draw most of its members from the poor.

Sources of Homogeneity

Why has class and ethnic homogeneity been so widespread in religious congregations? There are several reasons. First of all, societies as complex as those of the United States and Canada naturally contain a wide variety of age, class and ethnic/racial subcultures. To the extent that each of these is preoccupied by a different set of issues, they may each have a different "sharpest anguish" for religious virtuosity to address. People from upper socioeconomic levels, who could easily have afforded to pursue a college education and a career without entering a community, may no longer feel the need to belong to an apostolic order. Instead, they may prefer a religious virtuosity that emphasizes primarily spirituality and contemplation. (This preference may explain the rising population of new contemplative groups in late twentieth-century America and elsewhere—groups that appear to attract mostly middle-class whites.) On the other hand, lower socioeconomic classes may desire ways to develop and use their talents in God's active service. The apostolic versions of religious life might still appeal to these social groups. Many of the new immigrant cultures are also more conservative than Euro-Americans, and may prefer elements in their version of religious life which the latter would wish to discard. If a community pressures its Latina or Asian applicants to drop their "outdated" beliefs and customs, they may alienate them instead of attracting them. Persons from a different cultural background may simply prefer a kind of religious life different from the form which appeals to middle-class Euro-Americans—and vice versa.

Another reason for homogeneous communities is that many minorities may, like the college students in the *Sixty Minutes* segment, choose self-segregation as a form of cultural affirmation. Members of the dominant majority rarely realize how completely the mainstream culture reflects their worldview, and how very difficult it is to hold on to an alternate culture in the face of such overwhelming pressure. Sometimes the only way for Latinos or African-Americans to avoid being submerged by the culture of whites—even well-intentioned whites who are honestly trying to give them space—is to withdraw and build their own spirituality. A recent study of Canadian denominations noted that the mainline United Church of Canada "has yet to find success in attracting ethnic diversity," and that the new immigrants who *have* joined the United Church "have tended to form their own congregations rather than join existing ones."[43] In other words, while the majority culture may benefit by enriching its schools, churches, and media outlets with the participation of ethnic minorities, *it may be more beneficial for the minorities to cherish and safeguard their distinctive cultures in separate institutions.*[44]

A similar phenomenon may be experienced in religious communities. The very fact that disproportionately few Black or Latino Catholics are entering religious communities indicates that neither the traditional, nor the liberal, nor the emerging new model of religious life is appealing to them.[45] If African-Americans or Latinos are to be attracted to Roman Catholic religious life, they may have to devise mono-ethnic communities that enflesh their own spiritual focus. Otherwise, many of the most committed Catholics from these "spiritually disenfranchised" groups will desert Catholicism for other, more congruent forms of virtuoso spirituality.[46]

A final reason for the homogeneity of religious communities may be that recruitment to *any* social movement group is most efffectively done through friendship and kin networks.[47] Religious orders have rarely, if ever, attracted their members primarily through media ads or vocation literature; a personal invi-

tation has been much more successful. Recruiting through kin
and friendship networks necessarily skews members' backgrounds to the social class or ethnicity in which these networks
are located.

Implications for Religious Communities

It may be, therefore, that cultural and socioeconomic homogeneity is natural, and even inevitable, for a community.
Certainly, the mere fact that so many older orders and congregations were *not* heterogeneous in composition should at least
give us pause. Striving for cultural or class heterogeneity may
simply not work. The objectionable aspect to homogeneity may
not be that congregations draw their members primarily from
one social category, but rather that, once having admitted the
assimilated second or third generation from another class or
ethnic group, *they bar them from opportunities for leadership or professional growth*. As one critic has noted: "The current trend at
multiculturalizing the American Church seems to me to be con-
cealing the obvious (and not surprising) fact that those who
really set the pastoral agendas...are still the Euro-American
Catholics."[48] It would be an instructive exercise for each member
of a religious community who reads this book to review mentally the ethnicity of his/her order's leadership, and to compare
the percentage of Irish-, German- or Polish-descended superiors
with the proportion of the entire community who are from that
ethnic group. Are Latinas, Italians, or African-Americans repre-
sented on provincial councils and in institutional administration in the same proportions as they comprise in the rank and
file? Rather than possibly wasting our time trying to attract persons from different backgrounds who may not even be interested in joining us, we might better expend our efforts in opening
to all of our current members the opportunities to use their talents in the fullest way possible for our congregation's newly
redefined goal. In the process, we may find that we have gained
a more multicultural membership by *not* trying to attract one,
than we did when we organized innumerable workshops on cultural diversity.

There is much evidence to support this assertion. Researchers
have found that the churches and denominations which made no

specific effort to become multicultural but simply welcomed anyone who ascribed to their beliefs, often ended up more diverse than groups that deliberately tried to incorporate rituals and beliefs other than their own.[49] A recent convention of the Evangelical Lutheran Church in America (ELCA), for example, was organized around multiculturalism:

> At least 80 percent of the hymns at the two festival services were in a language other than English. This when probably 99.999 percent of the delegates spoke English as their first, if not only, language. One church staff person said with mock seriousness, "The planners had two guidelines: 1) Do nothing that might be familiar to traditional Lutherans, and 2) thereby interfere as much as possible with whatever needs average Lutherans may have to sing, to praise and express themselves as Lutherans."[50]

Top-down attempts such as these to draw in minorities are "noble, but they are also incredibly naive," and often result in "erosion and alienation among the churches' traditional base" without ever attracting any new members from the other cultures.[51] Again, multicultural membership is more readily achieved by *not* trying specifically to achieve it:

> Churches that unite people across cultural boundaries can name the deeper religious source of their unity. For St. Joan of Arc Catholic Church, it's the liturgy and the sacraments around which black and white Christians gather....For Millard United Church of Christ, it's the pride of community ministry that brings together Anglo, Slovak and Mexican-American Christians. In the Rock of Salvation Church, it's typically "just Jesus." In each case, the source of unity is the central expression of the deepest religious faith.[52]

A similar prescription could apply to religious communities. Once a subgroup of an established order has chosen the particular focus which gives meaning and passion to their life together *as* a community, and once criteria for determining who is and who is not a member are set up, then membership should be open to *anyone* who wishes to commit him- or herself to that particular goal. Some new or refounded communities may discover that, without their necessarily intending it, they have attracted a wide variety of rich and poor, Anglo and Latino, American and foreign born members, all of whom are committed to the group's vision. The Disciples of the Lord Jesus Christ, a new religious community of some sixty members in Channing, Texas, is one of the most ethnically diverse communities I know of. Half of the members are Anglo, one-third are Latina (including Chicanas, Mexicans, South Americans, and one from Spain). There are three Filipinas, an African-American, one Japanese, three Koreans and three women from India. They came, not because the Disciples specifically attempted to become multiethnic, but because they were all active in the worldwide charismatic renewal. Other religious communities that hope for a more multicultural membership may find that the way to achieve one is to focus on something else.

Some communities, in contrast, may find that the particular focus they have chosen for themselves attracts only Latinas or only upper-class whites. *As long as the doors are truly open to any who share the vision, there is no shame if only certain socioeconomic or ethnic groups choose to knock at them.*[53] On the other hand, however, a mono-ethnic community may *believe* that its doors are open but, as time passes, it may more and more resemble an exclusive enclave from which potential entrants of other backgrounds are subtly discouraged.[54] Great discernment is obviously needed in this area.

CONCLUSIONS

Not only are the membership decisions discussed in this chapter difficult, they all involve potential pitfalls that could derail a new or newly-refounded community. Attracting sufficient numbers to be a leaven is well and good, but rapid growth carries its own, very real, dangers. (See below, chapter 10) Inclusivity, too, is good, but it is difficult to achieve without fatally blurring the community's boundaries. Some inclusive models may not be viable—admitting members of limited education, or advanced age, or physical handicaps, for example, may cause unforeseen difficulties. Cultural inclusion may not be attractive in our present separatist culture.

But for those who believe that the refounding journey is worth making, and who are willing—more than willing, joyfully anxious—to devote their lives to the quest, the important thing is to set out. If we truly begin, others will join us, others perhaps very similar to or very different from ourselves. Are we willing to risk travelling together?

Of course, more is needed than simply to set out. "The devil" as they say, "is in the details." We may have a clear idea of where we want to go but disagree profoundly on how to get there. Each detail of the route involves a choice. Some examples have already been mentioned: for example, the specific boundary markers that define a group's membership, and the particular mix of governmental participation levels to be established for core and extended members. But there are many other details as well. What rituals will be developed to nourish our vision? What vows (if any) will we profess and how will we live them? What prayers will we say, and when, and with whom? How will we interface with the rest of the laity? with the church hierarchy? with local parishes? What standard of living (working class, middle class, poverty level) will we adopt, and how will we earn whatever money we will need to support ourselves at that level? Chapter 8 will be devoted to examining some of the ways of answering such questions.

A CHECKLIST FOR THE JOURNEY

• Why do we wish to exist as a community?

• *What is the difference between being a member of our community and not being a member?*

• *What kinds of membership categories will we have, if any?*
  – *Who will be eligible for each of these types of membership?*
  – *How,* specifically, *will the daily life of a member differ from that of a non-member? A core* member from that of an extended* member?*
  – *What rights and responsibilities will the core* members have? the extended* members? the temporary* members? Who will be eligible for election to what kinds of positions? Who will be eligible to vote? What financial links will exist between the members and the community?*
  – *What will be the formation/incorporation stages for core* members? for extended* members? How long will each take? Who will determine when they are successfully completed? Who will train the new core* members? The new extended* members?*
  – *What leavetaking rituals will be devised for the end of temporary* membership? What incorporation rituals will mark the beginning of membership?*

---

*Applicable only if these membership categories exist

8

Decision #3:
How Do We Get There?

As anyone who has ever planned a vacation knows, there is more involved than simply choosing a destination. Our group of traveling friends must also decide what route to take, and what stops or scenic detours to make along the way. Should they fly, take a bus, or drive themselves? Should they sign up for a guided "package tour" or design an experience more tailored to their own interests? Making these secondary decisions could result in very different kinds of vacations.

Similarly, whatever basic goal or defining purpose ultimately arises for religious life in the twenty-first century, those who follow its call will have to engage in intensely active ideological *work* as they design the manifold components of their lifestyle. As chapter 2 has pointed out, every ideology for virtuoso spirituality must also specify the behaviors involved in it. What vows (if any) will be taken and what specific daily practices will these vows entail? What works (for sustenance and/or for ministry) will the group's members perform? What will their prayer look like—not only in its frequency/duration and in whether the members pray alone or together, but also in its specific spiritual "flavor"? (In my interviews with new communities, I have encountered groups with a predominantly charismatic orientation, others strongly influenced by Eastern hesychastic prayer and icons, and one group consciously attempting to integrate Native American spirituality with Christianity's ancient wilderness tradition.) What will the community's relationship be with the hierarchy and the other laity? With the local parish? What stance will they take vis-à-vis

121

the larger secular society—will they consider it a source of danger and a temptation to be avoided, or a divine milieu to be leavened and praised?

In building up this new ideological frame, a community's members will have to avail themselves of all the tools with which any new worldview is constructed. New concepts will have to be developed. Old concepts will have to be revived and refurbished, with new content added to their meaning or new evaluations given to their worth. New packages will have to be assembled, linking together beliefs and practices formerly assumed to be opposed to each other. New myths and rituals will have to be created to enflesh and enact the ideology in daily life.

Doing this ideological work is absolutely essential. The more countercultural and prophetic a community's stance is and the more it departs from both the accepted liberal and conservative frames for religious life to address the hungers of twenty-first century society, the more crucial it will be that its members are absolutely convinced of the worth and value of their new vision. For this reason, several studies have found, the members of new social movements always spend a very large amount of time together in ideological construction work, as "they jointly develop rationales for what they are or are not doing."[1] Only thus can they construct the overall "plausibility structure" that will justify sacrificing their own personal goals to that of the larger group. If such an ideological structure is weak or non-existent, the community will not long survive.

CONSTRUCTING AND MAINTAINING A NEW IDEOLOGICAL FRAME

New and Redefined Concepts

The new paradigm or ideological frame for religious life will be expressed in a vocabulary that is quite different from the old. Some entirely new concepts will be added, reflecting the influence both of secular disciplines and of other religious traditions. The previous, liberal version of religious life, for example, used the writings of psychologist Carl Jung and the Myers-Briggs Personality Type Indicator to shed new light on the spiritual life.

The sixteen Myers-Briggs personality types became a standard jargon ("I'm an ENFP—what are you?"). Books were written and workshops given describing the prayer styles and spiritualities most congruent with each type.[2] The Enneagram, borrowed from Sufi mysticism, was similarly used. In somewhat the same manner, future models of religious life may borrow and "Catholicize" concepts from the ecological movement, New Age Spirituality, or Protestant evangelicalism.

Concepts may also be reappropriated and refurbished from within the previous traditions of Catholic virtuoso spirituality. Mary Margaret Funk, OSB, describes one such "retrieval and reappropriation" within the Benedictine monastery of which she was prioress.[3] During her time in office (1985–1993), the entire community engaged in an intensive effort to reclaim the tradition of monasticism for the twenty-first century. Some aspects of the process—those involving a new form of the daily office, lectio divina, and monastic poverty—appear to have been successful; others (most notably the retrieval of monastic obedience and asceticism) were strongly resisted and eventually postponed.

It is important to note that the reappropriation and redefinition of old (and often discredited) ideological elements will usually result in opposition from those for whom these elements still carry their old conceptual and emotional overtones. For example, St. Benedict had condemned "gyrovagues," the wandering and undisciplined hermit virtuosi of his day who competed with each other in feats of asceticism and meddled—sometimes disastrously—in secular and ecclesiastical affairs.[4] Subsequent generations of Benedictines and other monastics retained this suspicion of any virtuoso spirituality carried on outside of cloister walls. When the mendicant orders developed in the thirteenth century, the monks assumed they were just another type of gyrovague and that their spirituality was thus illegitimate.

Reappropriations of discredited and "outdated" elements of religious virtuosity may meet a similar fate today. There is growing evidence, for example, that wearing a religious habit does not mean the same thing, or carry the same emotional freight, for the young members of new religious communities that it does for either the conservative or the liberal religious orders of the past. Not one of the young people I interviewed in these communities (all of them swathed in cowls, veils, scapulars and floor-length robes) considered their dress to be a sign of their superior status, much less a denial of their sexuality, both of which connotations critics had ascribed to the pre-Vatican II habits.[5]

> We don't want asexual people; we use our sexual energy to touch all our brothers and sisters. We can give the time laypeople can't give.
>
> We're at the full service of people. It is a deeper commitment—not that we're holier or that God is more pleased with us.
>
> They will not just love me, they will love my God and they will see my God in me. Because that's the love that I want to bring them—who cares about me, Debbie, but when they can touch God through me, that's the important thing.
>
> It was like, I wanted to evangelize and I said, "Well, if I look like this, people will have to think of God and I don't even have to open my mouth." So, for me, that *sign*, that's the value.[6]

After the past thirty years, when—whether through their own choice or because of external pressure—religious have been outwardly indistinguishable from the rest of the laity, it is the *visible sign value* of the habit which the new groups appear to value. For them, the habit is not a sign of separation and superiority, but of faith, hope and the love of God:

> Czech Ursuline Sister Caterina Havlova described life in the "concentration convents" of the Stalinist period. After 1968, they lived underground, with new novices not even telling their parents. It was too risky...."Today, the sight of sisters in religious garb, who radiate the happiness that comes from their faith, encourages people in their search for God and helps them understand the need for truth, trust and collaboration in charity." Clearly, the wearing of the habit means something completely different in ex-Communist countries.[7]

This is precisely the point. Whether or not a refounding community adopts a habit, fasting on bread and water once a week, incensing icons during prayer, or any other discrete element drawn from the previous models of religious life can be either life-giving or retrograde *depending on the meaning they attach to this element and on how it supports or detracts from their ability to attain their stated goal or purpose.* It is a mistake for outside observers to conclude that, because some practice had connoted elitism, rigidity, infantilism, or other negative characteristics under former models, that it necessarily does so today. It may, but then again, it may not. New and refounding communities must be free to adopt and modify the practices that most reflect their basic charism—unhindered by either the strictures of traditionalists ("That's never been done before!") or the dismissiveness of the liberals ("Only the psychologically immature would consider reviving *that* unhealthy practice!"). Of course, with this freedom comes a corresponding responsibility. The members of the new community must be willing constantly to reexamine their motives, lest they drift into precisely the sorts of detrimental attitudes and practices which their critics attribute to them.

New models of religious life, therefore, may contain some elements that are totally new, as well as other elements that appear ancient and thoroughly outmoded. Even the most traditional element, however—in any model that is viable and healthy—will *not* be merely a carbon copy of the past. As in other types of ideological change, any traditional values, concepts, or practices which may be adopted by new or refounded religious congregations will have slightly different connotations or slightly different emotional overtones than they had in the past. But this is not the only way in which a new ideological frame differs from an older one.

Rearranged Packages

As was noted in chapter 3, a group's separate concepts or beliefs are bound together in an ideological "package," whereby endorsing one element usually means accepting the others with which it is associated. Even though there may be no logical connection between a given position on one issue and the prescribed stance regarding any other topic, if a person is for (or against) Issue A, it is considered "only logical" that he/she would be for (or against) Issues B, C, and D. When the defects of an existing ideological frame become apparent, therefore, the first reaction is often to devise a counter-frame by simply negating the elements of the former. Table I illustrates this.

TABLE I	
Original Frame	*Counter-frame*
A	not-A
B	not-B
C	not-C
D	not-D

The development of such a counter-frame may then be mistakenly identified as a new ideology.

Such is not really the case, however. A truly new ideological frame would not conform to the preestablished packages. Some ideas or beliefs would disappear altogether and entirely new ones would be added. Others will be subtly changed, and packages of the retained and redefined elements would be "inconsistent" under former models. Table II illustrates this:

TABLE II		
Original Frame	*Counter-frame*	*New Frame*
A	not-A	a
B	not-B	not-B
C	not-C	X
D	not-D	ɵ

Thus, for example, a new or refounded community may adopt a habit—but wear blue jeans and sweatshirts when not at prayer or ministry. A group may espouse an extremely contemplative lifestyle—but not cloister. Non-inclusive language may be used in the Office by a combined community of co-equal male and female members—headed by a woman. The possible configurations are endless.

If members of existing conservative or liberal religious congregations are put off by certain individual aspects of a new or refounded community's ideological frame, they will be further disconcerted by the "illogical" way in which these aspects are combined. New groups often find that neither conservative nor liberal religious accept their vision. For this very reason, it is necessary that they constantly reaffirm its plausibility among themselves. The most effective way to do this is by constructing new myths, metaphors, and sacred stories.

Myths, Stories, and Legends

New beginnings are always mythic. An essential part of all ideological development is to have "a story that invigorates":

> The mythic stage is that of laying foundations. There does not exist a well-thought-out plan, but there is a powerful vision that unites the founding group and energizes it for action. It is as if the group is carried along by some, perhaps unnamable, supernatural force...
>
> The story arising from this type of experience we call myth; it is not a legendary, fanciful tale with no foundation in reality, but a story loaded with emotion and meaning which grasps those who tell [it].[8]

A primary characteristic of almost all new religious communities—as well as of established congregations—is that they experience their foundation periods in just such mythic ways. One founder received prophetic confirmation from Catherine Doherty:

> Anyway, so Catherine Doherty said, "Tell me, Father, where are you from?" I said, "I'm not a Father." She said, "That's too bad, because you are called to be Father of many." ...So I proceeded to tell her about the community I envisioned. A priest would be the sacramental minister. The laypeople would be involved, vowed laypeople would have a voice in the community. She said, "Yes, this is God's will." In 1983, when I went back,...we were told our community was the only one Catherine Doherty had encouraged to be founded.[9]

Another founder, a parish priest, received a similar call from the "messages" received by several members of his parish's prayer group.

> One day, she told me, "The Lord says He has a special work for you—will you do it?" And I said, "Well, whatever the Lord wants, you know, I'll do." Thinking, I'm going to get asked to lead the fund drive for the diocese, or something....Well, that was on a

Wednesday. On Sunday, between Masses, she called me over and said, "I know what your special work is." And I said, "What?" and she said, "You're going to establish a religious order." And I immediately said: "I like what I am, I have absolutely no desire to be a religious, I never did—and now I'm going to establish a religious order?"...So that's how it came about. The very day that [she] told me that, she had breakfast with the other woman who had had voices—because they lived in the same area of [the parish]. The other one—her name was Sue—said to Judy (she was the one who told me), "You know, I have a message for Father Joe, but I'm afraid to give it to him." And Judy tried to tell her not to be afraid and she said, "No, I'm just afraid to tell him." And so Judy says, "Well, what is it?" And Sue said, "I'm supposed to tell him he's not going to be a diocesan priest for very much longer." Now is that a confirmation or not? On the same day, on the *same day*.[10]

Practically every community can cite similar "divine coincidences." The two founders of one U.S. group, now modeled after the Monastic Fraternities of Jerusalem in Paris, each stumbled upon the French community's new Rule book in two separate cities during the same weekend. Each read it and was moved by it on the way home, and discovered on Monday that the other had done the same thing.

After the founding, the mythic stories continue. Money for a mortgage payment comes providentially, just when it is needed, "from places I never heard of before." Even tragedies can become part of God's plan:

Well, their founder...apparently had a heart attack and he was suffering some respiratory problems. And he was unconscious just a little bit too long before the brothers found him. And so he's in a coma. And so now they love him so much. They get him up every morning, they massage him, they put on his habit and they sit him in his wheelchair....And I really think—I hope he didn't ask God for that blessing, for that grace, but I really think he's offering up his sufferings for the brothers. And they're doing very well....There's about ten or eleven of them now.[11]

Stories such as these, in their telling and retelling, confirm the divine plan for the community and give approval for its particular ideological frame.

Implications for Refounding Religious Communities

Ideological frames are most effectively rooted in our minds through myths and metaphors, in stories and songs.[12] Lack of such ideological supports is a major defect of modern culture: "We have no vision, no models or metaphors to live by. Only the saints and the mystics live well in a time like this."[13] The primary way, therefore, that any group builds up its plausibility structure, its ideological frame, is to repeat its myths and stories to each other—over and over and over again. Men and women in religious life currently do this, even if they are seldom aware of the deeper purpose which these retellings serve. Members of liberal religious congregations recount tales of comic or ridiculous novitiate requirements—or horror stories of tyrannical superiors and impossible mission assignments—as a way of reminding themselves how vastly preferable their current version of religious life is. Members of conservative congregations share accounts of this or that lay person who congratulated them for still wearing a habit, or of the inability of liberal communities to attract new members. Again, such stories support the chosen ideological stance of those who tell them. Reading material and retreat experiences serve similarly to reinforce the community's worldview: newspapers such as the *National Catholic Reporter* and publishing companies such as Ignatius Press primarily reach like-minded readers.

But, while such symbol sharing is essential for the support of an ideological frame, it also tends to fossilize it:

> Symbols were adopted based on what was survived together. The recalling of these stories became the ritual. However, if this is all that occurs in a community, no counter-symbols or new experiences can penetrate this atmosphere. This forms an old-(although age may not be a factor) girl or old-boy mentality in a congregation, and the community then becomes an enclave. There is a tacit agreement among its members not to invest energy into creating a common future, but merely to continue as they are.[14]

Members wishing to refound an existing community must consciously devise new stories to support their vision, new myths to enunciate God's transcendent plan at work in their lives. They must then deliberately substitute these new symbols for the tired myths and stories that bind them to the past—whether that past be the 1950's or the 1960's.[15] One way to do this would be through regular faith sharing sessions in which members recounted and explored how God had validated (or challenged) their new way. In the initial, precarious times of founding or refounding a community, this should be done *at least* daily. Daily rituals, songs and other customs would also help to support a new ideological frame. Chapter 10 will provide some concrete examples of how this might be done.

Conclusions

In order to exist as a concrete entity, a religious community must not only have a common, overarching goal or purpose (as difficult as this is to achieve in our pluralistic environment), but they must also develop a well-articulated set of concepts, myths, beliefs and practices, linked together in coherent ideological packages, which validate this purpose and enflesh it in their daily lives. Such a comprehensive ideological frame must be constructed and reconstructed, revised and renovated, almost continuously during the initial years of the community's founding or refounding. The process is intensely demanding, and will absorb, directly or indirectly, a major portion of the members' lives.

But all of this discussion has been rather abstract. What are some of the elements of religious life that we will have to reconstruct? How did they change during past refounding periods and how might they change today? The following section will attempt to answer these questions for two of the main components of the apostolic model of religious life: the vows and common life.

COMPONENTS OF RELIGIOUS LIFE: THE VOWS

In the years since the Second Vatican Council, the meaning and the validity of poverty, obedience and chastity/celibacy have been thoroughly explored by numerous psychologists and theologians.[16] I am not qualified to add to a discussion in either of these disciplines. I cannot say whether a psychologically healthy celibacy is possible, or what the most valid theological interpretation of obedience is. What I would like to offer here is a *sociological* interpretation of the vows. By such an interpretation, I do not mean an analysis of factors in the larger society that call religious to modify their traditional ideas of the vowed life. This, too, has been done, and quite competently, by writers such as Marie Augusta Neal, SNDdeN, and Diarmuid O'Murchu, MSC.[17] Instead, I wish to focus on how the meanings of the vows have changed in previous refounding periods, and on how these changes have contributed to the internal viability of the various models of religious life. By such an analysis, I hope to discover the essential sociological elements which must be present in any vow—whether the traditional poverty/chastity/obedience triad or some new commitment—that becomes part of refounded religious life, *in addition to* whatever psychological and theological requirements the reformulated vows must also meet.

A Brief Historical Overview

The various refounding periods within the history of Roman Catholic religious life have often been marked by changes in the meaning and the importance given to one or the other of the vows.[18] Obedience, for example, was exercised differently by the abbot-father of an autonomous monastery in the early Middle Ages than it was by the absentee abbot who nominally supervised dozens of far-flung twelfth-century Cluniac houses, or by the Dominican prior of the mendicant period, an elected official "with strictly limited rights and functions."[19] From the point of view of the subject, obedience might entail complete submission of one's very will to the superior, or it might permit spirited dissent. (The early medieval Benedictines and the sixteenth-century Jesuits ascribed to the former definition of obedience; the medieval Dominicans to the latter.) Obedience might be considered the most important vow, surpassing even chastity in importance,[20] or it might be widely discarded. Similarly, the external observance of poverty has sometimes required a religious to give away all of his or her possessions and experience actual want, while at other times it simply meant holding an impressive amount of wealth communally rather than individually. Again, poverty was the most important vow for some religious orders; others deemphasized or even discarded it altogether.

Even chastity, the one vow consistently taken by all religious communities in the Catholic tradition, has varied in the types of additional behaviors it entailed, and in who were most apt to practice it. At one time, only middle-aged individuals were expected to make such a vow, once their children were safely grown. At other times, only the young did. In some eras, women were considered too carnal ever to be able to vow chastity; in the nineteenth century, on the other hand, popular culture denied that women had any sex drive at all. Since all "normal" nineteenth-century women were therefore immune to sexual temptations, the vow of chastity was reinterpreted to mean restricting their other appetites.[21] Religious virtuosi of one period showed their fidelity to the vow by being able to sleep with members of the opposite sex without succumbing to temptation; at other times, vowed religious would not be permitted even to be in the presence of such living occasions of sin.

The wide variations in the meaning and importance attached to the three vows by quite successful and valid past models of religious life mean that there is no *sociological* reason why any new or refounded community need adopt one particular version of them instead of another. Whether or not a community adopts *any* vow, and what the adopted vows are considered to mean, should depend on three basic tests: 1) whether and how the vow enfleshes and supports the basic goal or vision of the community, 2) whether and how the vow enables the individual members to grow in their self-gift to God and neighbor, and 3) whether and how the vow serves to give a corporate identity and focus to the group. Psychological and spiritual writers have addressed the second of these questions quite competently; they have devoted less attention to the other two. It is true that one basic purpose for a vow is to enable or further one's personal response to God, and that any vow which detracts from an individual's psychic health should be reinterpreted or discarded. But unless a vow also contributes in some concrete way to the *community's* fundamental goal and its collective identity, there is no reason to require it of all the members—even if some individual religious may continue to make vows for their own individual growth and/or sanctification.

A Sociological Analysis of the Vows

Why should members of a religious community, *as members of that community*, make any vows at all? On an individual, personal level, of course, vowing poverty, celibacy, obedience, or something else may be a way of seeking a particular interior attitude or focus that facilitates one's spiritual growth. Thus, a personal vow of poverty might call an individual to develop an attitude of detachment from worldly possessions and a dependence on God. Obedience might help someone to practice a spirit of open listening for the will of God in daily events. And celibacy/chastity might free someone for a single-hearted focus on God. Indeed, without such interior personal dispositions, any external observances of the vows would be hypocritical and useless.

But one need not be a member of a religious community to take this kind of vow. Indeed, many writers have argued that *all* Christians are called to lives of detachment and discernment by the very fact of their baptism. "Poverty," stated one writer as early as 1966, "needs to be seen as an integral part of the Christian vocation, common to both lay and religious."[22] And should not *all* Christians be actively open to discerning the will of God? What is different about the vows taken by members of a religious community?

"The vows," one recent author states, "are to be a concrete sign in the world." And this does not apply only on the individual level: "the religious community *as a whole* is a sign."[23] Therefore, whatever vows the members of a new or refounded community decide to take as part of their membership in the community must have a communal as well as an individual component. It is the *community* that is to be a sign to the larger society, a corporate witness of the way its virtuoso spirituality answers that society's deepest longings. If there are only individual signs, there is no need for the community to exist. The vows, insofar as they enflesh this communal sign, must contain communal as well as individual aspects.

There are, basically, two ways in which any practice can be said to be "communal" in nature. A given category of persons may all individually perform the same activity. In some cultures, for example, religious virtuosi do not live together or interact with each other in any way. But each one may shave his/her head, or abstain from meat, or renounce sexual activity. This is one way that a given component of virtuoso spirituality could be communal. The second way would be for the virtuosi to engage in related activities that are linked together by some visible common goal. Operating a hospice for dying and homeless AIDS victims, or a printing house that disseminates spiritual literature, involves many different tasks in pursuit of a common enterprise. So does collectively limiting consumption in one's local house, or working together for neighborhood (or world) peace. If the vows are to have a meaning beyond the individual level, they, too, must have one of these two communal manifestations. Otherwise, while taking a vow may be a good and praiseworthy thing for an individual to do, the vows would contribute nothing directly to the life or functioning of the community.

In the end, of course, all three tests must be applied to any vow(s) which the community decides to adopt. If a vow has *only* a common external component and supports neither the spiritual growth of the individual members nor the living out of the community's basic vision, it is worse than useless. But a vow that denotes merely an internal disposition of detachment or listening will not be sufficient either. Currently, for many religious, the living out of the traditional three vows has drifted toward one or the other of these two extremes.

Celibacy

At the present time, the vow of celibate chastity is the only one which can be said to have a communal external dimension. Members of religious congregations do not marry, date, or engage in sexual intercourse. Since this requirement is expected of all who enter a religious community, it can truly be said to be a distinguishing mark of these groups. Several contemporary theologians have considered consecrated celibacy to be *"the* defining characteristic of religious life."[24] This appears to be the teaching of the magisterium as well: the Under Secretary of the Congregation of Religious, Father Jesus Torres, has recently stated that celibacy is the only distinctive characteristic of religious.[25] The adoption of celibacy is thus "communal" in the first of the above two meanings: a common individual behavior practiced by all those who follow "the religious life."

In a world inundated with sexual messages, celibate chastity is the aspect of religious life which makes the most striking impact on outside observers:

> It is the aspect of a priest or religious that makes the most concrete impact on them, for it opens up a world of surprise. After getting to know a priest or a religious for a while, young people never fail to ask: "Why can't you get married?" Celibacy intrigues people because it is out of the ordinary; it is a symbol of the knowledge of God and its novelty.[26]

In their celibacy, members of religious communities continue to be a visible, *communal* sign to the larger society—even if that society is often somewhat confused about what the sign means.

There are also practical sociological reasons for communal groups to adopt celibacy. Several researchers who have studied such groups have noted that the exclusive loyalties demanded by marital and family ties are extremely disruptive to the unity of the larger community.[27] For this reason, successful communities have typically required their members to practice either promiscuity (the policy of the Oneida community) or celibacy (the policy of the Shakers). The arrival of children, too, often causes split loyalties, since most parents naturally feel a greater concern for the well-being of their offspring than they do for that of the larger group. Thus, Dorothy Day is known to have advised against including families with children in Catholic Worker houses: the competing demands of family were too great.[28]

Still another reason for requiring celibacy relates to the nature of virtuosity itself. A compelling argument might be made that artistic and intellectual virtuosi—the Michelangelos, Van Goghs, Mozarts and Picassos of the world—make less than ideal spouses. The driving inner fire that compels them to address their age's burning questions in their painting, poetry, music, or philosophy, also leaves them with less time and emotional energy for their wives (or husbands) and children. *A fortiori* then, religious virtuosi, engaged as they are in the most consuming of all quests, will find it difficult or impossible to divide their time with family demands.[29]

Sociologically, therefore, it would appear that any community of religious virtuosi will have to require its core members to be celibate. Of course, merely mandating this external requirement is not enough. An intellectually and emotionally engaging connection must be made between the daily practice of celibacy and the transcendent goal or vision of the community. (See Test #1, p. 132, above) And both the daily practices and the larger ideological justifications for them must also be conducive to each individual member's personal and spiritual development. (See Test #2)

In other words, it is not enough for celibacy to be commonly practiced, it must also be theologically meaningful and psychologically healthy. The recent national survey conducted by Nygren and Ukeritis appears to indicate that a majority of U.S. women religious, at least, do find in celibate chastity a deeply spiritual meaning.[30] This same survey, however, found that celibacy was *not* perceived as meaningful by a large percentage of male religious. And persons outside religious communities, both Catholic and non-Catholic, remain unsure why anyone would take such a vow. It would appear, then, that more "ideological construction work"—by theologians, psychologists and the members of the new and refounded religious orders themselves—is needed in order to make this vow, not a mere necessity for communal functioning or an unexamined inheritance from past models, but rather a consuming fire in each individual's life and a coherent witness to the world.

Even after this ideological development is done, however, there will still be practical considerations regarding the vow of celibacy/chastity that will have to be worked out. Communities that allow for different modes of membership (see chapter 7, above) will have to decide how the vow applies to each type. Will married lay associates be asked to vow chastity? If they are, what will their chastity mean, and how will it differ from the marital chastity demanded of all baptized Christians? Will it be possible to vow celibate chastity for a temporary period and then switch to a vow of marital chastity later? Or will having a *temporary* vow of celibacy reduce its power and importance, since the corresponding marriage vows are *not* temporary? What ritual celebrations will be devised to mark the taking of a vow of celibate chastity? Of marital chastity? What rituals will mark the dissolutions of such vows or the change from one to the other? As with the vacationing friends mapping out the intricacies of their route, building even such an easily defined and probably necessary practice as celibate chastity into a new community's ideological frame will involve a host of separate, and very specific, decisions. Decisions involving other vows will be much more complicated.

Poverty

Having a vow of poverty poses many more difficulties for a new or refounded community than the vow of celibacy does. Celibacy has at least retained a common external component, and it is still widely assumed to be an essential requirement of any new or refounded version of religious life. Neither of these assertions is true for the vow of poverty. To begin with, poverty has essentially lost its communal expression in post-Vatican II religious life. The practice of celibacy is fairly unambiguous—it is relatively simple to tell what behaviors would constitute infidelity to this vow.[31] The practice of poverty, on the other hand, is not so clear cut. Does poverty imply actual material deprivation? If so, what level of deprivation is required—can members of a religious community live in a middle-class neighborhood, own a stereo, eat steak, or drive a late-model car? Are the nightly "happy hours" observed in some men's communities violations of poverty? Is wearing jewelry or earrings? Or perhaps poverty's primary requirement is serving the materially poor and/or working for redistributive justice. If so, what proportion of one's time should be devoted to these activities—is it enough to volunteer once a month at a homeless shelter and write a letter or two to Congress for Bread for the World?

Prior to Vatican II, the practice of poverty, like celibacy, required a uniform set of behaviors from all the members of a religious congregation. The actual standard of living in the community could be quite high, provided that the individual members asked "permission" before they used anything. Perhaps because this imposed standard was perceived by religious to be superficial and overly limiting, there has been a pronounced reluctance to define *any* common practice as indicative of vowed poverty in post-Vatican II religious life. As one 1969 author noted, poverty "is seen in many ways; a community possession of goods; care of the poor and downtrodden; the spirit of *anawim*, of emptiness before God without reference necessarily to the question of material possession; the lack of concern for providing material goods (an unnecessary bother that is relieved by the vow); actual physical poverty, and so forth."[32] Since then, still *further* interpretations have been advanced for the vow: standing with the poor and oppressed, for example, or working for social justice, or even ecological stewardship of all creation.[33]

Because of the wide variety of observable behaviors potentially included under the vow of poverty, the communal sign value of the vow has been diluted. One 1981 survey of Catholic laywomen found that they did not perceive sisters to be living a life of poverty and simplicity. Nor did they think religious women were adequately serving the poor.[34] The more recent Nygren and Ukeritis survey found that both male and female religious displayed only a "moderate" level of commitment to work with the materially poor.[35] For most religious, the vow of poverty has been identified primarily with an interior disposition of detachment and dependence on God. *But all Christians are called to possess these virtues.* To limit a vow to a "common" internal disposition is either a waste of time (because anyone can claim to have such a disposition) or impossibly tyrannical ("You *must* feel *this* way"). If there is nothing about the vow of poverty that distinguishes a religious community, then there is no reason for the community to require it of its members.

Thus, new and refounded communities must first of all decide whether to adopt a vow of poverty at all. There have been a few versions of religious life (notably some groups of medieval canons)[36] which did not include such a vow. As with any element of their ideological frame, poverty should be included *only* if its common practice supports or enhances the basic vision or purpose chosen by the community. The members must be able to articulate—passionately—why such a vow is absolutely essential in living their life.

For any community that chooses to make a vow of poverty, there are a large number of possible interpretations to choose from. A refounded group within an established tradition will probably wish to choose and adapt a version from within that tradition. For example, refounded Benedictine groups might be more likely to select some form of communal sharing or peace-making[37] as their way of living poverty, while Franciscan groups may be more apt to choose living with, and as, the poor. Other groups may devise entirely new interpretations. In any event, it must be clear how the common *vow of poverty* taken by the religious congregation differs from the *spirit of poverty* expected of all Christians, and also why it is absolutely necessary for the group's vision.

Even after these decisions have been made, the "nuts and bolts" of communally living the vow in daily life must still be worked out. The community may choose a common practice, or practices, for all members to perform individually: limiting material consumption by forgoing meat, a car, a TV, or whatever, restricting dress in some way, or tithing each member's time and money to the materially poor. It should not be necessary to add, of course, that any such common individual behaviors would have to be chosen by the members themselves and not imposed by the leadership.

The second way for a vow to be practiced communally is for all the members to devote themselves to a specific work or project. An apostolic community may choose to refocus its ministries on some particular group of the poor. A community oriented around spirituality and prayer may covenant to live in poor areas and share their spirituality with the people there. In either case, paradoxically, the more stringent the demands their vow of poverty makes and the more visible their common practices are, the more likely a community will be to attract new members.[38] In fact, the experienced members of a new or refounded community will probably have to "rein in" the enthusiasm of the young so that whatever sacrifices are chosen to enflesh the practice of poverty will be sustainable in the long run.

Communities with different types of membership will also have to work out the interpretation of poverty that will be applied to each group. Married couples with children will be understandably reluctant to practice the same degree of material poverty that may be expected of core members, or to move their family into an inner city school district. But, again, unless the "vow of poverty" taken by the married members is in some readily observable way

distinct from the spirit of poverty expected of all Christians, there
is no reason to require it. A community may decide that only the
core members will vow poverty, and that the extended members
will confine themselves to supporting the core in their efforts,
and perhaps "rotating in" to live poverty with the core for limited
periods of time. Or an apostolic core community devoted to serving the poor in some way may expect its extended members to
work with them for a specified number of hours a week.

Finally, whatever version(s) of communal poverty may be chosen by the members, the vow's underlying rationale, its link with
the transcendent reason for the order's existence, will have to be
clearly specified and constantly reinforced in the members'
minds. Daily rituals to emphasize the sacredness of poverty will
need to be devised: a group that has renounced TV or automo-
bile ownership, for example, might want to substitute a nightly
prayer or a faith sharing service with the poor of the neighborhood during the hours when the TV would have been watched, or
a morning prayer/leavetaking ritual as the members walk to the
bus stop. A community which ministers to the materially poor
will have to devise some way to witness—to members and to non-
members—how what they are doing differs from social work.
Rituals, myths, story-telling, and external signs of clothing
and/or home furnishing styles might all be used for this purpose.
Usually, such daily ideological supports are devised naturally,
gradually, and from the "grass-roots" up, as the community lives
out its charism. But it would be helpful to recognize the importance of such practices and to cherish and nurture them when
and as they develop.

Obedience

Of the three traditional vows, obedience needs the most ideological "work" before it can be adopted by a new or refounded
community. The difficulties with the vow predate Vatican II.
Whereas the vows of poverty and chastity were basically uncon-
tested in the theological and psychological literature aimed at
religious communities before 1960, articles critiquing or defend-
ing the vow of obedience appeared quite regularly during this
period. Many writers noted that this vow was the most difficult
for 1950's youth, and frequently deterred them from entering.[39]

With their increased psychological knowledge, other writers began to question whether obedience might be actually detrimental to mental health.[40] Obedience also clashed with professional independence:

> Observers have noted that it was in ministry settings, actually, that sisters had the opportunity to exert the autonomy of adults, in contrast to the dependence and docility expected in the convent. Instances abound. The administrator of a large teaching hospital not only ran the institution effectively but dealt with her peers in the field and with civic officials. The college president oversaw governance, finances and curricula. The scholarly anthropologist conducted field research with grant funding. The high school drama coach staged the annual musical to which an entire town flocked. All these women then returned to the convent, where they had to ask permission to stay up past 9 P.M....[41]

Finally, the aftermath of World War II called into question the very value of obedience: "After disclaimers of guilt by obedient Nazis at the Nuremberg trials, religious men and women can no longer honestly idealize total submission to the will of another human being as a good."[42]

Under such assaults, the traditional interpretation of obedience quickly collapsed after Vatican II. *And no new communal practice has been advanced to replace it.* Today, the vow has been almost completely reduced to its internalized component: obedience is "reverent listening to God's voice," a "life lived with alertness to the Spirit," a "means to develop as an adult," or even "the actualization of one's own destiny."[43] In one 1989 survey of U.S. sisters, 50% chose "my own inner spirit" when asked where they would turn to hear God's voice—a far greater percentage than those choosing "my community gathered together to deliberate a question" (30%).[44] Only 11% continued to believe that "a truly obedient religious need seek no source other than her Rule and the will of her superiors to know what she should do."[45]

Today, therefore, obedience is "the least appreciated" of the traditional three vows.[46] This is to be expected. Of all the new attitudes and values which arose in the nineteenth century (and which were *not* addressed by the version of religious virtuosity which Catholicism developed at that time), belief in the worth of the individual and his/her personal fulfillment is perhaps the most deeply rooted in American life today.[47] *Monarchical religious obedience, resuscitated unchanged from the sixteenth-century apostolic model for religious life, never addressed the new ideas about the rights of the individual which flowered after 1776 and 1789.* And we are now reaping the result. When the marginalized, peripheral populations from which nineteenth-century religious life had traditionally drawn its recruits finally became assimilated to twentieth-century culture, it became more and more obvious how truly out of step the traditional notion of obedience was.

Of course, poverty, celibacy and obedience are *all* countercultural. In terms of mainstream cultural values, it makes no more sense to renounce sex or possessions than it does to renounce personal freedom. But celibacy at least involves a commonly-agreed-upon behavior, even if much work still remains in enunciating why this behavior is worthwhile. The problem with poverty is that there is an overabundance of possible behaviors that have been advanced to mark the practice of the vow, and it is difficult for a religious community to choose among them. Once the choice has been made, however, there is a certain amount of support, in at least some sectors of mainstream culture, for each of the interpretations. Obedience, in contrast, lacks *any* common expression that is at all valued, either by the mainstream culture or by the majority of the members themselves.

And yet, just as Western mainstream culture needs the witness of poverty and celibacy to balance its obsession with consumerism and sex, so, too, the unfettered individualism of modern society needs to be balanced by *something*. As several prominent writers and social critics have pointed out, American culture defines freedom as "freedom from" external restrictions. "Freedom for"—what one should *do* with one's freedom—is rarely addressed.[48]

> What goals should an individual have once he or she has been liberated? Here the culture is silent except to uphold the right of each individual to do whatever he or she chooses to do, as long as he or she does not hurt anyone. This focus on personal freedom, to the exclusion of a vision of what this freedom is for, creates an

atmosphere of malaise, or lack of meaning and purpose in the lives of many people.[49]

This malaise and lack of purpose can create a dangerous backlash, too. Disconnected and autonomous individuals are the most vulnerable to the attraction of dictatorial leaders and totalistic cults.[50]

In religious life, too, there has been a tendency to fluctuate between the two extremes: to be either "a loose aggregation of individuals with private agendas or a faceless corps of bodies without souls."[51] It is the balance between the two—not independence or dependence, but *inter*dependence—which our society most urgently needs, and it is precisely this balance which neither the traditional concept of obedience nor its post-Vatican II, internalized antithesis has been able to supply. We need a totally new vow here, whether or not we retain the term "obedience" to refer to it. As with the other vows a new or refounded religious community chooses to adopt, "obedience" cannot be a mere internal attitude. It must have a common *external* component: one which daily touches the lives of each community member, which energizes and excites their efforts for the community's transcendent goal, and which supports each member's personal growth into the love and the likeness of God. It is a daunting task.

And a new or refounded community cannot stop with "merely" defining a vow that meets the above criteria. The daily "nuts and bolts" of the vow must also be devised—and revised—in a continuous process of trial and error. What structures will be erected for community governance? How will visioning and/or task leaders be selected and what authority will they have? Who will call the members and leaders to accountability, and how often and in what manner? What rituals will celebrate the voluntary subordination of one's individual goals to the community's, and what rituals will mark the cessation of this subordination? Even the most mundane decisions—how long a term of office should be and whether its occupant may succeed him/herself—have profound and long-lasting implications.

The task of ideologically redefining such an elusive and disvalued concept may seem impossibly hard, and many will decide to abandon it altogether. Two conditions, however, may combine to make the development of this vow not only feasible, but an actual joy. First of all, the overarching purpose of the community, if adhered to passionately enough, will greatly facilitate the development of whatever vow of obedience, interdependence, or communal self-giving most naturally flows from it. "The real issue...may not be so much the lack of obedience as it is the lack of purpose in the group."[52] Secondly, the ongoing development and revision of such a potentially explosive vow can be greatly enhanced by the regular utilization of an in-depth discernment process, preferably facilitated by someone from outside the community. The community will need to force itself to examine—and reexamine—hard questions. Is our leadership getting too inbred or maintenance-oriented and losing touch with the original vision? Are some individuals or subgroups being unjustly ignored and their God-given talents thwarted for the sake of "the greater good"? Are there certain issues that both the members and the leadership are studiously ignoring—the "elephant in the bathtub" that everyone is pretending isn't there? A mini-discernment process should probably be built into the daily life of the new or refounded community, with a facilitated process once a month. As a side benefit of all this discernment, the members will get to know each other more deeply, which is, of course, a necessary precondition before one can hear the Spirit's voice in one's brothers and sisters.

Conclusions

Vows of poverty, celibacy and obedience are, of course, not the only vows a new or refounded community may decide to adopt. Monastic groups may wish to vow stability. Other communities may choose mutual charity, non-violence, or service to the poorest of the poor. Whichever vow(s) a community chooses to adopt, however, must meet the three tests outlined on page 132: they must enflesh and support the basic vision or purpose of the community; they must be conducive to the psychological and spiritual growth of the individual members, and they must in some visible, common, and concrete way be different from the duties required of all Christians. Unless a vow does these things, and does them daily in some manner, a community should not bother with it.

COMPONENTS OF RELIGIOUS LIFE: COMMUNITY

The American Sociological Association is divided into sections, each of which focuses on some particular topic within the discipline. A few years ago, Lynn Lofland, the president of the ASA's section on Community, wrote an editorial in its newsletter.[53] In it, she suggested that the members ban all use of "the C word" in their writing. Community, she stated, is fuzzy and vague in its meaning: one researcher counted 95 different usages, ranging from "the community of Greenville" to "the gay (or African-American, or medical) community." A second difficulty is that the term is loaded with emotional overtones: like motherhood and apple pie, it elicits almost universally warm and uncritical feelings of approval—even from supposedly neutral and scientific sociologists.

I would argue that we are experiencing similar difficulties with the concept of "community" in religious life. On the one hand, we have used it to refer to several different realities. For some, "community" refers to a lifestyle—usually the lifestyle which they are living at the present time, and which they are unwilling to change. For others, "community" means a common set of beliefs and values, independent of lifestyle, even though it is not clear how these beliefs and values will be sustained without some lifestyle practices to enflesh and support them. For still others, "community" simply means the congregation. To quote Lewis Carroll's Humpty Dumpty, the word seems to mean what we want it to mean.

Lofland's second difficulty also applies to religious life. However we define "community," we accept its goodness uncritically. If a particular lifestyle has negative side effects, either for the individual members or for the congregation as a whole, then it must not be a *real* "community." Both of these misconceptions reduce the usefulness of the concept for newly-founded and refounded religious congregations.

The Spirit of "Community" and "Community" Lifestyles

Whatever definition(s) of "community" a new or refounded religious congregation chooses to adopt, the same general principles apply as applied to the vows. "Community" must first of all enflesh and support the common vision or purpose of the group. Without a common and underlying "community" *spirit* any "community" *lifestyle* will be dead and barren. On the other hand, we are not non-material angels. Without some lifestyle practices to support our common spirit, it will soon wither and die.

The form(s) of "community" must also be—or strive to be—psychologically healthy for the members. It is here that Lofland's second difficulty with the term come into play. *No "community" lifestyle is without potentially detrimental side effects for those who engage in it.* Groups of eight to ten (or more) living under one roof can degenerate into mere hotels of nodding acquaintances. Alternatively, they can, like malignant cancers, devour the individuality, creativity and psychic strength of their members. Two individuals in an apartment can become a codependent couple (critics in my congregation and others call them "marriages"), who exclude outsiders and feed each other's neuroses. And what "community" do these two individuals belong to—their own dyad or the larger congregation?[54] Finally, persons living singly can become self-centered and narcissistic without the daily "shoulder-rubbing" and compromises involved in living with other people. None of these forms of community is perfect. What I have found, however, is that, whenever the religious who are living in one of these forms of "community" have its defects pointed out to them, they react defensively by listing all the abuses and unhealthy situations that arise from the *other* forms, which therefore cannot possibly be "real communities" since they possess these defects. Again, we see the assumption that "community" is an unalloyed good. This tendency to respond to criticisms by criticizing others only short-circuits the self-examination that new or refounded groups must conduct of their own "community" life.

"Community" Lifestyles and Religious Life

Over the centuries and across cultures, religious virtuosi have engaged in widely varied "community" lifestyles. Some of these individuals did not live together, and may rarely have even seen each other. If a common cultural definition existed for virtuoso beliefs and practices, a man or woman might simply decide to become one, don whatever clothing or symbol (e.g., a shaven head) signified their choice, and begin to practice the prescribed activities, without ever associating with another virtuoso. Hindu sadhus and the wandering holy men of nineteenth-century Russian Orthodoxy engaged in this kind of common life. So did many of the fourth-century Christian hermits and the medieval anchoresses.

Other religious virtuosi formed communal associations. Like the individual hermits and anchoresses, they shared a common self-definition, beliefs and practices, but they also met periodically to reinforce and reaffirm them. Other than these periodic meetings, which may have been as rare as once a year or as frequent as several times a day, the members carried on their separate lives. Some of the Beguines, the sixteenth and seventeenth-century Jesuits and Angela Merici's Ursulines (before their enclosure by Charles Borromeo) appear to have followed this type of "community" life.

Finally, of course, there is the intentional community. According to its official sociological definition, an intentional community is one in which the members live together, and often work together as well. Because this was the most common model for religious life in the nineteenth and early twentieth centuries, some people assume that it is the only way religious life can be lived. Others, who remember its many deficiencies, are equally sure that authentic religious life can *never* be lived this way. Both views are equally wrong.

This is only the most brief outline of one dimension along which "community" lifestyles for religious virtuosity have varied in the past. There are other dimensions as well: 1) How much leeway there is for the individual virtuoso to define his/her activities, or 2) How much contact is prescribed or permitted with the outside world. The lifestyles can merge into each other: members of a communal association may be expected to pass a novitiate or renewal period in an intentional community before returning to their separate lifestyles. Wandering hermits may likewise apprentice themselves to a guru and live in community with his/her disciples before setting out on their own. Some Hindu and Buddhist monks wandered alone for most of the year, but lived together during the rainy season. Medieval anchoresses, apparently the most solitary of individuals, often maintained an extensive, long-distance correspondence with other like-minded virtuosi. Where a new or refounded congregation locates itself along these dimensions, and the particular mix of "community" lifestyle practices it chooses to adopt, are key decisions in the ongoing development of its ideological frame.

Making the Choice

As with the living of the vows, the living of "community" involves a host of very specific decisions. Will the group live together? Will there be an upper (or lower) limit to house size if they do? If the members do not live together, how often will they meet? What will be the purpose and content of these meetings? Who will plan and coordinate them? What common ritual activities (if any) will be performed? How separate (if at all) will "community" members be from "non-community" members? Again, the same three criteria apply: the communal practices must flow essentially from the basic goals, meaning and values of the group, they must be as psychologically healthy as possible, and they must in some way be distinguishable from the brotherly/sisterly love expected of all Christians.

A wide range of variations in "community" are theoretically—and historically—compatible with Roman Catholic religious life. But not all will be equally attractive today. Studies of the successful new religious communities indicate that most require a much more intense common life than is offered by many established congregations.[55] This is probably because young prospective members have not experienced the intentional community lifestyle, with all its good and bad points, that current members remember from their own novitiate and early years on mission. These young people are thus more likely to idealize it and to discount its liabilities. Also, the "sharpest anguish" of modern Western culture, as chapter 6 has pointed out, is precisely a "lack of community."[56] New members seek this "community," they hunger for it. Meanwhile, many present congregations have found that their older members were so traumatized by previous experiences of intentional community living that they strongly resist any attempts to revive it, even if failing to do so means that their congregation will die for want of new members: "Today, there are some religious who are eminently successful at apostolic work, whose mem-

ories of their religious formation days are so bitter that they hope
never again to live in [intentional] community."[57]

Whether the older members of a community like it or not, the
hunger of prospective members for "community" is very real.
Whatever forms of "community" lifestyle are adopted by the new
or refounded congregations, therefore, they will probably have
to demand much more common involvement than is currently
the case. Members may choose to live again under the same roof.
Alternatively, they may live apart but gather very frequently: at
least weekly and preferably more often. Many current members
have lost the skills for this type of life, even if they desire to recreate it: "Because of the emphasis given by religious to the
renewal of apostolic works in these past thirty years, the renewal
of their forms of conversation, worship and mutual service in the
average local community has been mediocre."[58] So both new and
old members will be starting something new for them.

I wish to emphasize again that no way of living out the communal spirit is without its dangers. And most religious are more
attuned to the dangers of the form which they have *not* adopted
than they are to the dangers of the form under which they live.
Likewise, no one "community" lifestyle is uniquely required of
Catholic religious life.[59] What is important is that the lifestyle
enflesh and support the basic purpose and values of the congregation, that it continue to foster psychological and spiritual
growth among the individual members, and that it sufficiently
differentiate the members as a group so that prospective recruits
see a reason for joining them. Today, this is more likely to
demand a lifestyle with frequent—probably daily—interaction. A
century hence, such may not be the case.

CONCLUSIONS

A recent study of the first generation of Jesuits noted that St.
Ignatius and his followers had no idea of the final form their
order would eventually take.[60] Likewise, St. Francis of Assisi
ended up founding an order that looked very little like his original conception. Initially, both founders were overly bound by
their previous mindsets: Francis thought he was starting a com-

munity of hermits; Ignatius envisioned a group of wandering mendicant preachers. Only gradually did the revolutionary implications of their new visions unfold—even to the founders. An ongoing dialectical process of adaptation and challenge exists between every new religious order and its environment; orders that fail to adapt do not survive.

The same is true today. Whatever new version of religious life ultimately develops in this country, it will likely be very different from what has been standard in the past. And it will develop gradually, by trial and error, adaptation and readaptation, as the new communities learn from each other and from their mistakes. Liberal communities, Merkle notes,[61] are more comfortable than conservative ones with this kind of open-ended process. Conservatives are vulnerable to the temptation to canonize past models, and may not change sufficiently to meet the needs of their new environments. Without sufficient adaptation, conservative communities may not die out completely, but they will remain stuck at the level of "minimal survival," peripheral and irrelevant to the church of the twenty-first century.[62]

The important thing is to attempt *something*. A richly detailed and developed new model for religious life, such as has only been hinted at in this chapter, cannot be developed by sitting down and thinking it out ahead of time. It must be *lived*—and lived daily. It is here that the liberal orders find difficulty. "The liberal model allows for…the trial and error search…but it is less successful in dealing with the second step, the testing of experience."[63] Once we have a communal destination, we must set out. The road, it is said, is made by walking it. Had Francis or Ignatius stopped to work out every detail of the way before starting, they would never have developed the revolutionary models they did.

There is one further question we have to ask. How will the larger church—both the hierarchy and the other laity—react to what we are doing? How can we enlist their support? What is the most effective way to locate new members? To accumulate sufficient financial resources? Dealing with questions such as these will be addressed in chapter 9.

A CHECKLIST FOR THE JOURNEY

- Why do we wish to exist as a community?

- What is the difference between being a member of our community and not being a member?

- What kinds of membership categories will we have? What will distinguish them from each other? From non-membership?

- *What vows (if any) will we take?*
  - *How are these vows essential to our basic purpose or goal?*
  - *What daily rituals will celebrate these vows? What rituals will mark first/final profession?*
  - *What rituals will celebrate the dissolution of these vows?*
  - *What common practices do we choose to enflesh these vows in our daily lives?*
  - *If there are different categories of membership, what vows will apply to each category?*

- *How will we live "community"? Will we live together or not? Pray together? Work together? How often will we gather to deepen our community bonds? What will we do at these gathering times?*

- *Why is this form of community living necessary to our basic purpose or goal?*

- *What are the liabilities of this form of community living? How will we attempt to neutralize these liabilities?*

9

Decision #4:
What Do We Need for the Journey?
(And Where Can We Find It?)

According to Resource Mobilization Theory (see chapter 4, above), there is an almost infinite number of longings and dissatisfactions circulating among the members of any society. Whether any of these will develop into a successful movement, however, depends on the resources which a given group can muster to support its cause. Similarly, a wide variety of new and refounded religious communities may initially develop, they may meet the needs and hungers of society and even have well-thought-out daily practices, but their success or failure will also depend on their ability to locate and tap certain key resources. This chapter will list the "supplies" necessary for a refounding journey, and will give some suggestions on how, and where, such resources might be obtained.

PERSONNEL RESOURCE #1: NEW RECRUITS

The most valuable resources of any social movement are the persons involved in it, and a wide range of sociological studies have focused on how movement organizations recruit and retain their membership. If religious life is to have a future beyond our individual life spans, then we, too, must spend a significant amount of time, thought, and effort in locating our successors and inviting them to join us. This, Merkle notes, is the true meaning of generativity: not merely being involved in one's own creative activities, but rather having an "interest in the next generation or in the deeper elements of life which require long-term commitment and investment."[1] If we truly and passionately believe in the new vision we have chosen for religious life, then we will, of necessity, take steps to insure that it will not die when we do.

In the past few decades, many religious have avoided thinking about ways to attract new members. The massive decline in the number of young people entering religious life seems far beyond the ability of any individual religious, or of any individual religious community, to reverse. Faced with such an apparently irresistible and society-wide trend, we feel like King Canute commanding the tide to reverse itself. Why even bother trying?

The Drying Up of Traditional Recruitment Sources

Traditionally, women and men who felt a call to religious life were persuaded to enter a particular religious order primarily through the operation of four major incentives: a personal invitation by the present members, the innate benefits of the life itself, the urging of family, clergy, or lay sodality members, and the operation of institutionalized recruitment "funnels." As this section will show, all four of these incentives have been seriously diminished, if they have not disappeared altogether.

Many of the religious communities of previous eras, and especially the apostolic communities of the past two refounding periods, made conscious and continual efforts to attract others to join them. The sixteenth-century Jesuits, for example, required each of their local communities to appoint a "promoter" especially charged with the task of recruitment, and *all* Jesuits were repeatedly urged to recruit "as many as possible and the very best."[2] In the nineteenth-century United States, congregations of sisters would open private academies with the express hope of obtaining new members from among their graduates.[3] Faculties of the various schools run by a congregation would informally compete to see how many young women they could send to the motherhouse each year; parishes in a diocese boasted of the number of their young people entering seminaries or novitiates.[4]

Invitational efforts of this extent rarely occur today. As far back as the late 1960's, the expansion and consolidation of community-

run academies into diocesan-supported high schools had the side
effect of diminishing the opportunities to invite new members:

> Often in these schools, priests and brothers, sisters from a variety
> of religious congregations, and married and single lay faculty pro-
> vided an education for young men and women together....
> Frequently within the faculties there was an unspoken agreement
> that it was inappropriate to "recruit" a student for religious life or
> to join a particular congregation....At the same time, the decrease
> in academies and small colleges and the growth of large consoli-
> dated high schools and urban colleges lessened opportunities for
> students to enter into relational intimacy with communities of sis-
> ters, brothers or priests.[5]

More recently, the lack of role clarity felt by many religious has
also discouraged them from recruiting new members. A few
have even questioned whether it is moral or ethical to invite persons to join a group that is so uncertain about its future and in
such a disadvantageous power position vis à vis the church hierarchy.[6] For others, the congregation has ceased to be their primary source of reference, as they become more and more
involved in professional or ministerial pursuits. For these religious, the prospect of their congregations' demise through a
lack of new members may not be sufficiently threatening to spur
them to devote any time to recruitment activities. Still other religious remain in their communities primarily because of a "sense
of affiliation" and their friendships with other members.[7]
Already-established groups of friends usually have little incentive to seek new members, and may even be perceived by outsiders as an exclusive clique. For all of these reasons, therefore,
religious today are less likely to invite new members to their
communities.

Such unwillingness is deadly, as studies of other communal
groups have demonstrated. Several historians have observed
that, when the Shakers stopped believing in their founding ideology, they became reluctant to seek new converts. This put them
at a serious disadvantage when compared to their evangelical
competitors, who still had a strong sense of clarity about their
mission.[8] Gradually, mainstream American society came to
regard the Shakers as anachronistic and dying:

> That this opinion was shared by the Shakers themselves is evidenced by the historical and apologetic tone of their later writings, and their...insistence that, despite the inevitable decay of institutions, essential Shakerism could never die.[9]

A similar vocabulary occurs in the rationalizations offered by many religious today. It does *not* bode well for their communities' future.

The second incentive to enter religious communities in the past was the innate attractiveness of the life itself. Becoming a priest, brother, or sister was often the only way a young working-class man—or a young woman of *any* social class—could receive an education or an opportunity to use his/her talents.[10] This is not to imply, of course, that such individuals were entering only for selfish reasons of personal interest. The opportunity to develop and use one's God-given talents in God's own service is a worthy motivation to enter religious life. Since such a lifestyle was also perceived as "the way of perfection" and superior to marriage, it attracted a large number of idealistic and fervent young people who wanted to give their absolute best to God.[11]

While these motivating attractors may still operate in other parts of the world, they emphatically do not in Western Europe and North America. Many other career paths—in secular professions as well as in church service—are open to young men and women today.[12] Furthermore, the life of a sister, brother or religious order priest is no longer perceived as holier; if anything, the opposite is true. Popular news and entertainment media depict religious as immature and childish at best (*Sister Act*, *Nunsense*), or as psychologically damaged and sexually predatory at worst. Recent surveys in both North America and Europe have shown that Catholic laywomen have negative opinions of sisters, viewing them as weak, ineffectual, and irrelevant:

> The interviewees, when asked specifically about religious life, described it in negative terms as being "unreal" and "out of touch with reality." Celibacy and long-term commitment clearly presented "big problems" for them. They seemed to reject or discount the idea of religious community as a valid way of life for today.[13]

The third incentive was that young people in previous eras were invited, or even pressured, by their relatives, the clergy, and others in their society to enter religious life. Parents were proud and thrilled when one of their children became a sister, priest, or brother; one of my own earliest memories is of a framed poem hanging on my grandmother's living room wall, entitled "I'm the Mother of a Nun." That my aunt had become a Sister of Charity was obviously a source of pride for my grandmother. In some subcultures, families even experienced increased social status if a child entered a religious order. In other cultures, a religious vocation might be a way in which a family could evade the onerous duty of providing doweries for its surplus daughters.

> Obviously, such familial self-interest could lead to abuses: Only too clearly, the interests of the girls themselves were confounded with the piety, or the self interest, or both, of their families.... "One goes," wrote Jean Cordelier in 1643, "to the clothing of a girl who has been trained to respond according to the wishes of her father and mother, not her own wishes. They dress her like a little goddess....They assemble her relatives, they ask her, My daughter, do you wish to be a religious? Her conscience says no, but her mouth, betraying her heart, says yes."[14]

On the other hand, many who originally entered because of such familial expectations later discovered in themselves a true vocation to religious life.

Bishops, priests, and other laity also served as "recruiting agents" for many religious orders. The Utah Sisters of Mercy had no problem "finding recruits into their ranks...since missionary priests channeled vocations to them from different parts of the country."[15] The editor of the Catholic newspaper, *Our Sunday Visitor*, did the same for the Victory Noll Sisters.[16] Several nineteenth-century lay missionary societies in France, Bavaria, and Austria published glowing reports of the work of religious congregations in North America, thus encouraging hundreds of young people to emigrate and join these communities.[17]

Again, outside actors rarely recruit members to religious orders today. According to a 1993 *Newsweek* poll, only 44% of the U.S. Catholics surveyed would want their child to become a priest or nun.[18] This appears true in other countries as well:

At the time of Vatican II, the family which had a member in a religious order was considered "respectable" and had status in local [Irish] society....Today, twenty-five years later, the picture is very different. A sister's life is looked upon as somewhat stunted and one that even good Catholic parents would not encourage their daughters to pursue.[19]

Families are also smaller today, and more scattered. Parents with only one daughter may be less supportive of her religious vocation than parents with five daughters. Nieces with an aunt in a religious community on the other side of the continent may rarely see her.[20]

At one time, there were also many institutionalized recruitment channels which funneled candidates to religious orders, often without a lot of specific recruitment efforts on the orders' part. The importance of schools as a seedbed for vocations in the United States has already been mentioned; such institutions were equally important in Ireland and on the continent during the nineteenth century. Schools also served as recruitment channels during the preceding growth periods of religious life. After the Jesuits opened their first schools in 1548, for example, over 50% of their novices came from these establishments.[21] Many of the recruits to the thirteenth-century mendicant orders came through the medieval universities, where the friars dominated the faculty positions.[22]

Another institutionalized source of vocations can be found in the popular books that were written about famous persons in religious life. St. Athanasius' fourth-century biography of Anthony the Abbot resulted in a "flood of converts" to the eremitical life; Jacques de Vitry's *Life* of Mary of Oignies attracted hundreds of women to the Beguines.[23] In the early to mid-twentieth century, the popular *Autobiography* of St. Thérèse of Lisieux attracted many women to Carmelite monasteries, and Thomas Merton's writings had a similar result for the Trappists.[24] Again, most of these institutionalized channels have since been shut off. No new book or film draws seekers to religious life today. Most congregation-run schools and academies have been closed, consolidated, or shifted to lay operation.

New Recruitment Strategies for Refounding Communities

If a new or refounded community wishes to survive beyond the life spans of its current members, therefore, it must either revive the incentives that previously operated to attract new entrants or else develop new ones. The one thing that absolutely must be revived is *the vigorous effort on the part of every individual member to invite new recruits to the community.* As numerous previous studies have noted, the strongest single predictor of whether a religious group grows or not is the amount of time and effort it devotes to this recruitment process.[25]

At a minimum, therefore, the members of any new or refounded community should tithe their waking hours to activities which in some way relate to membership invitation. I am not exaggerating here. Every sister, brother or priest in a religious community should be devoting at least ten hours a week to recruitment-related efforts. Obviously, this does not mean going from door to door as if one were selling Girl Scout cookies, or even giving five vocation talks a week in parochial high schools. Initially, at least, most of the time would be devoted to participation in workshops and in ongoing internships to learn *how* to invite different categories of persons to religious life. For some, it would also include "hanging out" with and getting to know a given group of young people, perhaps offering them the opportunity for participating in a prayer group or helping in ministerial activities one afternoon a week. For still other religious, it might include writing or producing more positive media presentations on religious life than currently exist. As a repertoire of different invitatory activities is built up, regular sessions to compare their relative effectiveness would also be necessary.

Undoubtedly, readers of the preceding paragraph have already thought of a host of objections. "Such activities would be discouraging and futile—no one joins religious life any more. We would be doing all that work and, at the end, we would be totally depressed by our inevitable failure." "We are all so busy with our various ministerial activities that we are hard pressed to find a single night each week when we can spend time with our other community members. When would we ever find ten hours to devote to invitation activities?" And, most tellingly, "You'd have to be young and on fire to be willing to give that much time. We are old and tired and disillusioned, and we doubt very much that it's worth it." Or, "Are you trying to make Moonies out of us?"

Such objections are serious ones. But the need for intensive and ongoing invitation efforts by every member of a new or refounded community is also serious—deadly serious. No community will survive without such efforts, for two reasons. First of all, there are few other incentives operating to attract people to Roman Catholic religious life. If we do not do the inviting, it will not be done. Secondly, as the previously-mentioned studies of the Shakers have shown, the willingness to recruit others is the most basic indication that a group really *believes* in what it is doing. If we are not willing to devote time to inviting new members, then we may not have the kind of "fire" which chapter 6 has shown to be the fundamental grounding of any new or refounded community.

How, therefore, can we answer the objections that invitation activities would be futile, take too much time, and sap our already limited energy? To begin with, all sorts of activities involve more failure than success: losing fifty pounds, breaking an addiction to drugs or alcohol, door-to-door proselytizing, and selling Mary Kay cosmetics, for example. Through trial and error, those who have succeeded at these failure-prone endeavors have developed a set of techniques to help others do the same. The most essential of these techniques is to insure that the struggle is never solitary. Mormons and Jehovah's Witnesses work in pairs in their door-to-door missionary work. The presence of a fellow believer strengthens the belief system of the missionary in spite of almost constant rejection. Each member of Alcoholics Anonymous is assigned a "buddy" whom he/she can call, day or night, for support and encouragement. In addition to such supportive pairings, most groups also have weekly motivational meetings, when larger numbers gather to share struggles and rejoice in successes. "Judy lost five pounds this week!" "Mary sold another $5,000 worth of cosmetics and is now eligible for her pink cadillac!"

There are strong inhibitions in North American and Western European culture which discourage us from talking about spiritual things. "As several writers of the Quinn consultation papers noted, we are very reluctant to talk about our deepest experiences of prayer and union with Christ. Yet how can we expect anyone to be drawn to this aspect of our life if it is not joyfully shared with them?"[26] Learning to share our spiritual lives with strangers is, for most of us, easily as difficult as losing fifty pounds. Perhaps we could learn from Weight Watchers and Alcoholics Anonymous how to devise motivational meetings to share useful strategies, celebrate our successes, and reignite our enthusiasm after our failures. Continued participation in such meetings would be a significant part of a community's weekly tithed time.

In our modern society, when so few external incentives are present to attract new entrants, regular and intensive recruitment activities by *all* members are absolutely indispensible. How else will any religious seekers take us seriously? But such activities have a second, equally beneficial, effect. *Participation in recruitment efforts is the ongoing "fuel" that keeps one's own fervor alive.* Many researchers have observed that belief often follows behavior rather than preceding it:

> If social psychology has taught us anything during the past twenty years, it is that we are as likely to act ourselves into a way of thinking as to think ourselves into a line of action. Individuals are as likely to believe what they have stood up for as to stand up for what they believe in.[27]

In contrast, many of today's religious have retreated to a psychological "maintenance mode" with regard to religious life. They would find it too painful to leave their congregations, but they no longer possess the enthusiasm to seek out and invite new members. *Such an attitude is deadly.* "By their own admission," Nygren and Ukeritis state, "members of religious orders see indifference and a lack of passion to be a major threat to themselves as persons and to the broader scheme of religious life in relation to other social systems in society."[28] One vicar for religious whom I interviewed wondered:

> Where did we lose our passion? I still have mine. I still believe in it and I can say that I would repeat these vows again....But I need to find out where we lost our passion. And that is my struggle. [Interviewer: And is that your impression, that a lot of religious in

this diocese have lost their passion?] Yes, some. They are lovely people. They are lovely and gracious. But that fire, that passion—like some of the holy founders and foundresses, they had *passion*. I want to know where we lost our fire. Is there a spark?[29]

Paradoxically, the way to reignite the spark is to behave as though it were already burning. In a sort of reverse chicken-and-egg scenario, recruitment efforts may come first and then the enthusiasm to recruit will follow.

A third beneficial effect can arise from increased invitation activities. The involvement of so many individuals in weekly motivational meetings, ongoing mentorships, brainstorming about recruitment tactics, and faithsharing their own spiritual searches, will also help in the ongoing ideological redevelopment discussed in the preceding chapter. The more individuals engage in such ideological work, the more creative their efforts are likely to be. Since we do not yet know what precise version(s) of religious life will speak to twenty-first century cultures, it is necessary that we develop and test as many as possible.

Other Sources of Recruits

Inviting new members one individual at a time—while utterly necessary for all three of the reasons listed above—is not the only way to attract new members. New or refounded communities should also try to supplement their members' personal efforts with additional recruitment channels. In previous refounding periods, for example, it was quite common for several members of a family to enter the same community: as many as 25% of some nineteenth-century religious congregations in Ireland, France and the United States were related to each other, as were 31% of women in seventeenth-century Quebec communities.[30] St. Bernard arrived at Clairveaux with thirty relatives and friends, all of whom entered along with him.[31] The kin and family networks of current members may be valuable sources of new entrants, and creative ways—nephew/niece overnights, sister/blood sister retreats, etc.—might be explored to tap these groups.

Targeting groups rather than individuals is especially important when a community attempts to attract entrants who differ in age, social class, or ethnicity from the majority of its present members. One lone twenty-five-year-old, however warmly and personally invited to a religious community, may well hesitate to join it if the next youngest member is forty-five. A single Latina might feel a similar reluctance to enter an Anglo community. In these cases, communities may have greater success if they begin by establishing an ongoing relationship with some group—a city-wide youth organization, an African-American prayer group, or a base community of ex-migrant workers—rather than with individuals. They may also wish to establish quasi-autonomous houses or provinces in which entrants from the new generation, class, or ethnic group can comprise a significantly large proportion of the membership and not feel swamped by the middle-aged, middle-class, or middle-American members of the larger congregation.

There are other kinds of groups with which it is often helpful to cultivate relationships. Both in this country and in Europe, some of the most successful new communities have close ties to the charismatic movement, which publicizes these communities in its publications and funnels its most fervent members to them.[32] The Focolare movement channels young men to the Blessed Sacrament Fathers in Holland; the Neo-Catechumenate sends interested applicants to the Marists and Capuchins in Italy.[33] The advantage of such an arrangement is that another group—a very enthusiastic and committed group—is willing to add its invitational efforts to those of the religious community. A disadvantage, as DiIanni points out, is the problem of "double belonging" or "dual loyalty."[34] Are the new members Capuchins first and Neo-Catechumens second, or vice versa? Furthermore, the spirituality of (e.g.) recruits from the Charismatic Renewal will differ from that of the older community members, which may lead to misunderstanding and division. On the other hand, if both sides are willing to learn from each other, such "spiritual culture clashes" can result in a creative renewal of the community's own charism.

It must be acknowledged, however, that *all* successful recruitment efforts will carry at least some element of threat to the members who have already lived decades in the community. If a congregation is not to die out, it must, sooner or later, attract and retain a relatively large group of newcomers, who will *not* be identical clones of those they replace. When the time comes, the

Vatican II generation of religious will have to relinquish the reins to their "Generation X" successors; Anglo religious to Latins, liberation theologians to charismatics. This will be painful. Religious today are middle class in culture and highly educated: 64% of U.S. sisters have advanced degrees beyond their bachelor's.[35] Many have been thoroughly "liberalized" by Vatican II and its aftermath. Some may actually prefer that their congregation die out rather than be "taken over" by interlopers who are less educated, who appear to be more conservative, or whose burning issues are not their own.

The Pros and Cons of Third-World Recruitment Efforts

Today is not the first time that religious congregations have operated in societies whose members showed little interest in joining them. To the Sisters of Mercy in Red Bluff, California, for example, it had become "painfully obvious" by 1906 "that there were very few young Catholic women in Northern California who were sufficiently educated in their religion and willing to embrace the religious life. No one had entered and stayed for twenty years!"[36] Nineteenth-century communities—and there were many—who found local vocations lacking did not hesitate to look overseas for new members. Most often, "overseas" meant Ireland, where a combination of social and economic conditions severely limited the other options of women and made religious life attractive to them.[37]

Similarly, many religious communities today may find that there are far more young men and women from Nigeria, Pakistan, Korea, or the Philippines who are interested in entering their communities than there are Americans. Among the young men and women of these and other developing countries, many of the former attractions to religious life still hold true. Entering a community often provides social status and the opportunity for a professional education to young people—especially young *women*—for whom other options are limited. In South Asia, especially, dowry requirements are so high that girls may experience intense pressure from their families to enter a religious community instead of getting married—pressure which these young women are culturally ill-equipped to resist. In many instances, of course, these young men and women do have true vocations to religious life. But there are added incentives for them to enter which no longer apply in North America and Western Europe.

On the positive side, Third World entrants can be a valuable source of renewal and revitalization for established religious congregations. Looking at a founder's charism through a different cultural lens can bring about new insights, and the youthful enthusiasm of these members can spark renewed fervor in their elders. This assumes that these members, as they mature and gain experience, are allowed full participation in congregational leadership, and are given the opportunity to interpret the community's charism through the lens of their own culture. In such a situation, embracing a trans-cultural membership could be a valuable witness in our increasingly Balkanized society.

But other aspects of late-twentieth century Catholicism differentiate us from previous eras when religious communities sought the majority of their entrants abroad. First of all, in the nineteenth century, newly-arrived Irish, German, or Polish religious were not very different in culture from the first generation Irish-American, German-American, and Polish-American Catholics they met in the New World. This is not the case with the Filippino, Nigerian or Pakistani religious of today. A real culture gap may prevent their effective ministerial service in North America or Western Europe (although, obviously, their continued ministry in their home countries would not present this problem). Such a culture gap may also make it more difficult for American or Western European religious to relinquish the reins of governance to their Third World members when the time comes. Still another problem arises when Third World entrants view religious life as a "step up" in status. One new Franciscan community in the United States, intensely committed to living in poverty among the inner city poor, finally had to allow a number of their Nigerian candidates to leave. These men had come to America for an education and the opportunity to develop their talents in God's service, *not* for a ministry of simple presence to the homeless and drug addicted of the inner city.[38] Similar clashing expectations may arise in other communities.

Conclusions

One of the most important and vital resources of any religious community is its present and future members. If we truly believe that religious life should survive, if we are glad that we entered and wish others could enjoy the riches we have received, then we have an obligation before God to invite others to take our place. Merely leaving brochures—in English or in Spanish or both—in the back of church is not sufficient. Expecting the appointed Vocations Director to do the bulk of the recruiting is not sufficient. We must personally share our joy and our faith with others whom we invite to enter; we must meet frequently within our congregations to encourage each other; we must network with other communities to share what works and what doesn't. Without an invitation effort of this magnitude, a community will not survive. And it won't deserve to.

PERSONNEL RESOURCE #2: CHARISMATIC LEADERS

An equally valuable resource of a new or refounding community is its leaders. Several excellent works have already been written on the kind of leaders needed in this transition period of religious life. Such leaders must have an "ability to listen," a "creative imagination," and a "passionate commitment to refounding." They must be action-oriented, committed to hard work, have little need for affirmation, and great perseverance in spite of failures.[39] They must be achievement-oriented and activists who plan ahead, and who are not afraid to use their power.[40] Most importantly, they must be deeply spiritual and possess a mystical sense of God's support and presence.[41]

The type of person which these researchers are describing is a *charismatic leader.* For Max Weber and other sociological theorists, the word "charismatic" did not refer to membership in the Pentecostal movement. Instead, the word denoted a particular type of authority. Charismatic leaders derive their leadership ability from the force of their own personalities, and from their followers' sense—and their own—that they have been specially graced by God to fulfill their role.[42] In contrast, traditional leaders are obeyed because members of their family or tribe have always been obeyed. And bureaucratic leaders—the "typical" leaders of the Nygren and Ukeritis study—are those whose authority is based on the official rules and job descriptions attached to their position.[43]

Most founders/refounders of religious congregations in the past have been charismatic leaders. This appears to be almost an essential prerequisite for the role—especially in the most innovative groups. Only a charismatic leader has the ability to discard traditions, to transvalue established ideas, to say, "It was written, but I say unto you."[44] Such individuals serve as living models of the new vision, far more inspiring and attractive than the abstract philosophical articulation of the same vision would have been.

While there have been communities in the past that did not have charismatic founders,[45] the lack of such leaders often handicapped their later development. Several historians, for example, have noted that the reluctance of the Dominicans to accord charismatic status to St. Dominic (at least not to the same extent as the Franciscans had done to St. Francis) ultimately led to serious difficulties in articulating exactly what the order's basic ideological framework was.[46] The early Carmelites actually invented a charismatic founder, St. Simon Stock, whom modern historians doubt even existed.[47] Charisma can also be suppressed and short-circuited, which is equally harmful. The restriction and persecution of the charismatic founders of women's communities often resulted in the dilution or even the elimination of what was most innovative and prophetic about their visions.

Members with the potential for charismatic leadership are, therefore, tremendously valuable resources for any religious community today. Every congregation probably has several of these individuals but, as Arbuckle points out, these individuals are probably *not* currently its leaders and may be quite reluctant to become so.[48] Their personal gifts are their vision and their enthusiasm, and not necessarily their administrative or maintenance capabilities. Many in the congregation may consider them to be "fanatical" about their personal "thing," and they may even be disliked by some because of this. Established congregations tend to prefer "maintenance" leaders who will not rock the boat unduly, or "pastoral" leaders who are facilitating listeners to the members' concerns. When fostering charismatic leadership, therefore, communities might apply Arbuckle's axiom that "the new belongs elsewhere" and encourage its charismatic leaders to establish separate sub-communities in which their distinctive visions can be incubated, tinkered with, and developed.[49] This is not an abandonment of the charismatic individual, but rather an enthusiastic support: the group which forms around each leader's vision may be the nucleus of the refounded community. The larger congregation should uphold these groups by directing new members their way, as well as by providing whatever other resources they may need.

OTHER RESOURCES

While no resources are as important to a new or refounded community as its supply of new members and its charismatic leadership, there are other advantages which such groups should also have. In this section, we shall consider four: a recognized and valued "environmental niche," adequate finances, access to favorable publicity, and a stable relationship with the church's hierarchy. Some of these resources are more vital than others, but the lack of any one of them could seriously hamper a community's survival and growth.

A Recognized and Valued Environmental Niche

The external counterpart to the new ideological frame which redefines a community's goal and purpose (see above, chapter 6) is the recognition and esteem which this purpose receives in the church and in the larger society. In previous refounding periods, the meaning and purpose of religious life was widely understood and highly valued. Teaching and nursing congregations in nineteenth-century North America and in seventeenth-century France provided valuable services to Catholics at a time when alternatives were either unavailable or tainted with Protestant proselytization. Medieval monks and nuns provided valuable spiritual intercession with the Divine; the mendicant friars and later the Jesuits fought the incursions of heresy by evangelization and missionary work. Whatever the primary activity of the religious communities in a given period was, it was held in high esteem by some or all of the hierarchy, by the secular ruling elite, and by the lay masses. Because their meaning and purpose was so well understood and valued, the orders could expect other Catholics, and even non-Catholics, to provide them with financial support, favorable political intervention, land and property, and, of course, the always necessary new recruits.

As several studies have noted, the loss of role clarity among today's religious has been accompanied by a parallel loss of their "environmental niche" in late twentieth-century Catholicism.[50] Most surviving Catholic schools have few or no religious teaching in them and, especially in newer suburban areas, lay Catholics may not be convinced of the need for a separate Catholic educational system at all. Catholic hospitals have, on average, fewer than 1.5 sisters engaged in bedside nursing,[51] and the increasing governmental and economic restrictions on their functioning make them less and less distinguishable from non-Catholic hospitals. Catholic social work agencies are perceived as ministering primarily to non-Catholics—a holy work, surely, but one from which the average middle-class Catholic today gets little benefit. And few sisters or brothers are employed in these agencies, either. So what good are religious any more—why should the church bother with them? One recent study notes:

> As religious orders moved away from their mission to teach, heal and offer social services in parochial institutions, they were unable to identify a new niche for themselves in either the Church or society....Instead, many orders are struggling to redefine their purpose in more abstract, ideological terms such as "the witnessing of Christian values," "standing with the poor of society," and "dedication to fostering the mission in the world." But these redefinitions of purpose are more difficult to justify in terms of their necessity in society.[52]

When a religious community *does* choose a purpose that resonates with the needs of some subgroup within the Catholic community, they may find themselves opposed by competitors who claim a prior right to that niche. One new group of monks encountered intense resistance from neighboring parish priests who feared that the monks' goal of providing a variety of liturgical services to laypeople would draw parishioners away from their own churches.[53] Opposition from powerful actors on whose "territory" a new or refounded community is "poaching" can derail a refounding effort. Attacking these opponents, however, can have even worse repercussions.

Many writers claim that the new role of religious life is to be a prophetic witness to church and society. This may, in fact, be true. But prophecy, by definition, elicits intense opposition from whatever powerful elite group is being prophetically challenged. Any religious congregation which embraces a prophetic mission had better have the active support of a large popular following and/or of some powerful elites in order to counterbalance the antagonism of those they will inevitably offend. Mendicant friars such as St. Anthony of Padua could denounce the greed and laxity of the secular clergy only because they enjoyed papal support and were, moreover, intensely popular among the laity.[54] Bartolome de las Casas could oppose the slave-owning Spanish colonists only as long as he had church backing. In more recent eras, the prophetic stance of religious in El Salvador against that country's repressive government has enjoyed the active support of the populace, whose children refill the seminaries to replace those whom the military has martyred. The challenges of Polish priests and religious against Communist oppression were backed by both the Vatican and the people.[55] If religious communities in North America and Western Europe truly adopt a prophetic role as their defining purpose, they will offend people. They must, therefore, locate other people who appreciate and support their prophetic stance.

In contrast, focusing on evangelization, prayer and community might be a more appreciated niche in contemporary North American/Western European culture. While the market for retreat houses in many areas is already saturated, there are many elements of the Catholic/Christian population which these establishments do not reach effectively. It would take a fair amount of creativity to locate populations of (e.g.) public school teen-agers, twentysomething singles who are no longer in college, or inactive Catholic adults, and then to devise programs that would be appealing to them. But, if this could be done, evangelizing such populations would be a new niche which religious could fill in the church.

Financial Resources

Another reason why finding an environmental niche has been important in the past is that, traditionally, this was also the source of a community's financial resources. Early Christians brought gifts of food to the fourth-century hermits in exchange for their prayers; medieval nobles endowed monasteries for the same reason. Parents who sent their children to seventeenth- and nineteenth-century convent schools paid tuition for their instruction. If the money from tuition was not enough, seventeenth-century French convents might also receive donations from lay benefactors, who frequently gained increased social prestige or spiritual merit because of their generosity.[56] A valued environmental niche, therefore, serves the added function of providing the material sustenance of the community.

Today, interestingly, there seems to be a movement away from a community's connecting its sources of financial support to its basic goal or purpose. Most of the new groups I have studied make a distinction between their reason for existing and how they make their living. The monks at the Monastery of the Holy Cross work part time at whatever jobs they can find (one bagged groceries in a supermarket), but their *ministry* is their prayer and their provision of the most inspiring daily liturgies possible for the people of the city. The Little Brothers of St. Francis and the Franciscan Sisters of the Renewal were founded for an evangelization of presence to the poor of the inner city. Currently both of these groups depend solely on alms for their subsistence, but they expressed a willingness to work part time at whatever jobs they could find if money someday became a problem. The Teresian Carmelites have a primary ministry of communal prayer and some retreat work; they operate an in-house business support service for their financial needs. Similarly, in many established apostolic communities, fewer and fewer members work in their congregation's traditional institutions. Many simply try to give Christian witness in whatever job they happen to have, just as any lay believer would be expected to do. What makes them religious is not their work, but rather their community affiliation and vowed lifestyle.

Since this trend is occurring independently in both new and

established communities, it is likely to be part of whatever model develops for twenty-first century religious life. The *purpose* of religious communities will be to foster community and spiritual growth, both in the members themselves and in the larger society. Some few may make their living from this purpose—communities that give retreats, for example. But, at present, most community members appear to be accepting whatever money-earning opportunities the secular (or ecclesiastical) job market provides.

There are several potential liabilities to this development. Living totally on alms is well and good when all the community's members are young and another thing entirely when they become aged and infirm. Working in establishments not owned by one's community renders one vulnerable to the vicissitudes of the job market and the biases of one's employers. Whereas, in the past, elderly religious could expect to fill some sort of job in a community school or hospital for as long as they were physically able to do so, today's aging sisters often feel the bitter results of age and sex discrimination. Large institutions can also be powerful: in the current period of flux and instability in health care, for example, Catholic hospitals have a greater opportunity to influence the results than individual sisters or brothers working in small clinics could ever have. And the congregational institutions of the past provided some women religious with opportunities for professional advancement that, even today, remain essentially closed to their sex in the larger job market. Other than a dwindling number of women religious, how many female CEO's are there in U.S. hospitals?

Despite these liabilities, however, both new and established communities appear to be moving away from the former practice of receiving their material sustenance primarily through the operation of their basic goal or purpose. If this continues to be the case, they will have to take careful thought for how they will secure the financial resources necessary for their future. But financial resources are not the only resources a new or refounding community will require.

Public Relations

Seriously lacking to religious life in many countries today is the vital resource of a favorable public image. From *Nunsense* to

Sister Act to *The Father Dowling Mysteries*, women religious are
depicted as immature and childish featherbrains who need the
guidance of normal adults before they can function competently
in the real world. The picture appears to be getting worse rather
than better; the nuns in *Lilies of the Field* and *The Trouble with
Angels* showed at least some wisdom, and Hayley Mills and
Sidney Portier learned something from their run-ins with them.
In still earlier depictions (*The Bells of St. Mary's*, for example),
nuns were portrayed as strong and intelligent women, whom
priests and laity respected. Such is rarely the case today.

The current image also has a darker side. What sister, upon
being introduced as such, has not immediately been regaled with
stories of ruler-wielding grade school dictators whose sadism
sometimes seems to grow with each retelling? What male religious has not cringed at the assumption that a few pedophiles
are typical of all men in his community? Such negative depictions can be truly vicious: witness the play, *Sister Mary Ignatius
Explains It All to You*, for example.

No other group accepts being treated so contemptuously by
the popular media. African-Americans are not expected to be
amused by Stepin' Fetchit movies; feminists do not laugh at dizzy
blonde jokes. Hispanics objected so strongly to the "Frito
Bandito" commercials that the company pulled them from the
air. In a memory that remains somewhat painful even today, I
remember once being firmly told by a Japanese American that
the *Saturday Night Live* sketches of "Samurai Tailor" were really
not funny. What does it say of the self-image of women religious
when we laugh at such insulting portrayals? What does it say
about our lack of church support when these images are not
denounced by the clergy and hierarchy? Bishops would object to
a movie that portrayed diocesan priests as idiots; why not to similar portrayals of nuns?

What can we do to change these images? We can, of course,
register our objections to the current state of affairs—although
previous groups that have protested their unfavorable media
depictions are often accused of whining and being deficient in a
sense of humor. On a more positive note, we could mobilize our
resources to promote more positive images. The exploits of the
first priests and sisters on the Western frontier (my own commu-

nity's Sister Blandina foremost among them), as well as of the Civil War battlefield nurses, would make several wonderful miniseries. Made-for-TV movies have focused on dynamic lay teachers (e.g. Marva Collins and Jaime Escobar) who have goaded inner-city students to excellence, and *Sixty Minutes* recently profiled an elderly physician who treated Harlem residents for free. Why are similar presentations not done more often for the work of present-day religious?

Our resources to change our media image are greater than we realize. Many communities contain members who are the relatives or friends of national and local screenwriters, producers and actors. Many other communities taught such individuals in their schools. A concerted effort should be made to tap these connections. Perhaps national organizations such as LCWR or CMSM could coordinate such an effort. The payoff would be well worth the investment. Only if we are taken seriously and admired in the larger culture will its members even think of joining us.

In addition to improving the overall public image of religious life, individual communities must also take active steps to insure that their own mission and purpose is widely known. Local media ties should be cultivated for this purpose, and other ways of "getting the message out" about a community's charism and activities should be explored. Some congregations are doing this sort of public relations, of course, but much still needs to be done. One new community I interviewed—a small group with a well-thought-out and inspiring charism of evangelization and contemplative prayer—was concerned that so few new entrants were applying. I noted, "There are at least a dozen Catholic colleges in this city. Have you ever contacted their Newman Centers to see about starting weekly volunteer programs so that their students can accompany you in your street ministry work?" Well, no, they hadn't—they were relying on a single yearly ad in the vocation magazine *Visions.* An established contemplative community expressed similar concerns about their lack of new members but, when I asked them, admitted that they did not even arrange to have the schedule for their daily mass and the divine office posted at the neighboring Catholic parishes and colleges, although outsiders were graciously welcomed whenever they happened to show up for these services. If few people are aware of who we are, how can we expect them to decide to join us? In addition to their active involvement in personally inviting new entrants, therefore, the "tithe" of time devoted by every member of a new or refounding congregation should include locating and activating as many of these outreach channels as possible. We must put aside the false notion that letting others know who we are somehow violates the virtue of humble self-effacement. St. Francis, St. Ignatius, Theresa Maxis, Benedicta Riepp, and other founders and foundresses were not "too humble" to share their visions. Nor should we be.

Relations with the Church—and Its Hierarchy

Although individual religious communities may have been started by bishops, true refounding periods have never been initiated by the church's hierarchy. This is inherent in the nature of both groups. As I have noted above (chapter 5), the primary role of religious life has been to rearticulate Catholic theology and spirituality in answering the strains and social discontinuities of a new social milieu. The hierarchy, in contrast, is charged with ecclesial operation and maintenance—a more conservative, but equally necessary, work. Thus, communities begun by bishops have usually been established to meet a specific practical need in that bishop's diocese, not to develop new and more congruent models of religious life.

As part of their official role, church officials must actually cultivate a degree of skepticism regarding the most creative founding/refounding efforts. Many incompetent and even manipulative individuals may gather groups of people around them and claim to be founding religious orders. It is the canonical duty of the bishop to monitor the establishment of new religious communities in order to prevent abuses, but at the same time to respect any true call which a given group may be receiving from the Holy Spirit. Obviously, this is a fine line which is difficult to discern. The more innovative a group and the more charismatic its founder, the more likely it will be to experience ecclesial opposition. As one Vatican official has noted:

> Through various periods of its history, the Church has tried to block the beginning of new institutes or to render more difficult

the foundation of new religious families. The fact of such obstacles and difficulties notwithstanding, new institutes and new forms of consecrated life have arisen.[57]

Bishops have few organizational incentives to support the founding/refounding of a religious community within their dioceses in any active manner. According to the founder of one new group:

> No one can blame a bishop for trying to avoid extra work. There's so much on the average bishop's plate now that any more would seem cruel. And so, when a new community, following the directives of Canon Law, approaches their Ordinary, it's probably natural for him to groan a bit—more work. Unfortunately, many do more than just that. More than a few simply refuse to answer mail—my own experience will attest to that.[58]

Bishops get few personal or career benefits from supporting a new or refounded community. If such a group experiences financial difficulties, if its charismatic leader is accused (however unjustly) of starting a cult, or if the members seem to be adopting threatening practices such as feminist liturgies or activism for the poor, the resulting negative publicity may actually hurt a bishop's standing with the Roman authorities. Supporting a new community through its inevitable growing pains may simply appear to be another hassle, which a bishop may decide he does not need.

Clerical and episcopal support is, therefore, often difficult for a new or refounded community to obtain, and it may involve such a level of interference as to destroy whatever was innovative or attractive about the group in the first place. Furthermore, for refounding communities at least, the members may have such painful memories of past ecclesiastical oppression that they want no part of any official "support." In spite of all this, a community's good relationship with at least some level of the church hierarchy is a valuable resource which should not be lightly discounted. At least since the Middle Ages, few if any founding/refounding attempts have succeeded without the strong and active support of church officials.

Such support is necessary for several reasons. First of all, it lends stability to a fledgling community as the new group weathers the inevitable stresses that come with charismatic leadership.

(See chapter 10, below) Endorsement by church officials lends popular legitimacy and favorable publicity—both valued resources in any attempts to attract new members. Underground and unauthorized religious communities do exist without official approbation, but they are likely to be even more ephemeral than the new groups that enjoy such support.

Again, the focus on evangelization and prayer would be more likely to win clerical and episcopal support than the other foci which have been suggested for religious life in the twenty-first century. The pope himself has recently issued a call for a "new evangelization." Of course, a community should never adopt its primary focus just to win the support of a priest or a bishop—or even of the pope. But such support, when available, is an extremely valuable resource.

I believe that a continued membership in, and an active relationship with, the church is an essential component of religious life. Despite the remarks one occasionally hears from individual religious that they have no problem being a member of their congregations but that they no longer want to be members of the Catholic Church, these two memberships are essentially linked. As Doris Gottemoeller has noted:

> At religious profession we renewed our baptismal commitment, and thus signaled that membership in the church is intrinsic to the way of life we were choosing....To allow ourselves to be alienated from the church is to surrender our birthright: it is to deprive ourselves of life-giving nourishment; it is to be exiled from our true home. Furthermore, public estrangement from the church deprives its other members of the explicit witness of our lives, our truth, and our fidelity.[59]

One might argue that the "church" to which religious should belong is some sort of ecumenical, generic Christian church. But a small, beginning group with no one institutional sponsor ends up having to fend for itself. And most Protestant denominations have a weak or non-existent tradition of sponsoring religious communities. For most new communities, Catholic sponsorship will be the only option.

Finally, if my analysis of the role of religious virtuosity is correct and religious are to articulate the theology/spirituality of

Catholic Christianity in the cultural categories of twenty-first century society in the same way as the monastic, mendicant and apostolic orders did for their respective centuries, then they cannot divorce themselves from institutional Catholicism. If we abandon the church and develop our spiritual answers to societal strains apart from it, we will relegate Catholicism to a position of irrelevance in many of the most central sectors of future society—as it was irrelevant to many segments of nineteenth-century Western liberalism. And we will probably also condemn ourselves to irrelevance as well—without institutional support, it is unlikely that a religious community will outlive the lives of those who refound it.

What this appears to mean is that a new or refounded community must seek the acceptance and support of a group of individuals—the members of the church hierarchy—who either may not be inclined to give it to them, or worse, who may attempt to remake the community according to their own interests. Some officials may even prefer that the more creative and challenging of these "upstart" communities leave Catholicism, especially if they are attempting to exercise some sort of prophetic voice.[60] In previous refounding periods, bishops have deposed, excommunicated, exiled, and imprisoned founders and foundresses; they have appropriated infant communities' property and funds, and placed their entire membership under interdict. And yet these men and women did not leave the church that so unjustly mistreated them, nor did they waver in their own belief in their divine call and in their conviction that the will of God would be done. As the recently beatified Australian foundress, Mary McKillop, noted about her own public excommunication:

> I really felt like one in a dream. I seemed not to realize the presence of the bishop and the priests. But I felt, oh, such a love for their office, a sort of reverence for the very sentence that was being passed on me. I was intensely happy and felt nearer to God than I had ever felt before. The sensation of the calm, beautiful presence of God I shall never forget.[61]

One writer is of the opinion that the sufferings of the founding group have a "co-redeeming" quality: that their communities subsequently prosper in proportion to the number and severity of the founders' persecutions and trials, which often occur at the hands of the very church officials who should be supporting them.[62] I believe that the mystery is deeper than that. New forms of religious life that are meddled with, or even suppressed, by the hierarchy do not always prosper. Some are exterminated—the Beguines, for example. Some have their original charism deformed into something very other than what the founder/foundress had intended. The death or deformation of a vision is in some ways even harder for members and founders to accept than the congregation's organizational death. Notwithstanding the likelihood of such a demise, of injustices, of pain and misunderstanding, the very nature of Catholic religious life makes the support of church officials essential. Perhaps the "death" of one new religious community will seed its vision in another group at a different time and place. Or perhaps it won't. We may never know, but we have to seek church support anyway.

CONCLUSIONS

What do we need for a refounding journey? We need an all-consuming vision that resonates with the deepest felt strains and discontinuities of twenty-first century society. We need concrete daily practices—prayers, rituals, vows—that enflesh this vision in our community. We need members, and we need to be able to define exactly what distinguishes these members from non-members. We need sources of new recruits. We need, at least initially, charismatic leaders who are on fire with the vision and embody it for the rest of us. We need public and ecclesiastical support. Most of all, we may need a little "holy insanity" to believe that any group would possibly be able to find all these resources, even with the help of God. If we did not have the example of so many previous founders and foundresses who faced similar odds, we would probably despair. But our predecessors have proved it is possible. Who, initially, would have wagered a single penny on the likelihood that St. Francis, St. Dominic, St. Teresa of Avila, or Mary Ward would ultimately succeed in their endeavors?

Even to have fulfilled all of these prerequisites and to have set out on our refounding journey, however, is not the same as to have arrived at our destination. We may get sidetracked or lost; our "car" may break down; we may discover that we have overlooked something essential. The next chapter will give some hints on "troubleshooting" the difficulties which will inevitably arise during our refounding journey.

A CHECKLIST FOR THE JOURNEY

- Why do we wish to exist as a community?

- What is the difference between being a member of our community and not being a member?

- What kinds of membership categories will we have?

- What vows (if any) will we take?

- How will we live community?

- *Who is most on fire with our vision?*
  - *What are these persons' strengths and limitations?*
  - *In what ways/positions can these charismatic individuals best inspire the rest of us?*

- *Where can we find persons to invite to join us?*
  - *What actions will we take each day/week to invite these persons?*
  - *How/when will we meet to reignite our own enthusiasm and share our successes and failures?*
  - *What groups can we link up with to help us invite people?*

- *How can we get the message out about our vision?*
  - *What media contacts (church and secular) are possible?*
  - *What other publicity is possible?*

- *How will we earn our living? How will we provide for illness/old age?*
  - *How crowded is the environmental niche we seek to enter?*

- *How favorable is the local bishop to our refounding efforts?*
  - *What kinds of support would we like the local bishop to offer?*
  - *What other persons in the church (local and/or national) will support us?*
  - *How can we convince these individuals to be more supportive?*

10

Journey Disruptions:
Lost Route Retrieval
and Vehicle Maintenance

People who take vacation trips tend to follow one of two process-es. Some begin by visiting AAA and carefully mapping out their route, noting possible tourist attractions to visit along the way, reserving motel rooms in advance, picking up travelers' checks, and so on. Others simply decide to vacation in (e.g.) the Smokey Mountains, throw a few things in the car, and set out. For the lat-ter group, part of the charm of a vacation is the serendipity of being able to follow the opportunities that each day offers, unconstrained by a pre-ordained schedule.

I confess to being a member of the "preplanning" category, at least when it comes to vacations. Because of this subconscious bias, I have probably given the impression that similarly thor-ough preplanning should precede any attempt at a refounding "journey." The checklists following each of the last four chapters may have seemed like the "Things to Do Before Leaving" lists which I, and other preplanners, often make before starting on our vacations.

Nothing, however, would be more detrimental to the survival of a new or refounded community than to attempt to map out every stage of its journey before beginning. In fact, according to one study of the many utopian communes that sprang up in the nineteenth-century United States, it was the most carefully pre-delineated communal visions which were the most likely to be "irrelevant to the every day problems of initiating group life."[1]

181

Instead of planning our refounding journey in such detail, we must simply start out, inspired by our vision of where we want to go, but having only the vaguest idea of how to get there, who will join us, and what supplies we will need. And we must be open, as we journey, to the possibility that our originally envisioned destination may not be exactly where we are called to go. Once "on the road," we must engage in a continual discernment: making and remaking our itinerary, retracing our steps when we stray, refueling our community "vehicle" and repairing it when necessary, and picking up new supplies when we discover that we need them. This chapter will outline some of the many studies which have chronicled this process. Their findings may help us in fashioning our own journeys.

RECTIFYING ERRORS

Studies of other communal groups are unanimous in emphasizing the tenuous character of their beginning phases. "The initial periods of group life are...typically marked by confusion and disarray," states one author.[2] "Even the most organized nineteenth and twentieth century communes did not spring full-grown from a blueprint," notes another. "Instead, they went through periods of anarchy, chaos, non-direction, high turnover and open boundaries as they struggled to translate global ideals about community into specific behaviors."[3] Any religious who truly attempt to found or refound their community will make many, often serious, mistakes. Some of these mistakes will be so severe that they may easily destroy the entire project. This is a frightening prospect. Only those who never start out on the refounding journey—remaining content instead merely to talk, year after year, about someday doing so—will avoid mistakes. And that would be the greatest mistake of all.

Material Arrangements

One of the most common factors which can derail or divert a new community is unanticipated difficulties in meeting the concrete demands of its members' daily lives.[4] Zoning regulations, police harrassment, lack of available employment opportunities, or unexpectedly infertile soil may keep a new community in continual upheaval, forcing it to move repeatedly from place to place. Hostile neighbors, church officials and other established religious communities may accuse them of being a cult and refuse to support them.[5] Some may even actively persecute the group. On a more subtle level, the only location available to a new community may not be the one which is most appropriate for their developing charism. One new monastic group that I visited was established for the purpose of providing daily liturgical prayer opportunities for downtown workers. The community soon found, however, that the only available church and living quarters were too far from the center of the city for office employees to stop by before or after work. This seriously hindered them from pursuing their original goal. The members of another group were only able to find remunerative positions as pastoral associates in a remote rural area, even though nothing in their original vision related to this type of ministry. The isolation of the area also made it hard for them to attract new recruits. It is often difficult to know how to interpret such situations. Sometimes these unexpected practical difficulties may be the Spirit's way of moving the group in a new and better direction. At other times, however, the compromises necessary to pay their medical insurance, to defuse opposition from the bishop and/or the vicar for religious, or simply to put a roof over their heads, may divert the new community from its original vision without substituting anything better. With its original charism compromised, the new community may gradually lose fervor or even dissolve.

Social Arrangements

If material arrangements are one of the two most common sources of failure for new communal groups, social arrangements are the other. Both Berger and Zablocki note that interpersonal conflicts were responsible for over half of all the communal dissolutions they studied.[6] Another difficulty is defining boundaries: Who is and who is not part of the new community? What are the responsibilities, rights and duties of members vis-à-vis the group? Several researchers note that most communes have had difficulty with the members' reluctance to commit themselves totally to the new way of life. These members often retained private property which they did not turn over to the group, kept outside jobs, or maintained friendships and family obligations that drew them away from the community.[7] Such outside ties made it easier to withdraw from the community when things got rough. In contrast, successful communities, even if they were "somewhat loose and open to possible recruits in early years," soon developed "a definable structure and definable admissions criteria" to determine who was a member and exactly what membership required.[8]

Still another social arrangement that must be worked out once the group has begun is to decide the amount of voice each member will exercise in community affairs. Again, this is a powerful source of dissension in many communities.[9] Americans instinctively assume that democratic forms of group governance are best. But at least one historian has documented the fact that many nineteenth-century utopian communities dissolved *precisely because* their members got so bogged down in endless "democratic" meetings over trivial petty rules that they lost sight of their original vision. "Most colonies encouraged democracy and pluralism, a virtue that had hidden costs....Democratic in intent out of a noble impulse to show absolute fairness to all voices on all questions, the penchant for talk came with a price tag. Special daytime meetings interrupted work...they leached away relaxation hours....At the least, frequent meetings simply became one distraction along the road to steady progress."[10] At the worst, entire communes could be "hijacked" by a vocal minority with discordant ideals. Lacking a means to deal with this minority, a commune's decision-making apparatus often became paralyzed. Some dissolved. Others abruptly changed course and alienated their founding members, who subsequently left.

Ironically, as Kanter has noted, the most enduring communal groups were highly centralized *as well as* highly participative.[11] Such a balance, obviously, is hard to achieve. A new community would benefit from "mentoring" by outside facilitators as they struggle to steer a viable course between democratic participation and group unity. Such mentors might be other, more established new groups which have already weathered similar difficulties, or they could be interested and experienced leadership figures from the original, parent community. With such help, a refounding subcommunity would have a better chance of survival. Still other difficulties, however, also await them.

Failure of the Group Myth

According to chapter 6, the most important prerequisite for founding or refounding a community is that the group have a compelling vision of what they want to do and why they want to do it. Without a consuming fire, a goal that makes their whole enterprise meaningful, they would probably not dare to begin a new community—and they would certainly not be able to keep up their enthusiasm for very long. But such a vision is also a source of danger. Previous groups have succumbed to what Kersten calls "visionary vision": they "immersed themselves so deeply in the brilliant glow of the future that they came away blinded to the prosaic obstacles that blocked their path to its glory."[12] The members' enthusiasm led them to oversimplify the magnitude of the tasks before them, or, even worse, to deny the existence of interpersonal discord and financial mismanagement that should have been plain to see. As the community collapsed about them, the visionaries continued to insist that all was well, because surely their noble and inspiring vision could not *possibly* be derailed by such petty difficulties.

The visionaries' eagerness to begin also made them prone to rashness. Often, they did not think through all the options available to them, and so settled on a location, a lifestyle, or a manner of earning sustenance that was less than satisfactory.[13] Many took on large mortgages without really planning how they would meet the payments, especially if some unforeseen calamity, such as bad weather, a recession, or illness were to strike. When unexpected difficulties did occur, tremendous strains resulted, which the communities were ill-equipped to meet.

While no new community should attempt to spell out solutions for every eventuality ahead of time, they should realize that some minor emergency or other will occur almost daily, and they should make plans for dealing with such eventualities when they arise. "In the absence of a carefully worked-out strategy for dealing with the day-to-day organizational procedures, most colonies fell back on traditional administrative formalities."[14] This bureaucratic "red tape" gave the illusion of doing something without actually addressing the causes of the problem, and, in the process, irritated and alienated the members. Bureaucratic demands also usurped the leaders' time and isolated them from the rank and file. As one former commune leader noted:

> Hardly ever could a...Servant...spend even half a day working alongside brothers in the garden or building. They devoted more and more of their time to an increasingly complex inter-[commune] correspondence with an exchange of reports in six, eight, ten, or more copies, as frequently happens with expanding business corporations. For this they needed a clerical staff....As the members gradually abdicated from an intimate knowledge and control of Brotherhood affairs, it became more difficult for them to discern and correct any wrong direction that a group of Servants might be taking.[15]

The vision decayed as bureaucratic procedures increased.

As with their social arrangements, the successful communities were those which somehow managed to strike a balance between maintaining the fire of their visionary enthusiasm, and yet not allowing it to blind them to the practical necessities of daily life. Refounding communities will need to achieve a similar balance today. Possibly they may need to solicit advice on this from other new groups, or from their parent congregation. Regular networking sessions may need to be set up where such information can be exchanged, successes celebrated, and failures remedied.

Conclusions

Most communal attempts failed, historians have found, not through a single, major mistake, but rather through the "accumulated minor details of life."[16] No community can possibly foresee and plan ahead for all the challenges it will face; it must set out "blind," so to speak. *The fatal mistake is to avoid dealing with these challenges when and as they arise.* Perhaps because of a misguided hope that if a problem's existence is denied long enough it will go away, unsuccessful communities ignored accumulating difficulties until it was too late. The increasing discrepancy between the stated ideals of the group, on the one hand, and what was really happening within it, on the other, ultimately became too great and the group dissolved, often in rancor and profound bitterness.[17]

To avoid this eventuality, any group wishing to found or refound a religious community must assume that it will make mistakes. Rather than letting this prospect deter them from ever setting out, they must begin their refounding journey anyway, in the context of an ongoing process of discernment. Perhaps the larger congregation that has "seeded" the new group might fill the role of "outside" facilitator in this process—meeting with the daughter community and helping it face and work through issues its members would rather avoid. This would be an invaluable service which was not available to most of the failed communes studied by historians, and would greatly increase a new group's chances for survival. Other discernment methods should also be devised—and practiced frequently and thoroughly. The sooner travelers are able to recognize that they are on a wrong road and begin to retrace their steps, the more likely it is that they will arrive at their destination.

The gradual accumulation of unfaced issues, however, is not the only thing which can derail a new community. Another source of difficulty is often the group's leadership.

PROBLEMS WITH CHARISMATIC LEADERSHIP

As the previous chapter has pointed out, most new religious communities were begun by a "charismatic" individual—one whose qualifications for leadership rested, not on family inheritance or bureaucratic appointment, but on the way he/she embodied the group's fundamental vision.[18] Charismatic leadership is necessary because, while bureaucratic or familial authority deals well with routine events, "in times of psychic, physical, economic, ethical, religious, [or] political distress," the leaders of a community must be "holders of specific gifts of body and spirit; and these gifts have been believed to be supernatural, not accessible to everybody."[19] In the tenuous times of founding/refounding a religious community, the vision of a truly charismatic leader—and the members' loyalty to that leader and to his/her vision—are necessary in order to transcend the inevitable stresses that would otherwise accumulate and cause great difficulty. But as valuable a resource as it is for a new community, charismatic leadership presents its own set of problems.

The Problem of Prolonged Charismatic Leadership

By its very nature, charismatic authority is anarchic and unstable. Because of this, a new community's period of charismatic leadership should probably last no longer than five or ten years. "As Weber pointed out, charisma, especially 'pure' charisma, is incompatible with the requirements of any kind of social organization with prospects for long-term survival."[20] Sooner or later, the charismatic authority of the leader must be "routinized" if the community is to survive.[21]

The reasons for this are many. First of all, charismatic leaders hold their authority because of the "graced" vision which they personally embody; not because of any formal election or appointment with a set term limit. "[Charismatic leadership] knows no agency of control or appeal...nor does it embrace permanent institutions like our bureaucratic 'departments'.... Charisma knows only inner determination and inner restraint."[22] Obviously, prolonged possession of such great power can be dangerous—for the members, for the community, and for the leader him/herself.

> When Rajneesh was still a university lecturer, he had to face the possibility that someone would challenge his arguments. In short, he operated in the ordinary world of verbal give and take. But as he became the center of a growing religious movement, he became removed from this world. He interacted only with his inner circle and with selected sannyasins and visitors in brief encounters on terms suitable to himself. He therefore could expect that no one would express anger to him in his presence, that everyone would agree with what he said, or disagree in the most agreeable manner possible.[23]

As the community increases in size and fewer members can have direct access to the founder, attempts may be made to emphasize his/her charismatic qualities through special symbols and rituals:

> As the communicative distance widened between [Rajneesh] and his followers, he became "present" everywhere in the movement

by symbolic means. He allowed himself to be photographed frequently, and pictures of him were predominantly displayed throughout the ashram. As the possibility for prolonged closeness to him grew remote, the significance of occasional closeness was symbolically magnified. [His] charismatic radiance became so intense that those who were drawn to him felt privileged simply to get an occasional glimpse of him from a distance.[24]

Too long an exposure to this kind of adulation could obviously lead to an induced messianic complex, especially in a leader who was already caught up in a compelling vision. As the cases of Jim Jones and David Koresh have made abundantly clear, prolonged charismatic leadership is psychologically unhealthy for those who wield it. Deprived for too long of the normal checks on their behavior, such leaders can lose touch—fatally—with reality.

Prolonged charismatic leadership is also unhealthy for a community's membership. The "totalitarian features or propensities"[25] latent in all such communities can combine with the members' self-sacrificing religious fervor to induce dependency and actual psychotic manifestations:

The charismatic commune is a dangerous place to live. There is probably no form of social organization in which the participants are more prone to behavioral influences over extended periods of time that go completely counter to actions they would take as isolated individuals.[26]

Prolonged charismatic leadership is also detrimental to the future of the community as an established group, since it inhibits the development of leadership skills in the other members. The longer the charismatic founder retains primary control, the less capable of governing themselves his/her followers will become, and the less promising will be the community's chances of surviving its transition to new leadership after its founder dies. Furthermore, as inspiring as the leader's original vision may have been, it will have to change and develop as the decades pass. If the founder continues too long as the sole charismatic repository of the vision, this development may be hindered.

Two kinds of leadership, therefore, are needed in a newly founded/refounded community:

> The first [phase] calls for leaders impatient with the past, and temperamentally disposed to an irreverent break with tradition.... However, phase two...calls for the opposite type: patient leaders, people temperamentally disposed of careful evaluating and building up.[27]

Each kind of leadership has its flaws; each kind is also necessary. The delicate point of transition from one to the other always has the potential of disrupting the group or deflecting it from its vision. In day-to-day, practical terms, how will the founder(s) train successors—how much autonomy will these successors be allowed to exercise, and how soon?

The Routinization of Charisma

Eventually, all charismatic leadership becomes "routinized."[28] This may happen while the founder is still alive. Several authors have described how the daily business of large and successful communal groups is gradually taken over by the leader's immediate staff. "The founder becomes dependent on a staff for the performance of necessary work, and the staff becomes dependent on the founder for policy directives and/or serving as the spiritual center of the movement."[29] Over time, the staff may acquire a large amount of informal power, and tensions may develop between the charismatic founder and the bureaucratic subordinates who manage the group's daily affairs. Some founders become "captives" of their staffs—mere figureheads in whose name the decisions are made. Other founders attempt to reassert their authority by constant shakeups, loyalty tests, pitting staff members against each other, appealing to the rank and file directly, or by other similar tactics.[30] Such attempts to prolong charismatic authority cause constant turmoil, which is yet another danger to the community.

At the latest, charismatic authority must be routinized when the founder dies. This is a key moment in the life of any community. How can the members nourish their commitment to the founding vision and their willingness to sacrifice their own interests in its behalf, now that the one who most clearly articulated the vision and its demands is gone? Elsewhere,[31] I have outlined the ways in which communities have typically bolstered their members' ideological commitment with affectional ties, together with the provision of concrete benefits for staying and/or penalties for leaving. Through such repeatedly-rediscovered techniques as common rituals, boundary maintenance against outside ideas, working and living together, shared sacrifice, and even mortification sessions, communities act to bolster their members' commitment once the charismatic founder is no longer present. Newly-refounded groups will differ in their ability to apply such commitment mechanisms, and those which are unable to do so will eventually dissolve.[32]

It is important to emphasize that a community's vision is no less authentic once these daily routines and supplementary commitment mechanisms are introduced. Devaluing the routinization process "smack[s] of an 'evangelical fallacy' that exalts 'the Spirit' over 'the letter.' ...I do not share the assumption that a dramatic vision is inherently more spiritual than the actions of an instructed conscience, or that a frenzied dance in the Spirit is more legitimately religious than reading and writing about the nature of good and evil."[33] Groups, like individuals, naturally pass through developmental stages. The charismatic stage is a community's infancy and childhood; routinization of charisma is its adulthood. Both phases have their strengths; to attempt to stop a community at its charismatic stage is to forego the benefits of the later stages. But each stage also has profound weaknesses and, ultimately, each bears the seeds of the group's destruction.

The Dangers of Routinization

The more effective they are in maintaining the necessary level of commitment, the more these communal mechanisms will simultaneously undermine it. As I have noted elsewhere,[34] practices such as sacrifice and mortification are psychologically dangerous. Boundary maintenance can lead to rigidity over minor matters, and thus result in an inability to make necessary changes. Ultimately, such mechanisms displace the group's ideological commitment, and members become prone to stay primarily because of their affiliative ties to other members, or because they have been isolated from the outside world so long that they fear returning to it.

The commitment mechanisms were thus a two-edged sword. Without boundary maintenance, common activities, sacrifice and mortification, communities were short-lived and ephemeral, subject to destructive schisms and heterodox excesses. But *with* the commitment mechanisms, religious orders became hollow shells held together, as generation succeeded generation, not by the members' commitment to the founding ideology (which, in any case, had become increasingly maladapted to the concerns of a changed socio-cultural environment), but instead by inertia, by in-group affiliative bonds, and by the personal benefits that could be gained from membership. Such communities abruptly collapsed when confronted with hostile persecutions or with new and enthusiastic orders built on some innovative model which the established orders could not match.[35]

Still other dangers result from successful routinization. If a community can successfully retain and mobilize its members for a common vision, it may ultimately amass extensive communal wealth from their sacrifices. Such wealth can be dangerous, as it often leads to laxity. One seventeenth-century French superior noted that "great temporal wealth ruins religious houses," and that "there is as much to fear from seeing them too rich as too poor."[36] Another historian observed that wealthy communities were likely to exhibit "endless feuds over money and possessions, minimal spiritual fervor among noble ladies of idleness, and the widespread adoption of a secular lifestyle."[37]

Another problem arises with the entrance of new members who have never known the founding generation. In the process of systematizing the behaviors and beliefs involved in the group's ideological frame and then imparting the resulting package to individuals who had not personally experienced the founding days, much may be lost or transformed. And if the order has been *very* successful in recruiting new entrants, it may have to impart this knowledge on a "mass production" basis that could stifle the creative spirituality which the order will eventually need when adapting to future conditions.[38]

The Tensions of Community Growth

As they grow and develop, all religious communities must navigate between sets of opposing poles. One of these tensions,

Oved notes, is between isolation and involvement. Movement by a new community to either extreme

> led to a serious erosion of communal life and its eventual destruction. Complete isolation led to a severing of ties with the outside world and to stagnation, while full adaptation to the conditions of existence and the rules of the outside world led to assimilation and loss of uniqueness.[39]

A related source of tension was between sustaining continuity with the founding vision and being open to change.[40] A certain amount of ideological inventiveness is necessary to meet new challenges, but the group must not drift so much that it becomes unrecognizable. Previous communities have usually erred on the side of continuity rather than change:

> In the history of the long-lived communes, a substantial gap developed between the rapid rate of change in the surrounding environment and the slow, controlled changes that took place in [the community]. The communes had two options open to them: to adapt to change, thus risking exposure to new ideas that might destroy "the old way" and erode the basis of [their] beliefs, or to increase and intensify their seclusion, ignoring events taking place in the world, and in this case risking stagnation....[41]

Again, the balance between these poles is a delicate one. Most new or refounded religious communities will constantly err on one side or the other, recovering from one overemphasis only to swing to the opposite extreme. The prospect of such detours, however, should not deter a community from setting out. Even with mistakes and misdirections, a community that *begins* its refounding journey has a better chance of arriving at its destination than one that never leaves the driveway.

"ARRIVING"

People who embark on a vacation trip are usually able to tell when they have reached their destination. And, once having completed their stay, they rarely find it difficult to evaluate whether their vacation was a "success" or not. If their original purpose was to relax and have a good time, did they have one? If they intended to tour the main Civil War battlefields or the chateaux of the Loire Valley, did they manage to do so? Did five days of uninterrupted rain prevent their getting a tan, or did the noisy and inebriated conventioneers in the hotel room next door disturb their sleep?

Evaluating the "success" of a new religious community is much more problematic. On the one hand, God's standards are not our standards. A religion whose founder was executed as a common criminal can hardly expect to measure the "success" of any of its endeavors the way rock stars list their platinum records or politicians count the votes they received in the last election. Indeed, the "failure" of a pioneering religious community may pave the way for later groups who learn from their experiences. St. Francis de Sales, for example, viewed the imposition of cloister upon the Visitation Sisters as the defeat of his original purposes. Despite this failure, the vision of the Visitation Sisters served as an inspiration to a host of later communities—and ultimately supplied St. Vincent de Paul with a way to get around the claustral restrictions that had hobbled the former community.[42] We may never in our lifetime learn whether the dissolution of one refounded community after only two years was "really" a failure—or whether another group's explosive growth in wealth, prestige, and number of new recruits was "really" a success—as God views such things.

Even on the material plane, it is difficult if not impossible to measure the success of any communal experiment. As one researcher who has extensively studied such groups pointed out, there exists no "single known set of criteria by which it is possible to judge the success of a communal society."[43] He then lists, and proceeds to demolish, several of the most commonly used of these criteria. All have relevance to judging the "success" or "failure" of a refounded religious community.

Did the Community Accomplish Its Stated Goal?[44]

On the surface, the most logical criterion for gauging a community's success would appear to be the one[s] adopted by the community itself. Surely, it would be unfair to judge a community for not living up to standards it had never said it would meet. Conversely, it would not seem unreasonable to question whether the group *had* fulfilled the goals its members had set for themselves.

Such an evaluation, however, raises both philosophical and practical questions. Many communal groups were founded to await an imminent apocalypse. If the end of the world does not come when expected, then the continued *survival* of a millennial community could be regarded as a failure. And what about the "successful" completion of the carefully-rehearsed mass suicide plan at Jonestown? Would the People's Temple have been a "failure" if the cyanide had not worked? Jones told his followers that a life of eternal bliss awaited them after a mere moment of pain, and that they should be anxious to make the transition.

Some might object that revolutionary suicide was not part of Jim Jones' *original* goals, and was a desperation measure designed to cover up the group's imminent failure. But many revered and "successful" communal groups also adopted their most salient practices after they were begun, and then concocted post-hoc religious justifications for the change. The Shakers, the Harmony Community and Amana, for example, were not originally communal at all. Several of the most innovative founders came to a full realization of their new vision only *after* several years of trying to build their religious community on some previous model.[45] Do changes of goals signify failure? "To what extent shall we allow a community to change its mind?"

Other difficulties also arise. Many communities, and the individuals in them, are equivocal about their goals—perhaps because they do not wish to expose their internal differences over exactly what these goals are. If one faction's goals win out over another faction's, is the community a success or a failure? Finally, some goals may be considered inhumane by outside standards. "Some contemporary communal sects, for example, are accused of physically brutalizing their members,...terrifying them with irrational and paranoid fears, inculcating them with vicious bigotry,...or even plotting the murder of outside opponents." Is it right to judge such communes "successes," if they achieve their goals?

Does the Community Conform to Some Objective Standard?

Some critics prefer judging communities by some common, objective standard, even if the communities' members themselves never intended—or even vehemently opposed—such a standard. For example, several writers have gauged the success of family communes by how closely they approached male-female equality.[46] Is this a fair standard to apply to (e.g.) a fundamentalist Christian community that explicitly denies the equality of the sexes?

The most commonly-applied external criterion is whether the community provides for the personal growth of the members. This, too, is difficult to assess. Every community *claims* to provide supreme personal growth and fulfillment for its members, whether as a direct goal in itself or as the inevitable side effect of its more transcendent aims. There is often intense social pressure on the members to attest to such growth. In his own field research, Wagner encountered "glowing testimonials of personal 'growth' from all members, even those secretly planning to leave the commune permanently. Letters from Jonestown reflected similarly ecstatic references to the members' personal fulfillment, even during what survivors later described as a time of endemic despair." Still another difficulty is deciding what definition will be used for "personal growth." How would we judge, for example, a religious community which eschewed a professional, "worldly" education for its members in favor of fostering their growth in prayer or contemplation?

A philosophical problem with the use of personal fulfillment to evaluate communal success is that many psychologists have seriously questioned whether *any* community can achieve its communal goal without sacrificing individual growth and development to at least some extent. "Freud, for example, maintained that any society, to the extent that it achieves its end efficiently, thwarts the individual's fundamental desires and produces personal misery. For Freud and other anti-utopian theorists, humankind may pursue either a perfectly-ordered society or genuine personal development, but not both at once." If this is true, then any religious community which aspires to some transcendent goal or purpose will necessarily infringe upon its members' personal fulfillment—and will thus "fail." And any religious community which places individual fulfillment first will become a self-help group whose primary function is "to serve the individualistic and narcissistic needs of its members."[47] Is such a community a success?

How Long Has the Community Existed?

One of the most straightforward and easily measured criteria for evaluating communal success is longevity, and many researchers have used this standard as their sole indicator. Again, there are problems. Longevity may be irrelevant to some groups—especially apocalyptic ones or "personal growth" communes whose purpose is to develop individuals so that they no longer need a communal crutch. Also, can we really evaluate long-lived communities as successful if their survival has been achieved through rigid commitment mechanisms that have usurped the founder's original vision? Communities in the Franciscan tradition, for example, have traditionally been relatively lacking in the commitment-maintenance techniques that so many other orders have employed. As a result, they have been exceptionally volatile, declining and dying—and also being refounded—at a faster pace than communities in other traditions.[48] Is a succession of renascent Franciscan communities more or less successful than (e.g.) the 1500-year-old monastery at Monte Cassino? Or are such questions meaningless?

How Large Is the Community?

Another common practice is to define a community's success in the terms of the number of its members, its wealth, or the influence it was able to exert on the surrounding society. This was commonly the way in which religious communities were tempted to evaluate themselves in the past. But such a criterion presupposes that "bigger is better," which may not be the case. Some communal groups, such as the Hutterites (at over 300 years of age, surely a "successful" community according to the longevity measure), strictly limit the number of persons in any one community, and split into two completely autonomous halves when they grow beyond that point. Traditionally, Benedictine, Carmelite, and a few other monastic groups have done the same thing. Beyond a certain numerical point, the members of a community lose contact with the center and a certain amount of bureaucratization sets in. Is this success or failure? Similarly, financial "success" may not be good for a community, if it leads to a dilution of the group's original ideals.[49]

I realize that, in chapter 7, I have argued that a sufficient, and relatively large, number of religious are necessary in order to be truly a leaven in society. This remains true. But it does not follow that each individual religious community has to be large. A community will have to discover for itself the pros and cons of various sizes for the fulfillment of its charism.

After reading the past few pages, one might conclude that it is essentially impossible to tell whether a given refounding attempt has succeeded or failed. At one level, this is true. But that must not deter us from trying. The definition of success may be uncertain, but there is, however, one absolutely sure definition of failure. And that is never to begin at all—to mouth platitudes about "dying with dignity" as we retreat into lethargy, to concoct alibis about "the worldliness of society today" and "young people's inability to make commitments," to cover up the fact that we have never really tried to refound our congregations. The ultimate failure would be to stand idly by while the next generation of religious virtuosi seek their call elsewhere.

Conclusions

Where does all this leave us? After generating 200 pages of text (and a superabundance of footnotes!) I would condense it all into one simple piece of advice: Start the journey. Flowery "Vision Statements" are not enough. Start the journey. The whole congregation will not take part. The whole congregation *should* not take part. As Hostie put it after studying a millennium and a half of refounding attempts: "Every *lasting* reform is rooted in the phenomenon of *a small group* that takes up again on its own account the way of foundation."[1] So find a vision which consumes and vitalizes you, one which you are willing to die for—and to live the rest of your life for—and start the journey. Don't wait until fifty, or twenty, or even ten people are ready to go with you. If others do not see religious going anywhere that is clear and distinctive, why on earth would they join them? Start the journey, alone if need be, and *then* invite others to come along.

Expect to "fail." Expect to fail several times. Expect to lose your way, to forget essential supplies, to suffer breakdowns (and breakups), to journey painstakingly for years only to face dead-ends and washed-out roads. Even if the larger congregation mentors your attempt, if they publicize your experiment and recruit new members for you, if they challenge you when you stray from your ideals and encourage you when you return to them—and this is precisely the role which established congregations *should* be playing to support their members' various refounding attempts—you will, quite possibly, *still* fail. Learn from your mistakes and try again...and again. That is what founders and refounders do. That is the crucifixion, the "Passover," to which they are called. The resurrection, we know by faith, will also occur.

from *Passover Remembered,*

by Alla Renee Bozarth

Pack nothing.
Bring only
your determination
to serve and
your willingness
to be free.

Don't wait for the bread to rise.
Take nourishment for the journey,
but eat standing, be ready
to move at a moment's notice.

Do not hesitate to leave
your old ways behind—
fear, silence, submission.

Only surrender to the need
of the time—to love
justice and walk humbly
with your God.

Do not take time
to explain to the neighbors.
Tell only a few trusted
friends and family members.
Then begin quickly,
before you have time

to sink back into
the old slavery.

Set out in the dark.
I will send fire
to warm and encourage you.
I will be with you in the fire
and I will be with you in the cloud.

You will learn to eat new food
and find refuge in new places.
I will give you dreams in the desert
to guide you safely home to that place
you have not yet seen.

The stories you tell
one another around your fires
in the dark will make you
strong and wise.

Outsiders will attack you,
and some who follow you,
and at times you will weary
and turn on each other
from fear and fatigue and
blind forgetfulness.

You have been preparing
for this for hundreds of years.
I am sending you into the wilderness
to make a way and to learn my ways
more deeply.

Those who fight you will teach you.
Those who fear you will strengthen you.
Those who follow you may forget you.
Only be faithful.
This alone matters.

Some of you will die in the desert,
for the way is longer than anyone imagined.
Some of you will give birth.

Some will join other tribes
along the way, and some
will simply stop and create
new families in a welcoming oasis.

Some of you will be so changed
by weathers and wanderings
that even your closest friends
will have to learn your features
as though for the first time.
Some of you will not change at all.

Some will be abandoned
by your dearest loves
and misunderstood by those
who have known you since birth
and feel abandoned by you.

Some will find new friendship
in unlikely faces, and old friends
as faithful and true
as the pillar of God's flame.
. . . .
So you will be only
the first of many waves
of deliverance on these
desert seas.

It is the first of many
beginnings—your Paschaltide.
Remain true to this mystery.

Pass on the whole story.
I spared you all
by calling you forth
from your chains.

Do not go back.

I am with you now
and I am waiting for you.

This is a portion of the poem, "Passover Remembered," from *Womanpriest: A Personal Odyssey*, by Alla Renee Bozarth, revised edition, LuraMedia 1988; also in *Stars in Your Bones: Emerging Signposts on Our Spiritual Journeys*, by Alla Bozarth et al, North Star Press of St. Cloud, 1990, and on the audiotape, *Water Women*, poems by Alla Renee Bozarth, Wisdom House Press, 1990. All rights reserved by the poet. (San Diego, CA: LuraMedia, 1988)

APPENDIX:

Journeystories

The following groups are fictional, although some are loosely based on actual new and refounded religious communities which I have visited around the country.* Each "journeystory" has been written to illustrate some of the trends–a spiritual and communal focus, varied types of membership–which I believe are reshaping religious life. All share the basic traits which new communities have found essential in the past: they have formed around a charismatic leader (or leaders) with an all-consuming vision, they have links to some institutionalized source of recruitment, and they are more demanding of their members than many of the readers of this book will find comfortable. Each story also includes a sampling of the problematic issues which still may need to be faced.

These are only a small number of the many stories that could be–and are being–written. A very useful preliminary exercise for refounding a religious community would be for the potential travelers to gather and create a journeystory for their own future religious life.

STORY #1: THE COMMUNITY OF ST. JOHN

Journey's Destination (The Primary Purpose of the Community):

The Community of St. John is based upon the words of Christ in the gospel of St. John: "By this shall all know that you are my disciples: that you have love for one another"(John 13:37). The members speak of their community as a living laboratory for the practice of all kinds of love—sisterly, brotherly, spousal, friend— and of each person as a unique song of God's love in the world.

History:

The two founders of the community were members of an established religious congregation, the Oblate Sisters of St. Scholastica (OSS). One, Sister Mary, had degrees in psychology and marriage counseling, and was in charge of the Marriage Encounter programs for the diocese. The second, Sister Ann, was

---

* The *names* are completely fictional. If there are real-life communities named Oblate Sisters of St. Scholastica, Poor Hermits of St. Francis, Community of St. John, etc., I am *not* referring to them.

on the pastoral team at the Newman Center of the local university. Mary was inspired by the depth of sharing she witnessed in the Marriage Encounter sessions, and began to urge that a similar process be initiated in all the local OSS houses. The larger congregation did not act on this suggestion, but Mary and Ann and the two other sisters they lived with began to hold monthly "Community Encounter" meetings themselves. Ann, a charismatic and dynamic young woman who was quite popular among the students frequenting the Newman Center, also began an ongoing Encounter program in some of the dorms and fraternity houses there.

Over time, the other two sisters living with Mary and Ann moved on. A third OSS sister joined them, and three college students asked to stay with the community for the summer. When the fall semester began, two of these students asked to remain with the group. Three more college seniors and two recent graduates joined the following spring. Since several of this new contingent were men, and since Mary's and Ann's convent had only six bedrooms, the group rented a second house near campus to which the men moved. The large living room and furnished basement of the new house began to be used more and more frequently for "Encounter Followup" sessions, as many of Mary's original Marriage Encounter participants wished to continue meeting on an ongoing basis. Gradually, the married couples began to share meals and liturgies with the college students who lived upstairs.

Who's Going? (Types of Membership):

There are several different types of membership in the Community of St. John. Some fifty couples comprise the Married Community. They meet each Wednesday evening at one of the core community's* houses (the group now owns eight throughout the diocese) for prayer, a communal supper with the core community, and an extended sharing session which follows a special format the members have devised over the years. Part of the sharing session is "Praise Time"—a time for mentioning aloud and celebrating the unique gifts of each member.

---

*This group calls itself the "Cor" Community—a deliberate pun on the Latin word for "heart."

The College Community (a name which is becoming some-what inappropriate, since many of its members are graduates and some have never been to college at all) is divided into two subgroups, the "interns" and the "externs." Over eighty externs live in the college dorms or in apartment houses around the city, and meet with the Married Community and the Cor Community on Wednesday evenings. The twenty or thirty interns live with the Cor Community for periods of three months to two years. During that time, they pay an agreed-upon maintenance to the local house. They take no vows, but are expected to live as the Cor Community lives while they are there.

The Cor Community takes vows of celibacy and "community." By the latter vow, they covenant to share all their material goods with each other and to subordinate their own personal desires to the needs of the group. The Cor Community members are rotat-ed by lot between the community's eight local houses every four or five years, since a fundamental principle of the community is that each person should endeavor to get to know and love all the others. The members of the Married and College Communities also shift to new core houses for their Wednesday meetings every few years.

All members are expected to participate in a formation pro-gram, in which they study and discuss the writings and tran-scribed talks of Sister Mary, Sister Ann, and Brother James (the priest at the Newman Center, who joined the group in its third year). The focus of these writings, and of other literature and seminars set up for the novices, is the group's philosophy of see-ing God even in personalities most alien to one's own. The Cor Community requires six months' live-in postulancy (which is waived for the interns who decide to join the group), and two years of novitiate before vows. Members of the Married and College Communities also make two years of novitiate, sharing in some of the seminars and retreats for the core novices, as well as in their own program (devised and run by long-time mem-bers of the College and Married Communities). The interns have no formation program as such, but they are expected to have been externs for at least one year before applying to be interns.

Ongoing formation is also required of all members. The Married and College Communities have bi-monthly Saturday retreats, which the Cor and the interns also attend. A large, week-long gathering also takes place each summer at a rural retreat center. All members plan their vacation times so that they will be able to attend. The relatives and children of the members are also invited to participate in the liturgies, seminars, discussion programs and just plain fun that goes on during that time.

How to Get There (Daily Routines and Practices):

All members participate in daily Lauds and Vespers. The Cor Community and the interns do this communally in the eight core houses, where they are joined by many of the externs of the College Community. While it is not formally stated, an extern is expected to link up with one of the eight houses (or, in a few instances, with a couple in the Married Community) and join them for either Lauds or Vespers several times a week. An extern who was routinely absent from these prayers would be challenged by the rest of the community. Married couples say Lauds and Vespers together in their homes with their children. All members are expected to spend time in personal prayer—thirty minutes for the Married Community members, as much as two hours for the Cor Community members. Members also attend daily mass at local parishes.

Lauds and Vespers are followed (or, in some cases, preceded) by the two common meals of the day. At breakfast, each member of the local house (or each family, in the case of the married couples) shares his/her plans for the day. At supper, each reports on the ways God has been present in their experiences. A period of "Praise Time" is also part of the supper sharing. The common evening meal and Vespers is usually followed by some "Together Time." Sometimes this is simply recreational, but each local house or individual member is also expected to choose and participate in one of the many service projects that the Community of St. John has adopted. Many members give Marriage Encounter and Engaged Encounter workshops in parishes and on college campuses, and they have developed an extensive conflict management program which they present for free in inner city schools. One core group has developed a parenting skills program for unwed teen-aged mothers. Another popular program is their "How to Build a Lasting Marriage" series. Many "twentysomething" singles and college students are leery of marriage because of the intensely painful experience of living through their own parents' divorces. The series is targeted at these people, who may not be engaged or even seriously dating someone yet. Participants often attend for several years, and "graduate" to the Engaged Encounter and Marriage Encounter workshops later.

The intense daily interaction, prayer, and sharing in the community inevitably leads to frictions. Part of the daily sharing session each evening is an intense time of soul searching, in which the local community members attempt to surface and resolve any unfinished issues of the day. Once or twice a year, a more serious disagreement will erupt in one of the houses. A special mediation team has been elected to help in such instances.

All of this takes time. The core group and the interns rarely hold more than half-time outside jobs, and even some of the married couples and externs have found it necessary to work reduced hours. The members are committed to living simply on less income, rather than sacrifice the time given to shared prayer and community development. There is also a strong community norm about sharing goods. None of the core members or interns may possess his/her own stereo or TV. (Many of the Married Community apply this standard in their houses as well.) The one TV set in most core houses is rarely used—Sister Mary calls it an "anti-community drug."

Supplies for the Journey (Recruitment and Other Sources of Assistance):

Most new members learn about the community through its extensive programs in parish Marriage Encounters and on the college campuses. A national Catholic magazine published an article two years ago on the group; currently three individuals and two young married couples from other states have joined them as temporary interns, intending ultimately to return to their own dioceses and begin similar communities there.

Relations with the previous bishop were good, but the current bishop is much less supportive. The community's governing council (Sister Mary, Sister Ann, Brother James, one married couple and a long-term extern member) have some doubts about the future. They would like to obtain official status as a Public Association of the Faithful, but the local vicar for religious interprets canon law as saying that they would have to do so as three or four separate communities, which they are unwilling to accept. Brother James also foresees trouble when he asks to be removed from diocesan status for full community membership, since the priest shortage in the diocese is severe.

Problems Along the Way:

The intensity of interaction and sharing which is expected of group members has alienated many in the diocese, as well as disturbing the relatives of some of the members. For a while, there was some brief publicity accusing the founders of starting a cult, and a diocesan investigation of the group was conducted. The investigation exonerated the community, but their reputation is still controversial. The members believe that the current bishop's "coolness" dates from this time. Other critics accuse the group of being too inward-focused, of engaging in a sort of narcissistic self-absorption instead of trying to alleviate the needs of the world. The members retort that the most basic need of early twenty-first century American society is alienation within families and isolation from friends and neighbors—which they are trying to ameliorate by their own lives and by the programs they offer. They are still quite sensitive about the issue.

The schedules of the members also present an ongoing difficulty in meeting the demanding round of communal activities. (One core group had to schedule its Lauds/Breakfast sharing at 5:15 AM, and its Vespers/Supper Sharing at 8:30 PM, in order to include everybody). The intense sharing has twice led to marriages between male and female members of the Cor Community, who then moved to the Married Community. While this outcome was joyously celebrated, the initial exclusiveness of the couples during their courtship had been a source of tension. The community still isn't sure how exactly to handle the problem of exclusive attractions in its communal core.

A major difficulty felt by the community is that, so far, its members have all been white and middle class. Several efforts have been made to invite Latinos and African Americans to join—especially from among the students and parents in the conflict resolution and parenting skills programs which the community runs—but, so far, none have done so. The community is divided on what, if anything, to do about this.

In a few months, some of the temporary interns are going to return to their home diocese and begin a similar community there. The Community of St. John is currently discussing how closely the two groups ought to be affiliated with each other and whether there should be any financial or government ties between them.

STORY #2: THE TREE OF LIFE COMMUNITY

Journey's Destination:

The members of the Tree of Life Community are dedicated to the intense belief that every human life, no matter how apparently "useless," is a supremely precious gift. They have pledged themselves to saving and/or bettering the lives of those whom the larger society would discard.

History:

The community grew from Holy Innocents Home, which was originally a shelter for unwed mothers and an adoption service for their babies. By the late 1970's fewer and fewer women were coming to Holy Innocents to have their children, and whole wings of the building began to stand empty. At the same time, there were a number of "unadoptable" infants and children with multiple handicaps who had nowhere else to go. The city approached the board of Holy Innocents in 1981 about serving as a facility to handle profoundly retarded and severely handicapped children.

The volunteer coordinator at Holy Innocents was Grandmother Jones, a dynamic African-American social worker who was devoted to "her babies." Under her inspiration, many of the volunteers began to gather for prayer in the morning and evening in the Holy Innocents chapel. Many of the paid workers joined them. When only two sisters were left in the convent wing, they invited Grandmother Jones to join them. One of Grandmother Jones' grown daughters, who was a nurse at Holy Innocents, and several of the other volunteers also moved into the former convent and began to live communally with the two sisters.

In the late 1980's, crack was introduced to the poor areas of the city, and many crack-addicted babies began to be born. With the support of the religious congregation that had operated Holy Innocents and the blessing of the Holy Innocents board, Grandmother Jones opened a second facility for these babies. Later, a hospice for homeless AIDS patients and a home for Alzheimer's victims were opened.

Who's Going?

While there are several types of membership in the Tree of Life Community, not all of the formal distinctions between them have ever been spelled out. Grandmother Jones has traditionally been impatient with such distinctions. She has a tendency to assume that everyone is as totally committed as she is. Still, over the years, some informal classifications have begun to form. Each residential facility has a core of people—men and women, married and single—who live in the building and devote themselves to caring for the residents. (The married couples tend to operate small group homes; the singles are more often found in the larger residences.) In addition, there are a large number of volunteers who join the core group for prayer and service. A number of married couples in the city have formally adopted some of the children; they form a third subgroup in the community. Finally, there are membership categories for the residents themselves—one for some of the mentally and physically handicapped "children" (who have by now reached early adulthood and still reside in Tree of Life facilities), and one for the dying AIDS patients. Except for the married couples who have adopted children, there is no permanent membership category—members make a commitment for two or three years and may renew it if they wish.

The formation of the core members has been heavily influenced by Jean Vanier's writings, and several have spent time in the various L'Arche communities. There are training sessions for the volunteers and an apprenticeship program for married couples who wish to adopt the children. The chief focus of the organized formation program, however, is deepening the prayer life of the members. Grandmother Jones and Sister Jane (her close friend and one of the two sisters in the convent wing who had invited the first group to life with them) are both adamant that prayer is utterly essential in order to be able to see God's love and purpose in those they care for. All members receive extensive and ongoing training in contemplative prayer forms and are expected to spend at least one hour a day in prayer.

How to Get There:

Each of the Tree of Life facilities, even the smallest group homes, has a chapel. The community prays Lauds, Sext, Vespers and Compline there each day. The format and the time of these services varies according to the schedule of the house and the physical and mental capacities of the members, but Lauds is generally before breakfast, Sext before lunch, Vespers before supper, and Compline before bedtime. Whenever possible, the volunteers join the core and residential communities for these prayers. Married couples who have adopted the children say similar prayers at home. The prayer times are joyous occasions, with brightly colored banners, singing, clapping, and even (sometimes) dancing. A common daily activity is preparing songs, music, artwork, poetry readings, etc., for these services. All take part in this creative activity, even the Alzheimer's patients and the smallest children. The community has compiled a songbook over the years, with the favorite songs the residents have "written." Outsiders visiting the Tree of Life liturgies are always profoundly touched by the universality of participation and the simple joy the members exhibit.

The members of the community do not have a formal habit, but all do wear the "Tree of Life Cross." This was designed by one of the early members who has since died of AIDS. It depicts a crucifix from which leaves and flowers are sprouting—both from the wood of the cross and from the body of Jesus. Core members wear a large version of this cross on a cord around their necks; volunteers and married couples have small pins with the same motif. The handicapped and AIDS members choose whichever version best suits them. (One young member has a Tree of Life bumper sticker on his wheelchair.)

Supplies for the Journey:

Initially, members were recruited into the core community through Holy Innocents' extensive volunteer program, as well as through the nursing and social work programs and the Newman Center at a local college where Grandmother Jones had extensive connections. More recently, the diocesan Right to Life Office began to publicize the group in the local parishes and several members were attracted through this route. A national Right to Life organization featured the Tree of Life Community in one of its publications, and so more and more of those who come to the community have an active background in the Right to Life Movement.

The local bishop actively supports the community. He himself was the NCCB coordinator of Pro-Life activities, and so he is delighted that such an effort has begun in his diocese. He actively searches out new ways to publicize the group.

Problems Along the Way:

There are pros and cons to the Tree of Life Community's growing connection to the Right to Life Movement. On the one hand, the movement publicizes the community and directs committed and enthusiastic potential members its way. On the other hand, the larger society's ideological baggage is beginning to cause a split in the community. Some of the members, especially those from the college networks and the AIDS community, are "put off" by what they see as the more recent members' single-minded focus on abortion. It doesn't help that a proportion of the former subcommunities are African-American and Latino, while the Right to Life members have tended to be white. The support of the bishop is also a mixed blessing, since it tends to skew the community to the Right to Life agenda. A growing debate is developing over the mix of activities which the group should engage in, in order to affirm life in all its aspects.

To date, the members have taken no vows. Some, however, are beginning to express a desire to ritualize a permanent commitment to the Tree of Life Community. There is much discussion over what form this commitment should take, as well as the relative rights and responsibilities of permanently committed members as compared to the rest of the community. The two sisters in the group are also under some pressure from their former congregation either to rejoin that community or else to regularize their status in the Tree of Life. Things are further complicated by the fact that Grandmother Jones is now in her seventies, and many in the community are beginning to wonder how the leadership of the community will look in the future. The diocesan officials are urging the members to write an official constitution and apply for status as a public association of the faithful (and, eventually, as a diocesan community). Such a move, however, would require the adoption of the three traditional vows of poverty, chastity and obedience, and would also mean that some of the subcommunities would no longer be considered "real" members. There is much resistance to this idea among some of the members, while other members strongly support it.

STORY #3: THE POOR HERMITS OF ST. FRANCIS

Journey's Destination:

The Poor Hermits of St. Francis draw their inspiration from the ancient rule which St. Francis of Assisi wrote for hermitages. They wish to live as contemplatives in the midst of the poorest persons in the city. They are emphatic that they are not social workers, nor do they provide any services to the poor other than their prayers and their presence.

History:

In the mid-1960's a group of male Franciscan tertiaries began an evangelization ministry to the homeless in a large midwestern city. They would visit the skid row and the flophouses, and pray with the men living there. Eventually, three of this group felt a call to live a more contemplative life and moved into an apartment in the district. They began to spend most of their days in prayer, continuing the street evangelization ministry a few after-

noons a week. A few others joined them, and an elderly woman
in the area left her house to the group when she died. They
applied to the bishop for status as a public association of the
faithful, and were approved in 1980.

Who's Going?

Currently, there are six men in the community. Following St.
Francis' original recommendation, they never intend to get
much larger. If two or three more men join, the group will split
into two autonomous hermitages and the second will move to
another city. They already have invitations from several dioceses,
should they ever get large enough to do so.

There is no female branch of the group. A few women did try
to begin a similar community in another house in the neighborhood, but left for safety reasons. Walking in groups of one or two
into such neighborhoods is even more dangerous for women than
for men. The men have reluctantly accepted this fact, and no
longer attempt to recruit women. A small group of associates pray
with the community once a month and help support their street
evangelization ministry, but these are not considered members.

Formation consists of spending three to six months as an
"Observer" (i.e., living with and as the community while discerning one's call), then another six months of postulancy and a year
of novitiate. Temporary vows are taken for five years, followed by
final vows. Those in formation take classes in lectio divina, centering prayer and the Franciscan history and tradition. They also
immediately begin to participate in the street evangelization program. If the group ever becomes large enough to split into two
hermitages, each hermitage will have its own formation program.

How to Get There:

The hermits practice an intense daily prayer schedule. They
chant the full liturgy of the hours, as well as spending at least
three hours a day in private prayer and eucharistic adoration.
Each morning, they walk to the local church for mass. Except for
the mid-day and evening meals and the evening recreation, the
community maintains silence in the house. They take the traditional three vows, including a solemn vow of poverty. In the spirit

of St. Francis, they have rejected the option of becoming ordained.

The community requires an equally intense practice of poverty. The hermits have no car, TV, radio, stereo. Not only do they not subscribe to any newspapers or magazines, they reject the offers of such periodicals from others. Personal poverty is also quite strict. Each member has only one brown habit, with another worn one to wear while the first is being washed. They do not shave, smoke, or use any personal hygiene products other than soap and water. They live entirely on alms and donations, although they are not rigid about this. When money once ran short, they took part-time jobs working in a warehouse, and they would be willing to do so again should the necessity arise. But they would take only menial, part-time work, to be more in solidarity with the poor.

There is no cloister. Neighborhood people can come to the door in the afternoons for a listening ear or a prayer, but no money or goods are given out. At least three afternoons a week, the hermits walk a short distance from their house to the city's skid row and homeless shelters, where they continue their street evangelization ministry. At such times, they simply befriend the poor—they say that there are other agencies which dispense food, shelter, and other services, but that no one but the Poor Hermits of St. Francis will pray with the homeless, learn their names, and become their friends. On other days of the week, some of the hermits visit AIDS patients in a local hospice, and, of course, at least one stays home in the afternoon to be present to the neighborhood people who call at the house.

Supplies for the Journey:

The hermits enjoy the good will of the bishop, who has been willing to grant them official status despite their small numbers. The numbers, however, show little sign of increasing very rapidly. The community lacks the routinized recruitment channels that direct interested applicants to the Tree of Life Community, the Community of St. John, and the Apostles of the Good News. They have taken out a small vocation ad in several Catholic publications, but this has had only sparse results.

Problems Along the Way:

The major difficulty the hermits have is with burnout. The intense poverty and the prayer schedule look romantic at first, but many recruits lose fervor after a few years, when the reality of spending the rest of one's life in such a demanding environment sinks in. Even two of the three founding members have left. When added to the lack of recruitment channels discussed above, this makes for a very precarious existence. The hermits are currently exploring the possibility of initiating temporary membership, but there are questions about whether these members would have equal status and decision-making responsibilities as the permanent members. There is a strong feeling among the hermits that they do *not* want to create any kind of "class structure" in the community.

STORY #4: THE APOSTLES OF THE GOOD NEWS

Journey's Destination:

The Apostles are two charismatic communities, one of men and one of women, dedicated to the evangelization of youth and other "unchurched" individuals.

History:

The Apostles were started by Father Peter, a Franciscan priest who became actively involved in the Charismatic Movement when it first began back in the late 1960's. As the chaplain at a large midwestern university, Father Peter helped catalyze the foundation of a charismatic covenant community on that campus, which still exists there.

By the late 1970's, however, some of the members of the covenant community began to express a desire to create a religious community. The most active in this effort was a young woman named Julie (who later became Mother Mary Julia of the women's community). After several false starts, which involved the group's bouncing between three dioceses in the early 1980's, the bishop of one southwest diocese invited them to come to his area, and provided the first "Motherhouse"—a run-down and vacant inner-city convent, which the Apostles later renovated with their own hands.

Mother Mary Julia and five of her followers moved there in 1983. Father Peter and the male Apostles joined them in 1984, moving into the adjacent rectory. The two communities received official certification as Public Associations of the Faithful in 1985; in 1990, both were chartered as diocesan communities. The celebrations marking this event were held in the newly-finished chapel of the group's retreat center—a project begun in 1987 and only recently completed. Both the men and the women Apostles now have larger motherhouses on the retreat house grounds.

Who's Going:

Currently, the women Apostles have thirty-seven professed members; the men have fifty-four. In addition, there are eight novices and three postulants discerning entrance into the women's community, and eleven novices and five postulants in the men's. While the Apostles are closely connected with charismatic covenant communities both in the southwestern city where they now reside and on the midwestern campus which they left, the members of these groups are not considered members of the Apostles. The various covenant communities across the nation (and around the world) do, however, channel potential members to the Apostles. Because of this, the Apostles are quite multi-ethnic in membership.

Formation includes six weeks of observership, six to nine months of postulancy, two years of novitiate, and three to six years of temporary profession. New entrants take classes in scripture and theology at their motherhouses, offered by the faculty members of a local Catholic college who are sympathetic with the charismatic movement. Since the group has a large Latino contingent, all of the Anglo members take Spanish and all of the Latino members who need to do so take English. Both groups are also studying Haitian Creole, in preparation for a foundation in Miami. Several of the male novices and temporary professed are studying for the priesthood at the diocesan seminary.

Formation also includes a mentored training program in evangelization work. Within a week of entering, the new observers are participating in the community's basic work of evangelizing: singing and playing guitars at youth liturgies and retreats, witnessing at local high schools and college Newman Centers, or even handing out literature on street corners and engaging the people there in discussion. (The Apostles say that all times and places are good opportunities for spreading the gospel.) The effectiveness of the new members' efforts is noted and discussed at weekly planning/feedback sessions. As the specific evangelization gifts (singing, writing, art, etc.) of each new member become more evident, they are paired with an older member who is also skilled in that area, and who acts as a mentor.

How to Get There:

The Apostles have chosen a "Contemplative-Active" lifestyle. Mornings are devoted to prayer: mass, Lauds, lectio divina, and an hour of eucharistic adoration. Afternoons and evenings are usually devoted to evangelization activities; the younger members also have classes during this time. The members who operate the retreat center and those who travel to other parts of the state to give parish missions have a different schedule while they are engaging in these activities, but they try to keep the "mornings for prayer/afternoons for evangelization" pattern as much as possible. In the evening, those of the group who are available gather for an hour of charismatic prayer, in which they each praise God for the blessings of the day and the blessings of the other members' gifts and presence.

Both communities wear a blue habit, sandals, and a cowl and scapular when praying and evangelizing, but they have blue jeans and similar attire for heavy work. The younger professed members also wear jeans for some of the youth ministry activities—hayrides, cookouts, volleyball games, and the like.

Supplies for the Journey:

As has already been mentioned, the Apostles receive most of their members through the charismatic renewal movement. The communities have been featured in several periodicals read by Catholic Pentecostals, and many charismatic prayer groups hold retreats at the Apostles' retreat center.

The communities have it written into their constitutions that they will never own institutions, nor will they accept a permanent assignment in a parish. A large part of their revenue comes from donations, and from whatever stipends they receive from their retreats and weekend parish missions. Mother Mary Julia and Father Peter are both emphatic that, if God wants them to undertake a particular project, the money for it will be provided. Neither group has health insurance (a condition shared by the Poor Hermits of St. Francis). Several local doctors donate their services, which have not been much needed, since the members are mostly young.

The bishop supports the group, but several of the priests and the members of other religious communities do not, viewing the charismatic movement in general with suspicion. Hence, there are a few parishes and schools in which the Apostles are not welcome. This is less of a problem than it was formerly, however, as the communities are gradually winning a reputation as respectable and *bona fide* religious congregations.

Problems Along the Way:

The Vicar for Religious was a member of an established religious community, and was intensely wary of what she perceived to be "cult-like" tendencies in charismatic groups. Under her insistence, when the Apostles gained diocesan status, the women's group was required to limit its leadership to two four-year terms of office. With their greater leeway under canon law, the men's group was able to avoid this limitation, even though the Vicar desired it. Consequently, Mother Mary Julia will have to leave office in 1998, while Father Peter shows no sign that he will do the same—in fact, he has been exercising more and more influence over the women's group as well as the men's. The Vicar worries that the women have no candidate with sufficient strength to stand up to Father Peter. The Latina members, especially, seem more likely to accept Father Peter's "natural" authority than the Anglo members do. This is causing a certain amount of division in the women's community. Mother Mary Julia, especially, seems worried about it. Father Peter is only 57, and so could potentially be the head of the male Apostles for another fifteen or twenty years. The Vicar also believes that this will not be healthy—either for Father Peter or for the community he heads.

STORY # 5: _____

JOURNEY'S DESTINATION:

WHO'S GOING:

HOW TO GET THERE:

SUPPLIES FOR THE JOURNEY:

Notes

1. INTRODUCTION

1. This argument is made, for example, by Raymond Hostie, in *La Vie et Mort Des Ordres Religieux* (Paris: Desclée de Brouwer, 1972), and Lawrence Cada, in *Shaping the Coming Age of Religious Life* (New York: Seabury, 1979).
2. See Jane Schulenberg, "Women's Monastic Communities, 500–1000: Patterns of Expansion and Decline," in Judith M. Bennett, ed., *Sisters and Workers in the Middle Ages* (Chicago: University of Chicago Press, 1989), p.213, for the decline of early medieval women's monasteries. See Ephrem Hollermann, *The Reshaping of a Tradition: American Benedictine Women, 1852–1881* (Ph.D. Dissertation, Marquette University, 1991), p.40, and Sharon K. Elkins, *Holy Women of Twelfth Century England* (Chapel Hill: University of North Carolina Press, 1988), p.45, for twelfth-century growth statistics.
3. Caroline W. Bynum, "Religious Women in the Later Middle Ages," in Jill Raitt, ed., *Christian Spirituality II: High Middle Ages and Reformation* (New York: Crossroad, 1987), p.123. See also C.H. Lawrence, *Medieval Monasticism: Forms of Religious Life in Western Europe in the Middle Ages* (London: Longman, 1989), p.228.
4. Ernest McDonnell, *The Beguines and Beghards in Medieval Culture* (New York: Octagon Books, 1969), p.119.
5. Thomas P. Rausch, SJ, *Radical Christian Communities* (Collegeville, MN: The Liturgical Press, 1990), pp.73–79. See also Lawrence Cada, *Shaping the Coming Age of Religious Life* (New York: Seabury Press, 1979), p.30.

Christian Communities (Collegeville, MN: the Liturgical Press, 1990), pp.67–69.

18. C. Wright Mills, *The Sociological Imagination* (New York: Pelican, 1970).
19. ibid., p.12. Italics mine.
20. Hostie, op. cit., p.261. Translation mine.
21. Rapley, op. cit., p.191.
22. ibid., p.84.
23. Quoted in Rapley, op. cit., p.191.
24. Rapley, op. cit., p.192.
25. According to David Nygren and Miriam Ukeritis in their Executive Summary of "The Future of Religious Orders in the United States," *Origins*, vol.22, no.15 (September 24, 1992), p.261, the Alexian Brothers, who were originally founded to care for medieval plague victims, have recently adopted AIDS care as a primary focus for their community.
26. Of course, I am not assuming that *all* of the members of an entire religious community will ever be persuaded to unite their energies in active response around a single concrete ministry or goal. As I stated in the last chapter of *Creating a Future*, I believe that this is extremely unlikely, bordering on impossible. In fact, if a religious congregation *does* claim to be united around a single focus, this would be a sign to me either that the focus was too vague to be of any real use or else that the leadership (or some faction of the membership) had imposed its vision on the entire community, and that the group's apparent unanimity was masking a lot of covert resentment and resistance. Instead, what is needed is for those members of a congregation (or of several congregations) who *do* share a common vision to join together to realize it, and for the larger congregation to support them (and, occasionally, to challenge them) in love. If there are several of these visionary subgroups within the congregation, so much the better. See chapter 7, below.
27. See Anne Munley, IHM, *Threads for the Loom* (LCWR Planning and Ministry Studies, 1992), for an excellent example of recent social analysis.
28. See Peter Brown's *The Body and Society: Men, Women and Sexual Renunciation in Early Christianity* (New York: Columbia University Press, 1988), Charles A. Frazee, "Late Roman and Byzantine Legislation on the Monastic Life from the Fourth to the Eighth Centuries," *Church History*, vol. 51, no. 3 (1982), pp.263–279, and Jo Ann McNamara, *A New Song: Celibate Women in the First Three Christian Centuries* (New York: Harrington Park Press, 1985), among

others, for religious life in the early church. See Schulenberg, Elkins, Bynum and Lawrence (op. cit.) as well as Lester K. Little, *Religious Poverty and the Profit Economy in Medieval Europe* (Ithaca: Cornell University Press, 1978), and Ernest McDonnell, *The Beguines and Beghards in Medieval Culture* (New York: Octagon Books, 1969), for medieval religious life. Rapley and Taylor (op. cit.) analyze seventeenth-century France; Clear, Langlois and Denault (op. cit.), as well as Marguerite Jean, *Evolution des commu- nautes religieuses de femmes au Canada de 1639 à nos jours* (Montreal: Fides, 1977), discuss nineteenth-century Ireland, France and Quebec, respectively. Works on American religious life in the nine- teenth century are quite numerous. Besides Ewens (op. cit.), they include Barbara Misner, *Highly Respectable and Accomplished Ladies* (New York: Garland, 1988), Mary Jo Oates, "Organized Volun- tarism," pp. 141–170 in Rosemary Ruether and Rosemary Keller, eds., *Women and Religion in America* (New York:Macmillan, 1983), and "The Good Sisters," pp.171–199 in Robert E. Sullivan and James M. O'Toole, eds., *Catholic Boston* (Boston Archdiocese, 1985), Margaret Thompson, "Discovering Foremothers," *U.S. Catholic Historian* vol.5, nos. 3,4 (1986), pp.273–290, and "Sisterhood and Power," *Colby Library Quarterly*, (Fall, 1989), pp.149–175, and James Kenneally, *The History of American Catholic Women* (New York: Crossroad, 1990).

29. William E. Biernatzki's *Roots of Acceptance: The Intercultural Communication of Religious Meaning* (Rome: Gregorian Pontifical Institute, 1991) uses this method. See p.48.

30. Wittberg, *The Rise and Decline*, op. cit.

2. THE "RELIGIOUS VIRTUOSO"

1. Max Weber, who originated the term, did not like it either: "In these contexts, every evaluative aspect must be removed from the concept of 'virtuosity' which adheres to it nowadays. I prefer the term 'hero- ic' religiosity because of the loaded character of 'virtuoso,' but 'heroic' is entirely too inadequate for some of the phenomena belonging here." Max Weber, "The Social Psychology of the World Religions," in H. H. Gerth and C. Wright Mills, eds., *From Max Weber: Essays in Sociology* (New York: Oxford University Press, 1958), p. 450, footnote #5.

2. In *Virtuosity, Charisma, and the Social Order* (New York, Cambridge

University Press, 1995), pp.190–191, Ilana Friedrich Silber lists five core characteristics of religious virtuosity:

1. it is a matter of free individual choice,
2. it entails "a search for perfection, an extreme urge to go beyond everyday life and average norms of achievement,"
3. this search for perfection is carried on in a disciplined, systematic fashion,
4. it implies a double standard of religious practice, a division between the virtuoso lifestyle and that of the average adherent, and
5. it is based on achievement, not inheritance.

3. See Silber, op. cit., p.221. Sandra Schneiders, IHM, uses this same analogy in *New Wineskins: Re-Imagining Religious Life Today* (New York: Paulist Press, 1986), p.34. See also her article, "Contemporary Religious Life: Death or Transformation?" in Cassian J. Yuhaus, CP, ed., *Religious Life: The Challenge for Tomorrow* (New York: Paulist, 1994), p.16, where she maintains that "the naked God-quest at the center of their hearts" is "the real meaning of religious vocation." Several other authors have also drawn a comparison between religious virtuosity and artistic virtuosity, most notably Andrew Greeley in *The Catholic Myth: The Behavior and Beliefs of American Catholics* (New York: Scribner's, 1990), p.36, and Max Weber himself, "The Social Psychology of World Religions," op. cit., p.287.

4. See Joan Fee et al., *Young Catholics in the United States and Canada* (Los Angeles: Sadlier, 1981), p.134, for parental influence on religious devotion. See Dean R. Hoge, et al., *Research on Men's Vocations to the Priesthood and Religious Life* (National Conference of Catholic Bishops, 1983), pp.23, 38, for a similar impact on seminary vocations.

5. Rea McDonnell, SSND, "Fundamentalism, Anxiety and Faith," *In-Formation*, vol.132 (March, 1991), p.2. Publication of the Religious Formation Conference.

6. Kenneth Woodward, *Making Saints: How the Catholic Church Determines Who Becomes a Saint, Who Doesn't, and Why* (New York: Simon & Schuster, 1990), p.346–352.

7. Thomas Bouchard et al., "Sources of Human Psychological Differences: The Minnesota Study of Twins Reared Apart," *Science* vol. 250 (Oct. 12, 1990), pp.223–228.

8. Max Weber, *The Sociology of Religion*, Translated by Ephraim Mischoff (Boston: Beacon Press, 1963), pp.166–67.

9. Mary Ann Donovan, SC, "The Spectrum of Church Teaching on Religious Life," in Robert J. Daly, SJ, et al., *Religious Life in the*

Church (New York: Paulist Press, 1984), p.214. See also Hostie and Rapley, op. cit.

10. Diarmuid O'Murchu, MSC, in *Religious Life: A Prophetic Vision* (Notre Dame, IN: Ave Maria Press, 1991), p.38, makes a similar point when he states that, if religious orders fail to produce an appropriate outlet, liminality will shift its focus elsewhere.

11. Thomas Rausch, SJ, *Radical Christian Communities* (Collegeville, MN: The Liturgical Press, 1990), p.33. On the other hand, Weber states flatly that, although Jesus' doctrine condemned the virtuoso spirituality of the scribes and Pharisees, his preaching demanded its own brand of virtuosity: "Nothing was further from Jesus' mind than the notion of the universalism of divine grace. On the contrary, he directed his whole preaching against this notion. Few are chosen to pass through the narrow gate, to repent and believe in Jesus." (Max Weber, *The Sociology of Religion*, op. cit., p.272).

12. Kenneth Woodward, op. cit., p.336.

13. Sally Cunneen, *Sex: Female; Religion: Catholic* (London: Burns & Oates, 1968), p.81.

14. Joan Fee et al., op. cit., p.140.

15. Rausch, op. cit., p.84.

16. Max Weber, "The Social Psychology of the World Religions," op. cit., p.287. Italics in the original.

17. Rausch, op. cit., p.12.

18. ibid., pp.87–88.

19. Michael Hill, in his *The Religious Orders: A Study of Virtuoso Spirituality* (London: Heinemann, 1973), p.67, states that there was always a covert tendency for members of religious orders to see themselves as superior to the laity.

20. Wade Clark Roof and William McKinney, *American Mainline Religion: Its Changing Shape and Future* (New Brunswick: Rutgers University Press, 1987), p.178.

21. ibid., pp.150, 231.

22. Edmundo Rodriguez, SJ, "Realities for Hispanics," *Company* (Fall, 1988), pp.9–10. See also David Martin, *Tongues of Fire: The Explosion of Protestantism in Latin America* (Cambridge: Basil Blackwell, 1990), Ana Maria Diaz Stevens, "Latinas and the Church," in Jay Dolan and Allan Figueroa Deck, SJ, eds., *Hispanic Catholic Culture in the U.S.: Issues and Concerns* (Notre Dame: University of Notre Dame Press, 1994), p.258, and Allan Figueroa Deck, SJ, "The Challenge of Evangelical/Pentecostal Christianity to Hispanic Catholicism," in Dolan and Deck, op. cit., p.413.

23. See Silber, op. cit., pp.49, 190-191.

24. Sandra M. Schneiders, IHM, *New Wineskins*, op. cit., p.34. See also Judith Merkle, SNDdeN, *Committed by Choice* (Collegeville, MN: The Liturgical Press, 1992), p.160.
25. This lack of clarity exists, first of all, in official church documents: Thomas Clarke's "Redeeming Conflict," in Madonna Kohlbenschlag, ed., *Authority, Community and Conflict* (Kansas City: Sheed and Ward, 1986), p.68, states "The *Constitution on the Church* of Vatican II, on which the new law of the Church and many other post Vatican II documents are selectively based, actually speaks ambivalently of the place of non-clerical religious in the Church. Where there is a question of the distinctive role of the laity within the secular, religious are not included, and in fact are spoken of as being, along with clerics, a distinct group. But in two formal statements which reflect a different long-standing view, it seems clear that, as non-clerical religious, women religious belong to the laity." According to Christopher O'Donnell, O.Carm., "Religious in the New Catechism," *Religious Life Review*, vol.33, no.5 (Sept.–Oct. 1994) pp.308,310, the new catechism is similarly vague. As a result, David Nygren and Miriam Ukeritis state in their "The Future of Religious Orders in the United States" (*Origins*, vol. 22, no.15, Sept. 24, 1992), there is a lack of role clarity among religious men and women. This, they found, was associated with lowered self-confidence and a sense of futility among those who experienced it most keenly.
26. Weber, *The Sociology of Religion*, op. cit., p.187.
27. Michael Hill, op. cit., p.23.
28. ibid., p.46.
29. Caroline Walker Bynum treats this topic in several books, notably *Jesus as Mother: Studies in the Spirituality of the High Middle Ages* (Berkeley: University of California Press, 1982), *Holy Feast and Holy Fast* (Berkeley: University of California Press, 1987), and *Fragmentation and Redemption: Essays on Gender and the Human Body in Medieval Religion* (New York: Zone Books, 1991). See also Woodward, op. cit., pp.161–184 for recent examples.
30. Weber, *The Sociology of Religion*, op. cit., p.193.
31. Lester Little, *Religious Poverty and the Profit Economy in Medieval Europe* (Ithaca: Cornell University Press, 1978), p.117, and Elizabeth Rapley, *The Devotes: Women and Church in Seventeenth Century France* (Montreal: McGill Queens University Press, 1990), p.172.
32. Max Weber, "The Social Psychology of World Religions," op. cit., p.88. See also Silber, op. cit., chapters four and seven.

33. Meredith McGuire, *Religion: The Social Context* (Belmont, CA: Wadsworth, 1987), p.128.
34. Wach, Joachim, *The Sociology of Religion* (Chicago: University of Chicago Press, 1944). Quoted in McGuire, op. cit., pp.127–28.
35. McGuire, op. cit., p.128.
36. A.O. Hirschmann, *Exit, Voice and Loyalty: Responses in Firms, Organizations and States* (Cambridge, MA: Harvard University Press, 1970), p.47.
37. Rea McDonnell, op. cit., p.8.
38. Thomas P. O'Meara, *Fundamentalism: A Catholic Perspective* (New York: Paulist, 1990), p.24.
39. ibid., p.86.
40. Sandra Schneiders, personal communication.
41. See Eileen Barker, "People Who Attend Unification Workshops and Do Not Become Moonies," in Rodney Stark, ed., *Religious Movements: Genesis, Exodus and Numbers* (New York: Paragon House, 1985), p.73. For Baptist figures, see Nancy T. Ammerman, *Bible Believers: Fundamentalists in the Modern World* (New Brunswick, NJ: Rutgers University Press, 1988), p.30.

3. IDEOLOGY

1. Clifford Geertz, "Ideology as a Cultural System," in Clifford Geertz, *The Interpretation of Cultures* (New York: Basic Books, 1973), p.193.
2. ibid., p.193. See Geertz, pp.196–97, and Karl Mannheim, *Ideology and Utopia* (New York: Harcourt, Brace, 1936), pp.55–56, for a list of sociologists who have been trapped into "ideological" denunciations of the term "ideology."
3. Geertz, op. cit., p.200.
4. Philip Converse, "The Nature of Belief Systems in Mass Publics," in David E. Apter, ed. *Ideology and Discontent* (New York: Free Press, 1964), p.207.
5. Geertz, op. cit., p.196.
6. David A. Snow and Robert D. Benford, "Master Frames and Cycles of Protest," in Aldon D. Morris and Carol McClurg Mueller, eds., *Frontiers in Social Movement Theory* (New Haven: Yale University Press, 1992), p.137.
7. Peter Berger and Thomas Luckmann, *The Social Construction of Reality* (New York: Doubleday, 1966), p.41.
8. Converse, op. cit., pp.207–209.
9. Greeley, op. cit., p.81.

10. Converse, op. cit., p.209.
11. See David Glassberg, *American Historical Pageantry: The Uses of Tradition in the Early Twentieth Century* (Chapel Hill: University of North Carolina Press, 1990), especially chapters 5 and 6. See also Adam Gamoran, "Civil Religion in American Schools," *Sociological Analysis,* vol. 51, no.3 (1990), pp.235–56.
12. Barbara Parker, "Your Schools May Be the Next Battlefield in the Crusade Against 'Improper' Textbooks," *The American School Board Journal* (June, 1979), pp.21–27.
13. Nathan O. Hatch, *The Democratization of American Christianity* (New Haven: Yale University Press, 1989), p.65.
14. Mannheim, op. cit., p.80.
15. Sidney Tarrow, "Mentalities, Political Cultures and Collective Action Frames: Constructing Meanings Through Action," pp.174–202 in Aldon D. Morris and Carol McClurg Mueller, eds., op. cit., p.189.
16. See Geertz, op. cit., p.216, and Converse, op. cit., p.211, for this analogy.
17. Mannheim, op. cit., p.2.
18. Berger and Luckmann, op. cit., p.78.
19. See Gary Wills, *Under God: Religion and American Politics* (New York: Simon and Schuster, 1990), p.132, and Nathan O. Hatch, op. cit., pp.78, 97.
20. William Thorkelson, "Landmark Study Finds Many Protestants' Faith Shaky," *National Catholic Reporter* (April 13, 1990), p.7. See also Roof and McKinney, op. cit., p.56, and Jean C. Lyles, "The Fading of Denominational Distinctiveness," in *Progressions,* Lilly Endowment Seasonal Report, vol.2, #1 (Jan. 1990), pp.16-17.
21. Nancy T. Ammerman, *Baptist Battles* (New Brunswick: Rutgers University Press, 1990), pp.248–252.
22. Berger and Luckmann, op. cit., p.84.
23. ibid., p.124.
24. William A. Gamson, "Political Discourse and Collective Action," pp.219–244 in Bert Klandermans et al., eds., *From Structure to Action: Comparing Social Movement Research Across Cultures*, Vol. 1, International Social Movement Research (Greenwich, CT: JAI Press, 1988).
25. Benett M. Berger, *The Survival of a Counterculture* (Berkeley: University of California Press, 1981), p.124.
26. Geertz, op. cit., p.231. See also Howard Zinn, *Declarations of Independence: Cross-Examining American Ideologies* (New York: Harper-Collins, 1990), p.7.

27. According to Geertz, op. cit., p.194, even Karl Mannheim, who invented the "non-ideological" concept of ideology, was uncomfortable with its apparent relativization of all truth.

28. ibid., p.212.

29. Berger, op. cit., p.178.

30. Quoted in Thomas Rausch, SJ, *Radical Christian Communities* (Collegeville, MN: Michael Glazier, 1990), pp.85–86.

31. Peter Brown, *The Body and Society: Sexual Renunciation in Early Christianity* (New York: Columbia University Press, 1988), pp.263, 382. See also his "The Notion of Virginity in the Early Church," pp.427–442 in Bernard McGinn and John Nyerdorff, eds., *Christian Spirituality I: Origins to the Twelfth Century* (New York: Crossroad, 1985), pp.429-435.

32. Michael Hill, *The Religious Order: A Study of Virtuoso Religiosity* (London: Heinemann, 1973), p.28. See also Caroline W. Bynum, *Jesus as Mother* (Berkeley: University of California Press, 1982), p.218, and *Holy Feast and Holy Fast* (Berkeley: University of California Press, 1987), p.115, and Jane Schulenberg, "Women's Monastic Communities, 500–1100: Patterns of Expansion and Decline," pp.205–239 in Judith M. Bennett et al., eds. *Sisters and Workers in the Middle Ages* (Chicago: University of Chicago Press, 1989), p.219.

33. Mary Ann Foley, "Women as Evangelizers in Seventeenth Century New France." Paper read at the History of Christianity Conference, Notre Dame University, March 27, 1992. See also Angelyn Dries, "The Americanization of Religious Life: Women Religious, 1872–1922," *U.S. Catholic Historian*, vol. 10, nos. 1 & 2 (1989), p.20, for the use of the soldier metaphor in nineteenth-century United States.

34. See also Ilana Friedrich Silber, *Virtuosity, Charisma, and the Social Order* (New York: Cambridge University Press, 1995), chapters three and six, for a discussion of ideologies of gift-giving and monasticism in Theravada Buddhism and medieval Christianity.

35. Hill, op. cit., p.189.

36. ibid., pp.169–178.

37. ibid., pp.194, 215.

38. Brown, op. cit., pp.202–208.

39. Hill, op. cit., p.40, makes this argument.

40. See Lester R. Kurtz, *The Politics of Heresy: The Modernist Crisis in Roman Catholicism* (Berkeley: University of California Press, 1986), pp.8–9, and Gene Burns, *The Frontiers of Catholicism: The Politics of Ideology in a Liberal World* (Berkeley: University of California Press,

1992), p.22, for the supposed incompatibility between liberal democracy and Catholicism. See *Religion Watch*, vol.5, no.3 (January 1990), p.7 for the increase in applicants to seminaries and religious orders in El Salvador.

41. Mark Juergensmeyer, *The New Cold War? Religious Nationalism Confronts the Secular State* (Berkeley: University of California Press, 1993), p.142.
42. Reported in *Religion Watch*, vol.10, no.7 (May, 1995), pp.6–7.
43. Susan D. Rose, "Women Warriors: The Negotiation of Gender in a Charismatic Community," *Sociological Analysis*, vol.48, no.3 (Fall, 1987), pp.245–258.
44. Meredith McGuire, *Religion: The Social Context*, 3rd ed. (Belmont, CA: Wadsworth, 1992), pp.126–127.
45. Kenneth C. Land, Glenn Deane and Judith R. Blau, "Religious Pluralism and Church Membership: A Spatial Diffusion Model," *American Sociological Review* vol. 56 (April, 1991) pp.246–248. See also Silber, op. cit., pp.122,135.
46. Raymond Hostie, *La vie et mort des ordres religieux* (Paris: Desclee de Brouwer, 1972), p.276.
47. Neither does Theravada Buddhist monasticism. See Silber, op. cit., p.106.

4. SOCIAL MOVEMENTS

1. John Wilson, *Introduction to Social Movements* (New York: Basic Books, 1973), p.8.
2. J. Craig Jenkins, "Resource Mobilization and the Study of Social Movements," *Annual Review of Sociology* vol.9 (1983), p.539.
3. Sidney Tarrow, *Struggle, Politics and Reform: Collective Action, Social Movements and Cycles of Protest*, Western Societies Program, Occasional paper #21 (Center for International Studies, Cornell University, 1989).
4. Doug McAdam, *Political Process and the Development of Black Insurgency: 1930–1970* (Chicago: University of Chicago Press, 1982), pp.27–28.
5. Aldon Morris, "Black Southern Student Sit-In Movements: An Analysis of Internal Organization," *American Sociological Review*, vol. 46 (1981), pp.747–767.
6. Bert Klandermans, "Mobilization and Participation: Social-Psychological Expansion of Resource Mobilization Theory," *American Sociological Review*, vol.49 (1984), p.586.

7. Tarrow, op. cit., p.79.

8. David A. Snow, et al., "Frame Alignment Processes, Micromobiliza-tion and Movement Participation," *American Sociological Review*, vol.51 (1986), p.464.

9. Bert Klandermans, "The Formation and Mobilization of Consen-sus," pp. 173–191, in Bert Klandermans et al., eds., *From Structure to Action: Comparing Social Movement Research Across Cultures* (Greenwich, CT: Jai Press, 1988), p.175.

10. Gamson, op. cit., pp.219–220.

11. The terminology in the next four paragraphs is taken from Snow et al., op. cit., pp.467–74.

12. ibid., p.467.

13. ibid., pp.474–475.

14. Nathan O. Hatch, *The Democratization of American Christianity* (New Haven: Yale University Press, 1989), pp.4, 220.

15. Kai Erikson, *Everything in Its Path* (New York: Simon and Schuster, 1976), pp.82ff, speaks of "axes of variation" in a culture—fault lines linking opposite values or traits. The entire society might move quite rapidly from one extreme to another along these fault lines—especially in times of social stress. Thus, for example, American cul-ture displays both a glorification of sex and an unusual degree of prudery in talking about it, as well as an obsession with law and order together with a lionization of certain "romantic" types of criminal. Thus, too, our extreme individualism and interpersonal isolation may make us more apt to form and join intensely commu-nal cults than members of a less individualistic society would be.

16. Jenkins, op. cit., p.538.

17. Tarrow, op. cit., p.52.

18. David A. Snow and Richard Machalek, "The Sociology of Conversion," *Annual Review of Sociology*, vol.10 (1984), p.182.

19. Caitriona Clear, *Nuns in Nineteenth Century Ireland* (Dublin: Gill and Macmillan Ltd., 1987), p.144.

20. Jenkins, op. cit., p.546. See also William A. Gamson, "The Social Psychology of Collective Action," in Aldon D. Morris and Carol McClurg Mueller, eds., *Frontiers in Social Movement Theory* (New Haven: Yale University Press, 1992), p.71.

21. Mary Ann Donovan, SC, "A More Limited Witness," in Laurie Felknor, ed. *The Crisis in Religious Vocations: An Inside View* (New York: Paulist Press, 1989), pp.90–92. See also Kenneth L. Woodward et al., "The Graying of the Convent," *Newsweek* (April 2, 1990), p.51.

22. Gary Wills, *Under God: Religion and American Politics* (New York: Simon and Schuster, 1990), p.18.
23. Tarrow, op. cit., p.4.
24. ibid., p.42.
25. Anthony F.C. Wallace, "Revitalization Movements," *American Anthropology*, vol. 56 (1956), pp.264–81.
26. Snow et al., Frame Alignment Processes, op. cit., p.477.
27. Tarrow, op. cit., p.44.

5. WHERE HAVE WE GONE BEFORE?

1. See, for example, Donald Reck, "Who Are We as Religious?" *Review for Religious*, vol. 45 (1986), p.50, Gerald Arbuckle, SM, *Out of Chaos* (New York: Paulist, 1990), pp.113–114; Sean Fagan, SM, "The Identity of Religious" *Religious Life Review*, vol. 32 (1993), p.74; Helen Rose Ebaugh, *Women in the Vanishing Cloister* (New Brunswick: Rutgers University Press, 1993), p.26; David Nygren, CM, and Miriam Ukeritis, CSJ, "The Future of Religious Orders in the U.S.," *Origins*, vol.22, no.15 (1992), p.263; Donna Markham, OP, "The Decline of Vocations," in Laurie Felknor, ed., *The Crisis in Religious Vocations* (New York: Paulist, 1989), p.184; and Mary Jo Leddy, *Reweaving Religious Life* (Mystic, CT: Twenty-Third Publications, 1990), p.73.
2. This argument is made by Eleace King, IHM, and Richard Deptula, OFMConv, *CARA Formation Directory, 1991* (CARA: Washington, D.C., 1990), pp.9–10; M. Marcelline Falk, "Vocations: Identity and Commitment," *Review for Religious*, vol.39 (1980), pp.357–365; Daniel Meenan, SJ, "On Dreaming Dreams," *Review for Religious*, vol. 43 (1984), pp.547–557; and Nygren and Ukeritis, "The Future of Religious Orders" op. cit., p.263.
3. Frank E. Manuel, "Toward a Psychological History of Utopias," in Frank E. Manuel, ed., *Utopias and Utopian Thought* (Boston: Houghton Mifflin, 1969), p.70; and Brian J.L. Berry, *America's Utopian Experiments* (Hanover: University Presses of New England, 1992), pp.228–229, make this argument for those religious virtuosi who have formed utopian communes. Albert DiIanni, SM, in his *Religious Life as Adventure* (New York: Alba House, 1994, p.121) holds that the "Church as communion" will be born "not out of the pockets of satisfaction within the Church but from its well of pain"— a similar observation to Manuel's and Berry's.
4. There are, of course, *many* candidates for "sharpest anguish." That

of India, Brazil or Bosnia will most likely not be the same as that of Western Europe or North America. And, to some extent, upper-middle class whites in the United States will experience different sources and foci of "sustained dissatisfaction" than do African-Americans in Harlem, unemployed mining families in rural West Virginia, or Mexican-Americans in South Texas. *Whatever form of religious life is devised for the coming century will be attractive only to the cultures or subcultures whose deepest needs and questions it addresses.* Ideally, therefore, we may need to create several very different forms.

5. See Thomas P. Rausch, SJ, *Radical Christian Communities* (Collegeville, MN: Michael Glazier, 1990), pp.41, 47–48, 51; Bryan S. Turner, *Religion and Social Theory*, 2nd ed. (Newbury Park, CA: Sage, 1991), p.101; C.H. Lawrence, *Medieval Monasticism* (London: Longman, 1989), pp.31–36, 127; Edward A. Wynne, *Traditional Catholic Religious Orders* (New Brunswick, NJ: Transaction, 1988), pp.108; Jane Schulenberg, "Women's Monastic Communities, 500–1100," in Judith Bennett et al., eds., *Sisters and Workers in the Middle Ages* (Chicago: University of Chicago Press, 1989), p.217; and Alan MacQuarrie, "Early Christian Houses in Scotland," in John Blair and Richard Sharpe, eds., *Pastoral Care Before the Parish* (Leicester: Leicester University Press, 1992), p.113, for documentation of the assertions in this paragraph.

6. See Rausch, op. cit., pp.70–71, and Ernest McDonnell, *The Beguines and Beghards in Medieval Culture* (New York: Octagon, 1969), p.137, for the Beguines. See Caroline W. Bynum, *Jesus as Mother* (Berkeley: University of California Press, 1982), pp.30–36, for the canons.

7. Judith D. Taylor, *From Proselytizing to Social Reform: Three Generations of French Female Teaching Congregations, 1600–1720* (Ph.D. Dissertation, History Department, Arizona State University, 1980), p.34.

8. John O'Malley, "Early Jesuit Spirituality: Spain and Italy," in Louis Dupre and Don E. Saliers, eds., *Christian Spirituality III: Post Reformation and Modern* (New York: Crossroad, 1989), p.7.

9. Elizabeth Rapley, *The Devotes* (Montreal: McGill Queens University Press, 1990), p.24.

10. Taylor, op. cit., p.166.

11. Raymond Hostie, *La vie et mort des ordres religieuses* (Paris: Desclée de Brouwer, 1972), pp.123–125, makes this point. See also Edward A. Wynne, *Traditional Catholic Religious Orders: Living in Community* (New Brunswick: Transaction, 1988), p.147.

12. Lester K. Little, *Religious Poverty and the Profit Economy in Medieval Europe* (Ithaca, NY: Cornell University Press, 1978), pp.173ff.
13. Little, op. cit., p.173.
14. Little, op. cit., pp.201–202. Italics mine.
15. Peter Brown, "The Notion of Virginity in the Early Church," pp.427–442 in Bernard McGinn and John Meyendorff, eds., *Christian Spirituality, vol. 1: Origins to the Twelfth Century* (New York: Crossroad, 1985), p.433. See also Rausch, op. cit., p.43.
16. Peter Brown, *The Body and Society: Men, Women and Sexual Renunciation in Early Christianity* (New York: Columbia University Press, 1988), p.170.
17. Jo McNamara, *A New Song: Celibate Women in the First Three Christian Centuries* (New York: Harrington Park Press, 1985). See also Brown, *The Body and Society*, op. cit., pp.260–276, and Pagels, op. cit., pp.80–83.
18. Elaine Pagels, *Adam, Eve and the Serpent* (New York: Random House, 1988), p.83.
19. C.H. Lawrence, op. cit., p.31. See also E. K. Francis, "Toward a Typology of Religious Orders," *American Journal of Sociology*, vol.55 (1950), pp.437–443.
20. Elizabeth Rapley, op. cit., p.11. See also Alan Figueroa Deck, SJ, "The Challenge of Evangelical/Pentecostal Christianity to Hispanic Catholics in the U.S," in Jay P. Dolan and Allan Figueroa Deck, SJ, eds., *Hispanic Catholic Culture in the U.S.: Issues and Concerns* (Notre Dame: Notre Dame University Press, 1994), p.425, for a description of the pre-Reformation Catholic viewpoint on these issues.
21. This point is made by John O'Malley, op. cit., p.9. See also Lewis Coser, *Greedy Institutions* (New York: Free Press, 1974), p.118, and Rapley, op. cit., p.9.
22. Ilana Friedrich Silber, in *Virtuosity, Charisma, and Social Order* (New York: Cambridge University Press, 1995), p. 47, makes the same argument for the role of religious virtuosity in Theravada Buddhism.
23. See Edward Shils, *Center and Periphery: Essays in Macrosociology* (Chicago: University of Chicago Press, 1975), for a development of the distinction between the "center" and the "periphery" of a culture.
24. One could argue that this was a defect—that religious life *should* also have been open to the lower classes as well as to the better off. It is true that the poor, and even, at times, the middle classes, were often unable to enter religious communities, especially during the Middle Ages. Today, one would hope that some version of virtuoso spiritu-

ality could be made available to the anawim of society. Still, as I will argue in chapter 6, a religious life that does not *also* speak to the needs and concerns of opinion leaders in the ideological center of society, forfeits a valuable opportunity to influence the wider culture.

25. Thus, the mendicant Charism drew recruits primarily from the rising merchant class, not from either the upper nobility or the peasants, whose concerns it did not address. Similarly, Eugene Hynes, "Nineteenth Century Irish Catholicism, Farmers' Ideology and National Religion: Explorations in Cultural Explanation," in Roger O'Toole, ed., *Sociological Studies in Roman Catholicism* (New York: Mellen, 1989), pp.15–69, notes that, since it was the Irish clergy who articulated a new identity and ideology for the tenant farming class, most recruits to the priesthood and religious life came from this class rather than from itinerant laborers or the urban poor.

26. For examples of religious orders that concentrated on peripheral customs and neglected basic frame transformations, see my *The Rise and Fall of Catholic Religious Orders* (Albany: SUNY Press, 1994), chapter 10.

27. Alberto Melucci, *Nomads of the Present: Social Movements and Individual Needs in Contemporary Society* (Philadelphia: Temple University Press, 1989), p.62.

28. See Peter McDonough, SJ, *Men Astutely Trained* (New York: Free Press, 1992), pp.154–155, David G. Schultenover, SJ, *A View From Rome: On the Eve of the Modernist Crisis* (New York: Fordham University Press, 1993), and Marvin R. O'Connell, "Ultramontanism and Dupanloup," *Church History,* vol.53 (1984), p.205. This retrenchment also occurred locally: see Peter Beyer's "The Evolution of Roman Catholicism in Quebec," pp.1–26 in Roger O'Toole, ed., *Sociological Studies in Roman Catholicism* (New York: Mellen, 1989), pp.21–26, and Hynes, op. cit., p.63.

29. Gene Burns, "The Politics of Ideology," *American Journal of Sociology,* vol.95 (1990), p.1129.

30. O'Connell, op. cit., p.207. Burns, op. cit., p.1133, and Joseph M. Becker, *The Re-Formed Jesuits* (San Francisco: Ignatius Press, 1992), p.140, make a similar point.

31. For example, both Hynes, op. cit., p.63 and Beyer, op. cit., pp.11–14, note that church writers in Ireland and Quebec glorified their countries' traditional rural culture as "true" Christianity and denigrated the rising industrial cities as alien and Protestant.

32. See Gene Burns, *The Frontiers of Catholicism: The Politics of Ideology in a Liberal World* (Berkeley: University of California Press, 1992), for a

fuller explication of this argument. See also Peter McDonough, op. cit., pp.148–161.

33. This was true even of the Jesuits—the archetypical apostolic order. See Peter McDonough, op. cit., pp.136–147.
34. DiIanni, op. cit., pp.23–26, also makes the point that religious life runs counter to the basic doctrines of the Enlightenment and the nineteenth century.
35. See Catriona Clear, *Nuns in Nineteenth Century Ireland* (Dublin: Gill and Macmillan, Ltd, 1987), pp.158–159, who argues that, because nineteenth-century Irish nuns so successfully addressed the symptoms of the economic system, an organized lay program of social welfare was delayed in that country.
36. Claude Langlois, *Le catholicisme au feminin* (Paris: Editions du Cerf, 1984), p.197, gives examples of this. See also Joseph Schmidt, FSC, "The Future of Religious Life," in Dolores Steinberg, OSC, ed., *The Future of Religious Life* (Collegeville, MN: The Liturgical Press, 1990), p.92.
37. Barbara Misner, OP, *"Highly Respectable and Accomplished Ladies": Catholic Religious Women in America, 1790-1850* (New York: Garland, 1988), p.20.
38. Langlois, op. cit., pp.185–199.
39. See Tony Fahey, "Catholicism and Industrial Society in Ireland," in J.H. Goldthorpe and C.T. Whelan, eds. *The Development of Industrial Society in Ireland* (Proceedings of the British Academy, 1992, vol.79, pp.241–263), p.254.
40. See the quotation from Bert Klandermans on page 48 of chapter 4.
41. Elizabeth Kolmer, *Religious Women in the United States: A Survey of the Influential Literature from 1950 to 1983* (Wilmington, DE: Michael Glazier, 1984), p.27, makes this assertion. See Mary L. Schneider, "The Transformation of American Women Religious: The Sister Formation Conference as a Catalyst for Change, 1954–1964" (Cushwa Center Working Paper Series 17 #1, Spring 1986), pp.6–7, for an example of resistance and confusion in the 1950's about how to respond to the pope's call.
42. This is, of course, the whole argument of Mary Jo Leddy's *Reweaving Religious Life: Beyond the Liberal Model* (Mystic, CT: Twenty-Third Publications, 1990). See especially pp.66–74. See also DiIanni, op. cit., pp.24–26.
43. David J. Nygren, CM, and Miriam D. Ukeritis, CSJ, *The Future of Religious Orders in the United States: Transformation and Commitment* (Westport, CT: Praeger, 1993), pp.241–242.
44. Nygren and Ukeritis, op. cit., p.158, make this assertion. See also

Judith A. Merkle, SNDdeN, *Committed by Choice* (Collegeville, MN: Liturgical Press, 1992), p.121, and Joan Chittister, OSB, "An Amazing Journey: A Road of Twists and Turns," in Cassian J. Yuhaus, CP, *Religious Life: The Challenge for Tomorrow* (New York: Paulist Press, 1994), p.85. According to Chittister, religious orders have "lost their sense of congregational purpose. The question 'Why stay?' has become the question 'Why come?'"

45. See Leddy, op. cit., p. 73 and Ebaugh, op. cit., p.87, for this argument. Marie Augusta Neal, SNDdeN, "Meeting the Challenges of the New Century" (in Yuhaus, op. cit., p.134), notes that sisters' individual preferences have become more salient than the institute's mission and charism in choosing a ministry.

46. Joan Chittister, OSB, "Religious Life Today: Response to Kerkhoffs," *Religious Life Review*, vol.32, no.4 (1993), p.203.

6. DECISION #1: WHERE DO WE WANT TO GO?

1. See the following sources for these demographic figures: Austin Flannery, OP, "Editorial," *Religious Life Review*, vol.31 (1992), p.343; David F. O'Connor, SJ, *Witness and Service* (Mahwah, NJ: Paulist Press, 1990), p.161; Arthur Jones, "Christian Brothers Search for Authenticity," *National Catholic Reporter*, vol.29, no.16 (February 19, 1993), p.15; Arthur Jones, "A Close Look at the Jesuit Order," *National Catholic Reporter*, vol.29, no. 16 (February 19, 1993), p.21; *Religion Watch*, "Counting Jesuit Losses," vol.4, no.3 (March, 1989), p.4. John Manuel Lozano, "Religious Life: The Continuing Journey," in Yuhaus, op. cit., p.154, cites similar figures.

2. "Imported Nuns," *Inside the Vatican*, December, 1993, pp.54–56. Of the 587 female postulants in Italy, 411 are foreigners.

3. "Imported Nuns," op. cit., p.56. See also the interview with Bishop Victor Dammertz during the Conference of Superior Generals in Rome (*Inside the Vatican*, January 1994, p.10).

4. Mary Jo Leddy, *Re-Weaving Religious Life* (Mystic, CT: Twenty-Third Publications, 1990), p.90.

5. See, for example, the first chapter in Anne Munley's *Threads for the Loom* (Silver Spring, MD: Leadership Conference of Women Religious, 1992). The majority of this chapter is composed of graphs on weapons production, median household income, AIDS deaths and the number of Federal and state prisoners.

6. For example, Louis DeThomasis, FSC, in his *Imagination: A Future for Religious Life* (Winona, MN: The Metanoia Group, 1992), pp.35,

41, 55, repeatedly identifies the "new paradigm" for religious life with creating more effective and responsive ministerial institutions.

7. Judith Merkle, SNDdeN, *Committed by Choice* (Collegeville, MN: Liturgical Press, 1992), p.133, makes this argument.

8. Robert Bellah, et al., *Habits of the Heart* (Berkeley: University of California Press, 1985), p.22. See also Bellah, et al., *The Good Society* (New York: Knopf, 1991), Wade Clark Roof, *A Generation of Seekers: The Spiritual Journeys of the Baby Boom Generation* (San Francisco: Harper, 1993), p.27, Robert Wuthnow, *Sharing the Journey* (New York: Free Press, 1994), pp.15, 21, 330, and Amitai Etzioni, *The Spirit of Community: Rights, Responsibilities and the Communitarian Agenda* (Southbridge, MA: Crown Publishers, 1993). Louis J. Kern, "Privatization, Midwifery and Synergistic Marriage," in Wendy E. Chmielewski, et al., eds., *Women in Spiritual and Communitarian Societies in the U.S.* (Syracuse: Syracuse University Press, 1993), pp.201–220; and Brian J. L. Berry, *America's Utopian Experiments* (Hanover: University Press of New England, 1992), p.237, notes that, in the past, utopian communities were established to counteract the individualism of American culture.

9. Douglas A. Walrath, *Frameworks: Patterns of Living and Believing* (New York: Pilgrim Press, 1987), p.22.

10. Norman Lear, "A Lonely Business," *Utne Reader*, no.59 (September/October, 1993), p.74.

11. Amitai Etzioni, "Review Essay on Communitarianism," *Contemporary Sociology*, vol.23, no.4 (July, 1994), pp.493–495.

12. See, for example, Carolyn R. Shaffer, *Creating Community Anywhere* (New York: Putnam, 1993), *The Graywolf Annual Ten: Changing Community* (Graywolf Press, 1993), or Vithal Rajan, *Rebuilding Communities* (Shelburne, VT: Green Books). Several organizations, such as the Communitarian Network and the American Alliance for Rights and Responsibilities, have as their primary goal the promotion of communitarian ideas.

13. See Osha Gray Davidson, "What, Exactly, Is Community?" *Utne Reader*, no.60 (November/December, 1993), pp.113–116, for a summary of these articles. See also Allan Winkler, "Communitarianism," *The Times of London Education Supplement*, April 15, 1994.

14. David A. Karp, Gregory P. Stone and William C. Yoels, *Being Urban: A Sociology of City Life*, second edition (New York: Praeger, 1991), pp.63, 189–216.

15. Sam Keen, "Peanut Butter Principles," in Charles Simpkinson and Anne Simpkinson, eds., *Sacred Stories: A Celebration of the Power of*

Stories to Transform and Heal (quoted in *Utne Reader*, no.62, March/April, 1994, p.120).

16. Quoted in Roof, op. cit., p.183. See also Christopher Lasch, *The True and Only Heaven* (in *Utne Reader*, July/August, 1994), p.34, and Wuthnow, op. cit., pp.34–35, 53, 171.

17. See Albert DiIanni, SM, *Religious Life as Adventure* (New York: Alba House, 1994), p.65, and Sam Keen, op. cit., for these quotations. See also Karen Armstrong, *A History of God: The 4,000 Year Quest of Judaism, Christianity and Islam* (New York: Knopf, 1994).

18. Roof, op. cit., p.243.

19. For a list of these books, see Valerie Takahama, "Spiritual Themes Flying High on Best Seller Lists" (*Cincinnati Enquirer*, March 20, 1994, p.E-1), and Steve Perry, "Filet of Soul: A Battery of New Books Seeks to Define the Indefinable," *Utne Reader*, no.62, (March/April 1994), pp.19–20. A survey in *Publisher's Weekly* (May 16, 1994) also notes a sharp upswing in the number of spirituality books sold (*Religion Watch*, vol.9, no.8, June, 1994, p.3, and vol.9 no.9, July/August, 1994, p.3). Sales for such books rose 56% between February 1993 and February 1994. Romance novels, the same article in *Religion Watch* reports, are also beginning to incorporate spiritual or paranormal themes. The number of such novels published in 1993 was twice the number published in 1992, and three times the number published in 1990. Kenneth Woodward, "On the Road Again," *Newsweek* (November 28, 1994), pp.61–62, notes that current self-help books are distinguished "by the authors' use of frankly religious language" such as "soul, sacred, spiritual and sacramental."

20. Helen Cordes, "Say Amen," *Utne Reader*, no.69 (May/June 1995), pp.22–24.

21. *Religion Watch*, (vol.9, no.4, February, 1994), a newsletter of religious trends, summarizes several current articles finding spiritual themes in movies (*Shadowlands*, *Ghost*, *Schindler's List*, *A River Runs Through It*), as well as "a spiritual yearning that harks back, consciously or not, to rock's gospel roots" in albums and videos by U2, Peter Gabriel., Matthew Sweet, and even Snoop Doggy Dogg. "Not since the peace and love era of the sixties...have religious themes been so conspicuously prevalent in pop." The recent compact disk of Gregorian chant by a group of Spanish Benedictines has sold 1.3 million copies, mainly among young people. (*Religion Watch*, vol.9, no.9, July/August 1994, p.3). A new phenomenon called "Gospel Rap" has emerged: According to *Newsweek* (November 28, 1994, p.64), one group recently sold 800,000 copies of its album. See also

Jay Waljasper, "Mystical Minimalists" (*Utne reader*, #66, November/December 1994, pp.22–24) for the influence of spiritual themes on modern composers.

22. Roof, op. cit., p.87, makes this point. Wuthnow, op. cit., pp. 3, 239, also expresses concern that the spirituality promulgated by the support/prayer groups he studied is a tamed, "feel good" spirituality without depth.

23. Erling Jorstad, "Concern for Spirituality Widespread Among Evangelicals," *Religion Watch*, vol.9, no.2 (December, 1993), p.3. There are recent indications that other Christian churches are experiencing the same thing; according to *Religion Watch*, vol.10, no.7 (May, 1995), p.7, there is a growing interest among Greek youth in Greek Orthodox monasticism.

24. Danny Duncan Collum, "A Western Eastern Way," *Utne Reader*, #66, (Nov/Dec, 1994), pp.32–34.

25. Allan Figueroa Deck, SJ, "Hispanic Ministry: Reasons for Our Hope" (*America*, April 23, 1994), p.13, cites this argument. See also Raymond Gamba, "The Role of Expectations in Religious Conversions: The Case of Hispanic Catholics," *Review of Religious Research*, vol.34, no.4 (1993), pp.357–371.

26. Gilles Kepel, *The Revenge of God*, trans. by Alan Braley (University Park, PA: The Pennsylvania State University Press, 1994), p.11, 192. Mark Juergensmeyer, *The New Cold War?* (Berkeley: University of California Press, 1993), p.180, makes the same point.

27. Paul J. Philibert, OP, *Living in the Meantime* (New York: Paulist, 1994), p.11.

28. Nygren and Ukeritis, op. cit., p.114. Nygren and Ukeritis also note (p.201) that the members of contemplative orders expressed greater role clarity.

29. Helen Rose Ebaugh, *Women in the Vanishing Cloister* (New Brunswick: Rutgers University Press, 1993), p. 101.

30. Rosemary Jeffries, RSM, "Commitment in Religious Life in the Post-Vatican II Era: A Study of Associate Programs" (Ph.D. Dissertation, Fordham University, 1991), pp.84–85, 92, 95.

31. Albert DiIanni, op. cit., pp.133–138.

32. Pascal Pingault, *Renouveau de l'eglise: les communautes nouvelles* (Paris: Fayard, 1989).

33. John Grindel and Sean Peters, "Religious Life Issues in a Time of Transition," *Review for Religious*, vol.51 (1992), p. 271. According to a 1985 survey by Donna Markham, OP, while the desire to live in community is a primary reason persons state for entering religious life, "women religious themselves do not give a significantly strong

endorsement" to the idea of community as witness. (Markham, "Psychological Factors Influencing the Decline of and Persistence in Religious Vocations," unpublished, p.12). DiIanni, op. cit., pp.138–141, and Joseph Schmidt, FSC, "The Future of Religious Life," in Dolores Steinberg, OSC, ed., *The Future of Religious Life: The Carondelet Conference* (Collegeville, MN: 1990) pp.89–90, all make a similar point. Judith Merkle, op. cit., p.155, notes that lay ministers are also looking for some sort of community support, and urges religious congregations to reach out to them.

34. This argument has reached the mainstream press: syndicated columnist William Raspberry, for example, recently argued that churches which are "endlessly involved in things that other agencies might do just as well" are neglecting their most distinctive and important work—that of serving as moral and spiritual centers (*Indianapolis Star*, February 14, 1995, p.A7).

35. Roof, op. cit., p.185. Nygren and Ukeritis, op. cit., p.151, found that most members of religious orders saw little connection between their work for systemic change on behalf of the poor, on the one hand, and their own personal and spiritual fulfillment, on the other.

36. DiIanni, op. cit., p.142.

37. Three of these groups are the Little Brothers of St. Francis in Boston, the Franciscan Brothers of Peace in Minneapolis, and the Franciscan Friars of the Renewal in the South Bronx. Of the thirty-four new French communities in Pingault's 1989 survey (op. cit.), at least nine cite such a ministry of presence.

38. Robert B. Reich, "Secession of the Successful," *New York Times Magazine*, January 20, 1991, pp.17–18, 42–45. Gregory M. Weiher, *The Fractured Metropolis* (Albany, SUNY Press, 1991), p.182, notes that the separate incorporation of suburban villages is done primarily to permit the residents to isolate themselves from the needs of the larger society. See also Evan McKenzie, *Privatopia* (New Haven: Yale University Press, 1994).

39. Nygren and Ukeritis, op. cit., pp. 160, 204, 229. Marie Augusta Neal, SNDdeN, "Meeting the Challenges of the New Century," op. cit., p.133, found in her most recent Sisters' Survey that only 44% of her respondents were willing "to do the actual work related to the elimination of the causes of poverty....In fact, in 1989, 77% of those sampled were not working with the poor."

40. DiIanni, op. cit., p.144, speculates that young people who come to religious life may "need to experience a religion of consolation before they can move to a religion of service." And Pingault, op.

cit., p. 26, notes that "among Christians, it is not enough to defend the oppressed or build a more human society, we must also create among ourselves the experience of brotherly [sic] love, the sharing of our goods and our whole lives,...forgiveness constantly renewed... [and] prayer rooted in daily existence." (translation mine)

41. Nygren and Ukeritis, op. cit., p.171, make this point. See also James Hennessey, SJ, "A Look at the Institution Itself," in Laurie Felknor, ed., *The Crisis in Religious Vocations* (New York: Paulist, 1989), p.35.

42. Mark Juergensmeyer, "The Monastic Syndrome in the Comparative Study of Culture," in Austin B. Creel and Vasudha Narayanan, eds., *Monastic Life in the Christian and Hindu Traditions* (Lewiston, NY: Mellen, 1990). See also Paul-André Turcotte, CSV, "Le recrutement dans les congregations religieuses canadiennes," *Sciences religieuses*, vol.9, no.4 (Fall, 1980), p.422.

43. DiIanni, op. cit., p.140, makes this argument.

44. Merkle, op. cit., p.21.

45. Both Peter McDonough, *Men Astutely Trained* (New York: Free Press, 1992), p.321, and Mary Jo Leddy, op. cit., p. 57, note an increased "shopping around" for a personal spirituality among members of religious orders. Joseph Becker, SJ, *The Re-Formed Jesuits* (San Francisco: Ignatius Press, 1992), p.288, notes the decline of a common Jesuit spiritual formation, while Paul-André Turcotte, CSV, *Les chemins de la difference* (Montreal: Bellarmin, 1985), p.103, notes the rise in individual prayer and the decline of common prayer in a Canadian men's order. In this, religious communities parallel a development in the larger American culture. (See Harold Bloom, *The American Religion*, New York: Simon and Schuster, 1992, pp.37,40)

46. Judith Merkle, op. cit., p.21.

47. The early hermits and medieval anchoresses would be two examples, as would various wandering Eastern ascetics.

48. Joan Chittister, OSB, "An Amazing Journey: A Road of Twists and Turns," in Cassian J. Yuhaus, CP, ed., *Religious Life: The Challenge for Tomorrow* (New York: Paulist Press, 1994), p.87, argues that only those religious communities "that form—and re-form—around a common vision and engage the support and gifts of every individual member to achieve it" will survive.

49. Grindel and Peters, op. cit., p.272. Italics mine. Merkle, op. cit., p.150, makes a similar point.

50. See Merkle, op. cit., p.47.

51. Nygren and Ukeritis, op. cit., pp.29–30.

52. See Leddy, op. cit., p.88.
53. David J. Nygren, CM, and Miriam D. Ukeritis, CSJ, *The Future of Religious Orders in the United States: Transformation and Commitment* (Westport, CT: Praeger, 1993), pp.183–184.
54. Fintan Sheeran, SSCC, "Struggling With Renewal," *Religious Life Review*, vol. 32 (March/April, 1993), p.87.
55 Nygren and Ukeritis, op. cit., p.181, make this argument.
56. Mission statement excerpts drawn at random from Eleace King, IHM and Thomas Ferguson, eds., *CARA Formation Directory, 1992* (Washington, DC: CARA, 1993).
57. DiIanni, op. cit., p.149.
58. ibid., p.150.
59. The Teresian Carmelites of Worcester, Massachusetts, who have not yet attained even the status of public association of the faithful, nevertheless attend meetings and workshops with the established Carmelite orders, and receive valuable mentoring and advice from them. The Little Brothers of St. Francis and the Franciscan Brothers of Peace value and maintain their links with the larger Franciscan Federation. Even if these experimental groups do not succeed, the support of the larger network of established communities may provide a safety net and/or opportunities for member transfer when the experimental group dissolves.
60. See Arthur L. Stinchcombe, "Social Structures and Organizations," pp.142–193 in J.G. March, ed., *Handbook of Organizations* (Chicago: Rand McNally, 1965).

7. DECISION #2: WHO'S GOING?

1. See Paul Philibert, OP, "Editor's Introduction" in Paul Philibert, ed., *Living in the Meantime: Concerning the Transformation of Religious Life* (New York: Paulist Press, 1994) for an example of the leaven assumption; see Jeanne Schweickert, SSSF, "Toward the New Millennium: A National Vision of Religious Life" (Chicago: Convergence, Inc. 1992), pp.33–34, and Marie Augusta Neal, SNDdeN, "Meeting the Challenges of the New Century," in Cassian J. Yuhaus, CP, ed., *Religious Life: The Challenge for Tomorrow* (New York: Paulist Press, 1994), p.135, for the assumptions on inclusivity and cultural diversity.
2. David Nygren, CM, and Miriam Ukeritis, CSJ, *The Future of Religious Orders in the United States* (Westport, CT: Praeger, 1993), p.10.

3. David Nygren, CM, and Miriam Ukeritis, CSJ, "Research Executive Summary: The Future of Religious Orders in the United States" (*Origins*, vol.22, no.15, September 24, 1992), p.264.
4. I am not being sexist here; single virtuosi with major impacts on their culture have almost always been male. Women have usually been denied access both to the preconditions for virtuosity and to the networks that spread a virtuoso's contribution to the surrounding society. Virginia Wolf's famous parable of "Shakespeare's Sister" is a good illustration of this.
5. Joan Chittister, OSB, "Religious Life Is Still Alive, But Far from the Promised Land," *National Catholic Reporter*, vol.30, no.16 (February 18, 1994), p.14.
6. I made this calculation in the following manner: according to Roger Finke's and Rodney Stark's *The Churching of America, 1776–1990* (New Brunswick, NJ: Rutgers University Press, 1992), pp.135 and 261, the number of women religious in the U.S. has averaged between 35 and 47 per 10,000 Catholics for all of the decades between 1880 and 1970. During that period, they had their most extensive influence on the American church. If we assume that at least half of that proportion of religious would be necessary for a minimal level of influence in Catholicism or in the U.S. at large, then there would need to be at least 1,000 religious in a diocese of 500,000. Dividing this number into small communities of 50 members each would give us 20 communities. Preferably, of course, there would be 30 or 40 such groups.
7. As early as 1980, over 100 congregations in the U.S. reported having Associate Programs. By 1992, over 50% of the 1,064 active and contemplative orders in the United States either had associate programs or were developing them (Rosemary Jeffries, RSM, "A Closer Look at What Lay Associate Programs Are Revealing to Religious Life," Unpublished paper). Almost all of these congregations were women's communities rather than men's–78% of the women's congregations either have or are interested in developing associate programs, as compared to only 45% of the men's (Rosemary Jeffries, RSM, "Commitment in Religious Life in the Post Vatican II Era: A Study of Associate Membership Programs," Ph.D. Dissertation, Fordham University, 1991, pp.65, 76–77). Many of the new religious communities also report having, or wanting to have, several types of membership: at least 19 of the 34 new communities listed in Pascal Pingault's *Renouveau de l'église: les communautes nouvelles* (Paris: Fayard, 1989) follow the core/extended membership model.
8. Quoted in Margaret Brennan, IHM, "A White Light Still and

Moving," in Cassian J. Yuhaus, CP, ed., *Religious Life: The Challenge for Tomorrow* (New York: Paulist Press, 1994), p.104.

9. Brennan, op. cit., p.104. See also Schwieckert, op. cit., p.34, and Jeffries, op. cit., pp.67, 69, 105–107, 112, for examples of these reservations.

10. John Manuel Lozano, CMF, "Religious Life: The Continuing Journey–Vision and Hope," Cassian J. Yuhaus, CP, ed., *Religious Life: The Challenge for Tomorrow* (New York: Paulist Press, 1994), p.159.

11. Lynn Jarrell, OSU, "Associates and Their Relationship to the Religious Institute," Unpublished paper, pp.6–7.

12. Interview notes, February, 1993. Similarly, none of the communities described in Pingault, op. cit., saw their core members as more essential to the group's identity/mission than the extended members were. According to the members of the Chemin Neuf community, for example: The complementarity of men and women on the one hand, and of married couples and consecrated celibates on the other hand, brings us more advantages than inconveniences, and the daily reality of our differences reminds us of our personal calling without separating us from the reality of the People of God which we are creating together (Pingault, p.74. Translation mine).

13. Jeffries, "Commitment," op. cit. See pp. 112–113, 119–120, 148–150 for the information in the following sentences. For a more recent study of one religious community, see Rosemary Jeffries, RSM, "Summary of Associate Survey for the Institute of the Sisters of Mercy of the Americas" (Privately published by the Sisters of Mercy, Mount St. Mary, 1645 Highway 22, Watchung, NJ, 07060, June, 1993). This second survey also reports only "lukewarm" acceptance of associate programs.

14. Jeffries, "Commitment," op. cit., pp.137–138.

15. Jeffries, "Commitment," op. cit., pp.132–133.

16. Jarrell, op. cit., p.7.

17. Nygren and Ukeritis, op. cit., p.235.

18. Jeffries, "Commitment," op. cit., p.54. Jeffries found a similar lack of expectations in her 1992 survey of the Sisters of Mercy (pp.6–7).

19. Jeffries, "Commitment," op. cit., p.186.

20. Jeffries, "Commitment," op. cit., pp.188, 186, 191. The 1992 Sisters of Mercy survey (Jeffries, "Summary," op. cit., pp.6–7) found a reluctance even to use the *word* "expectations" when referring to associates.

21. Jeffries, "Commitment," op. cit., pp.90–91.

22. According to Jeffries, "Summary," op. cit., p.1, only nine of the

Mercy regional communities had any associates in leadership roles within the associate program, and "only about 12% of Mercy associates reported being in any category of responsibility for the associate programs in their regional communities."

23. David Knoke, "Commitment and Detachment in Voluntary Associations," *American Sociological Review*, vol. 46, no.2 (1981), p.142.

24. Jeffries, "Commitment," op. cit., pp.156–158.

25. Tom Roberts, "Maryknoll Laity Form Own Group," *National Catholic Reporter*, vol. 30, no.36 (August 12, 1994), p.5. According to one participant in the founding assembly, "There is a sense of gratitude and completion. Finally, we can stand with the society and the congregation as adults, and it's a sacred gift."

26. Ian Robertson, *Sociology*, third edition (New York: Worth, 1987), p.167. Italics mine.

27. Nygren and Ukeritis, op. cit., p.241.

28. Quoted in Helen Rose Fuchs Ebaugh, *Women in the Vanishing Cloister: Organizational Decline in Catholic Religious Orders in the United States* (New Brunswick, NJ: Rutgers University Press, 1993), p.108.

29. John W. Padburg, SJ, "The Contexts of Comings and Goings" in Laurie Felknor, ed., *The Crisis in Religious Vocations* (New York: Paulist, 1989), pp. 26–27. This lack of corporate identity is also cited by John Grindel, CM, and Sean Peters, CSJ, in "Religious Life Issues in a Time of Transition," *Review for Religious*, vol.51, no.2 (March/April, 1992), p.269, and by Donna Markham, "The Decline of Vocations in the United States" (in Felknor, op. cit., p.184), as a major reason for members leaving, and new recruits not coming, to religious life.

30. A point made by Paul-André Turcotte, CSV, "Le recrutement dans les congregations religieux," *Sciences religieuses*, vol.9, no.4 (Fall, 1980, p.422), by Grindel and Peters, op. cit., p.271, and by Ebaugh, op. cit., p.109.

31. Nygren and Ukeritis, op. cit., p.235.

32. ibid., p.235. See also M. Marcelline Falk, OP, "Vocation: Identity and Commitment," *Review for Religious*, vol.39 (1980), pp.357–365.

33. Among them, John M. Staudenmaier, SJ, "Adult Commitment at Century's End," pp.116–137 in Felknor, op. cit., and Mary Ann Donovan, SC, "A More Limited Witness," pp.84–98, also in Felknor. Joseph Schmidt, FSC, "The Future of Religious Life," in Dolores Steinberg, OSC, ed., *The Future of Religious Life* (Collegeville, MN:

The Liturgical Press, 1990), pp. 93–94, makes the same recommendation for layers of membership that I am making here.

34. Even today, Jeffries notes ("Commitment," op. cit. pp.24–25, 60), there are a wide variety of associate programs—from foreign and domestic volunteers, to praying associates, to members of support groups, to associates in community living. Currently all of these groups have been labeled "associates," which leads to a great deal of confusion about what the term actually means.

35. Jeffries, "Commitment," op. cit., p.189.

36. Interview notes, May, 1994. I have been told that this is also the reason why the Maryknoll lay associates recently incorporated separately.

37. Robert Wuthnow, in his *Sharing the Journey* (New York: Free Press, 1994), p.332, found that local churches which were bound together by close friendship networks experienced less growth. It is reasonable to expect a similar outcome in religious communities.

38. See Margaret Susan Thompson, "Sisterhood and Power: Class, Culture and Ethnicity in the American Convent," *Colby Library Quarterly* (Fall, 1988), pp.149–175. Florence Jean Deacon, "Handmaids or Autonomous Women," (Ph.D. Dissertation, University of Wisconsin at Madison, 1989), pp.54–65 and Mary J. Oates, "'The Good Sisters': The Work and Position of Catholic Churchwomen in Boston, 1870–1940," in Robert E. Sullivan and James M. O'Toole, eds., *Catholic Boston: Studies in Religion and Community: 1870–1970* (Boston: Roman Catholic Archdiocese of Boston, 1985), especially pp.173–176.

39. See Mary Ewens, OP, "Lessons from the Quinn Consultation," in Dolores Steinberg, OSC, ed., *The Future of Religious Life* (Collegeville, MN: The Liturgical Press, 1990), p.63.

40. Thompson, op. cit., p.153.

41. Jeffries, "Commitment," op. cit., pp.78–80, 185, also notes that present associate programs attract persons who are basically similar to the vowed members: middle-aged or elderly, middle-class, single or widowed white women.

42. See C.H. Lawrence, *Medieval Monasticism*, second edition (London: Longman, 1989), pp.126, 231, 248, Carolyn W. Bynum, "Religious Women in the Later Middle Ages," in Jill Raitt, ed., *Christian Spirituality II: High Middle Ages and Reformation* (New York: Crossroad, 1987), p.126, Lester Little, *Religious Poverty and the Profit Economy in Medieval Europe* (Ithaca: Cornell University Press, 1978), pp. 68, 117–133, and Elizabeth Rapley, *The Devotes: Women and Church in Seventeenth Century France* (Montreal: McGill Queens

University Press, 1990), p.187, for the socioeconomic backgrounds of members of religious communities in previous centuries.

43. "How Multicultural Are the Churches? A Canadian Case Study," *Religion Watch*, vol.9, No.2. (December, 1993), pp.1–2.
44. See, for example, Arturo J. Perez, "The History of Hispanic Liturgy Since 1965," in Jay P. Dolan and Allan Figueroa Deck, SJ, eds., *Hispanic Catholic Culture in the U.S.* (Notre Dame: Notre Dame University Press, 1994), p.338, for a critique of multiculturalism as being "devastating for the Hispanic community."
45. As Jeffries ("Summary," op. cit., p.1) notes, the associates in most religious congregations are also similar in race and age to the vowed members—the associate programs have not significantly diversified the age or ethnic make-up of the communities that have them.
46. Laennec Hurbon, "New Religious Movements in the Caribbean," in J. Beckford, ed., *New Religious Movements and Social Change* (Beverly Hills, CA: Sage, 1986), pp.146–176, notes that the Apostles of Infinite Love had great success in Puerto Rico and Guadalupe because they encouraged the peasants' "traditional magico-religious system which had been endangered by the Catholic Church" after Vatican II. Ana Maria Diaz Stevens, "Latinas and the Church," p.258, and Allan Figueroa Deck, SJ, "The Challenge of Evangelical/Pentecostal Christianity," p.422, both in Dolan and Deck, op. cit., also make this assertion about Hispanics in general.
47. As I document at length in *The Rise and Fall of Catholic Religious Orders* (Albany: SUNY Press, 1994), pp.102–103, it has been common for several members of the same family to enter a religious order, whether that order was the twelfth-century Cistercians, the medieval Beguines, the seventeenth-century Quebec nuns, Mary Ward's "English Ladies," the nineteenth-century Irish and French convents, or the nascent nineteenth-century American communities.
48. Orlando O. Espin, "Popular Catholicism Among Latinos," in Dolan and Deck, op. cit., p.340.
49. See "How Multicultural Are the Churches?" op. cit., p.2.
50. ibid., p.2.
51. ibid., p.2.
52. Quoted in "How Multicultural Are the Churches?" op. cit., p.2.
53. There could, of course, be a religious community that was founded with the specific purpose of fostering integration in an ethnically fractured society. Such a community might have strong appeal if both sides of the fracture were Catholic and both felt the strain of

the division. Rwanda's Catholics might someday develop such a community. But currently, in the U.S. at least, the prevailing cultural trends appear to be the opposite: ethnic groups are affirming their own identity and seeking the "salad bowl" of pluralism rather than the "melting pot" of assimilation.

54. See Judith A. Merkle, SNDdeN, *Committed by Choice: Religious Life Today*, (Collegeville, MN: Liturgical Press, 1992), p.123.

8. DECISION #3: HOW DO WE GET THERE?

1. David A. Snow et al., "Frame Alignment Processes, Micromobilization, and Movement Participation," *American Sociological Review*, vol.51, No.4 (August, 1986) p.467.
2. For example, see Chester P. Michael and Marie C. Norrisey, *Prayer and Temperament: Different Prayer Forms for Different Personality Types* (Charlottesville, VA: The Open Door, Inc., 1984).
3. Mary Margaret Funk, OSB, "Retrieving, Reclaiming and Reappropriating Monasticism," in Paul J. Philibert, OP, ed., *Living in the Meantime: Concerning the Transformation of Religious Life* (New York: Paulist Press, 1994), pp.133–149.
4. C.H. Lawrence, *Medieval Monasticism: Forms of Religious Life in Western Europe in the Middle Ages* (London: Longman, 1989), pp.25–27, Simon Tugwell, "The Spirituality of the Dominicans," in Jill Raitt, ed., *Christian Spirituality II: High Middle Ages and Reformation* (New York: Crossroad, 1987), p.16.
5. See Catriona Clear, *Nuns in Nineteenth Century Ireland* (Dublin: Gill and Macmillan, Ltd., 1987), p.75, for the use of the habit to deny the wearer's sexuality.
6. These quotes were compiled from interviews with members of three different new religious communities, conducted between 1988 and 1994.
7. Peter Hebblethwaite, "Synod Women Get to Speak But Not Decide," *National Catholic Reporter*, vol.31, no.2 (October 28, 1994), p.8.
8. Diarmuid O'Murchu, MSC, *Religious Life: A Prophetic Vision* (Notre Dame, IN: Ave Maria Press, 1991), pp.89–90.
9. Interview notes, May, 1994.
10. Interview notes, October, 1994. Obviously, I make no claims as to whether these women *really* received divine messages or not. The important, mythic, aspect is that they *believe* that they had.
11. Interview notes, May 1994. The speaker is the founder of another

community. The man in this anecdote stayed with the speaker's community for some time before leaving to begin his own group in another city.

12. A point also made by Louis DeThomasis, FSC, in his *Imagination: A Future for Religious Life* (Winona, MN: The Metanoia Group, 1992), p.19.

13. Mary Jo Leddy, *Reweaving Religious Life: Beyond the Liberal Model* (Mystic, CT: Twenty-Third Publications, 1990), p.24.

14. Judith A. Merkle, SNDdeN, *Committed by Choice: Religious Life Today* (Collegeville, MN: The Liturgical Press, 1992), p.123.

15. Albert DiIanni, SM, makes a similar point in his *Religious Life as Adventure* (New York: Alba House, 1994), pp.101–103.

16. See, for example, pp.87–190 in Sandra M. Schneiders, IHM, *New Wineskins: Re-Imagining Religious Life Today* (New York, Paulist Press, 1986); Juliana Casey, IHM, "Toward a Theology of the Vows," in Carol Quigley, IHM, ed., *Turning Points in Religious Life* (Westminster, MD: Christian Classics, Inc., 1988); Elaine M. Prevallet, SL, "From the Inside Out," in Nadine Foley, OP, ed., *Claiming Our Truth: Reflections on Identity by U.S. Women Religious* (Washington, DC: LCWR, 1988); Donna Markham, OP, "The Decline of Vocations in the U.S.: Reflections from a Psychological Perspective," in Laurie Felknor, ed., *The Crisis in Religious Vocations* (New York: Paulist Press, 1989), especially pp.193–195; Diarmuid O'Murchu, MSC, *Religious Life: A Prophetic Vision* (Notre Dame, IN: Ave Maria Press, 1991), especially pp.118–173; Albert DiIanni, SM, "Celibacy, Cathedrals and Modern Psychology," in his *Religious Life as Adventure* (New York: Alba House, 1994), pp.49-70; Judith Merkle, SNDdeN, *Committed By Choice* (Collegeville, MN: The Liturgical Press, 1992), especially pp.79-114; and articles by R. Kevin Seasoltz, OSB, Luise Ahrens, MM, A.W. Richard Sipe, and Paul J. Philibert, OP, in Paul Philibert, ed., *Living in the Meantime* (New York: Paulist Press, 1994). There are, of course, numerous journal articles, too.

17. See Marie Augusta Neal, SNDdeN, "Meeting the Challenges of the New Century," pp.127–141 in Cassian J. Yuhaus, CP, ed., *Religious Life: The Challenge for Tomorrow* (New York: Paulist Press, 1994), and also her *From Nuns to Sisters* (Mystic, CT: Twenty-Third Publications, 1990), as well as Diarmuid O'Murchu, op. cit.

18. For a more thorough discussion of the points raised in this section, see my *The Rise and Fall of Catholic Religious Orders* (Albany, NY: SUNY Press, 1994), pp.118–141. See also Donald Senior, CP,

"Living in the Meantime: Biblical Foundations for Religious Life," in Paul J. Philibert, OP, ed., op. cit., pp.55–72.

19. E.K. Francis, "Toward a Typology of Religious Orders," *American Journal of Sociology*, vol.55, no.5 (1950), p.446.

20. Both Elizabeth Kolmer, ASC, *Religious Women in the U.S.: A Survey of the Influential Literature from 1950 to 1983* (Wilmington, DE: Michael Glazier, 1984), p.31, and Joseph Fichter, SJ, *A Sociologist Looks at Religion* (Wilmington, DE: Michael Glazier, 1988), p.106, make this assertion for early twentieth-century versions of religious obedience.

21. Caitriona Clear, in her *Nuns in Nineteenth Century Ireland* (Dublin: Gill and Macmillan, Ltd., 1987), p. 153, makes this point.

22. S. Helen Marie, "Having Nothing," *Review for Religious*, vol.25 (1966), p.704. See also David Knight, SJ, "Spousal Commitment and Religious Life," *Review for Religious*, vol.32 (1973), pp.85–86.

23. Merkle, op. cit., p.113. Italics added.

24. Sandra Schneiders, op. cit., p.114. Italics added. See also Mary Ann Donovan, SC, "A More Limited Witness: A Historical Theologian Looks at the Signposts," in Laurie Felknor, ed., *The Crisis in Religious Vocations* (New York: Paulist Press, 1989), p.95.

25. Quoted in Eoin de Bhaldraithe, "Nuns' Enclosure and Studies," *Religious Life Review*, vol.33, no.168 (Sept-Oct, 1994), pp.273–274.

26. Albert DiIanni, op. cit., p.55.

27. A point made by Lewis Coser in his *Greedy Institutions* (New York: Free Press, 1974), p.31, and by Benjamin Zablocki in his *The Joyful Community* (Chicago: University of Chicago Press, 1980), pp.169–170, among others.

28. See Harry Murray, *Do Not Neglect Hospitality: The Catholic Worker and the Homeless* (Philadelphia: Temple University Press, 1990), p.164.

29. Max Weber, "The Sociology of Charismatic Authority," in H.H. Gerth and C.W. Mills, eds., *From Max Weber: Essays in Sociology* (New York: Oxford University Press, 1958), p.248, makes precisely this point.

30. David Nygren, CM, and Miriam Ukeritis, CSJ, "The Future of Religious Orders in the United States: Executive Summary," *Origins*, vol.22, no.15 (Sept. 24, 1992), p.266.

31. Sandra Schneiders, op. cit., p.53, makes this point.

32. Joseph H. Lackner, SM, "Anomie and Religious Life," *Review for Religious*, vol.28 (1969), p.629.

33. See Juliana Casey, IHM, op. cit., pp.94–98, Judith Merkle, op. cit., p.56, and Diarmuid O'Murchu, op. cit., pp. 45, 160–161. Alexandra Kovats, "Reflections on the Vows from a Cosmic/Ecological

Perspective," *Information*, vol.146 (1992), p.22, suggests renaming the vow of poverty "the vow of cosmic reverence."

34. Donna Markham, OP, "Psychological Factors Influencing the Decline of and Persistence in Religious Vocations," unpublished paper, p.14.

35. Nygren and Ukeritis, op. cit., pp. 264, 270.

36. Francis, op. cit., p.443.

37. "Peacemaking" as an interpretation of poverty is not as odd as it sounds. There is an old medieval monastic tradition whereby poverty was interpreted to mean a knight-turned-monk laying down his knightly arms and renouncing violence—thus losing his secular status and becoming "poor in spirit." See Lester Little, *Religious Poverty and the Profit Economy in Medieval Europe* (Ithaca: Cornell University Press, 1978), p.68.

38. See Nygren and Ukeritis, op. cit., p.261, marginal citation: "Many people are looking for something they would be 'willing to put their life on the line for,' but many religious orders today are ambivalent about saying 'we want you to put your life on the line.'" See also, Eleace King, IHM, *CARA Formation Directory for Men and Women Religious, 1991* (Washington, DC: CARA, 1990), p.10, on the greater recruitment success of groups with a "convergent" focus.

39. See, for example, P. DeLetter, SJ, "Contemporary Depreciation of Religious Life," *Review for Religious*, vol.11, no.1 (1952), pp.34–41, and "Keeping the Rules," *Review for Religious*, vol.18, no.1 (1959), pp.13–24. Joseph M. Becker, SJ, in his *The Re-Formed Jesuits*, vol.1 (San Francisco: St. Ignatius Press, 1992), notes that the problems religious had with obedience began in the 1950's.

40. Historians Mary L. Schneider, OSF, "The Transformation of American Women Religious: The Sister Formation Conference as a Catalyst for Change, 1954-1971," Cushwa Center Working Paper Series, Series #17, no.1 (University of Notre Dame, 1986), and Becker, op. cit., pp.171, 190, 250, note this concern among 1950's religious communities. See also various articles in *Review for Religious*: Terence R. O'Connor, "Holy Obedience and Whole Obedience (1963, pp.634–47); Richard P. Vaughn, SJ, "Obedience and Psychological Maturity" (1962, pp.203–206); Sister Theresa Mary, CSC, "Religious Obedience and Critical Thinking" (1963, pp.541–554).

41. Lora Ann Quinonez, CDP, and Mary Daniel Turner, SNDdeN, *The Transformation of American Catholic Sisters* (Philadelphia: Temple University Press, 1992), p.116.

42. Marie Augusta Neal, SNDdeN, *From Nuns to Sisters*, op. cit., p.85.

43. Quotes taken from Donald Senior, op. cit., p.68; Merkle, op. cit., p.84; Neal, *From Nuns to Sisters*, op. cit., p.69, and Evelyn Woodward, *Poets, Prophets and Pragmatists: A New Challenge to Religious Life* (Notre Dame: Ave Maria Press, 1987), p.146.
44. Neal, "Meeting the Challenges," op. cit., p.133.
45. Marie Augusta Neal, SNDdeN, "American Sisters: Organizational and Value Changes," in Helen R. Ebaugh, ed., *Vatican II and U.S. Catholicism* (Greenwich, CT: JAI Press, 1991), p.108.
46. Senior, op. cit., p.61.
47. Donald Senior, CP, "A Biblical Perspective on Why They Left," in Laurie Felknor, ed., *The Crisis in Religious Vocations* (New York: Paulist, 1989), p.145, makes this point. See also R. Kevin Seasoltz, OSB, "Religious Obedience: Liberty and Law," in Paul Philibert, op. cit.
48. Robert Bellah et al., *Habits of the Heart* (New York: Harper and Row, 1985), pp. 23–25, makes this point.
49. Merkle, op. cit., p.19.
50. See John Lofland, "'Becoming A World-Saver' Revisited," *American Behavioral Scientist*, vol.20, no.6 (1977), pp. 805–818.
51. Joan Chittister, OSB, "An Amazing Journey: A Road of Twists and Turns," in Cassian J. Yuhaus, CP, ed., *Religious Life: The Challenge for Tomorrow* (New York: Paulist Press, 1994), p.81.
52. Chittister, op. cit., p.81.
53. Lyn H. Lofland, "Editorial," Community and Urban Sociology Newsletter, 1987, p.3.
54. See Patricia Wittberg, SC, "Dyads and Triads: The Sociological Implications of Small Group Living Experiments," *Review for Religious*, vol.49, no.1 (January/February, 1990), pp.43–51, for a further development of this topic.
55. See DiIanni, op. cit., p.138, and John Grindel, CM, and Sean Peters, CSJ, "Religious Life Issues in a Time of Transition: A Report to the Lilly Endowment," *Review for Religious*, vol.51 (1992), pp.267–275. My own interviews with new U.S. communities supports these authors' findings.
56. Of course, "community" is defined just as fuzzily on the secular, cultural level as it is in religious life. So there are many opinions on what, if anything, this "lack of community" means.
57. Paul J. Philibert, OP, *Living in the Meantime: Concerning the Transformation of Religious Life* (New York: Paulist, 1994), p.6.
58. ibid., p.6.
59. At least, no one lifestyle is required historically or sociologically. Canon law, however, may be another matter.
60. John W. O'Malley, SJ, *The First Jesuits* (Cambridge: Harvard

University Press, 1993). See especially pp.21 and 227. Lester Little, *Religious Poverty and the Profit Economy* (Ithaca: Cornell University Press, 1978) and Elizabeth Rapley, *The Devotes: Women and Church in Seventeenth-Century France* (Montreal: McGill Queens University Press, 1990) make similar assertions about the mendicants and the seventeenth-century French teaching congregations.

61. Merkle, op. cit., p.48.
62. Joan Chittister, OSB, *Women, Ministry and the Church* (New York: Paulist, 1983), p.30.
63. Merkle, op. cit., p.48.

9. DECISION #4: WHAT DO WE NEED FOR THE JOURNEY?

1. Judith Merkle, SNDdeN, *Committed by Choice: Religious Life Today* (Collegeville, MN: The Liturgical Press, 1992), p.51.
2. John W. O'Malley, SJ, *The First Jesuits* (Cambridge: Harvard University Press, 1993), p.55.
3. Margaret S. Thompson, "Sisterhood and Power: Class, Culture and Ethnicity in the American Convent," *Colby Library Quarterly* (Fall, 1989):149–175. See also Kathleen O'Brien, RSM, *Journeys: A Pre-Amalgamation History of the Sisters of Mercy, Omaha Province* (Omaha, NE: Sisters of Mercy, 1987), and Mary Ewens, OP, "Lessons From the Quinn Consultations," in Dolores Steinberg, OSC, ed., *The Future of Religious Life* (Collegeville, MN: The Liturgical Press, 1990), p.59.
4. See Daniel P. O'Neill, "St. Paul's Priests, 1850–1930: Recruitment, Ethnicity and Americanization," in Dolores Liptak, ed., *A Church of Many Cultures* (New York: Garland, 1988), p.76, for an example of this process.
5. Esther Heffernan, OP, "Religious Vocations of American Women: Membership in a Socio-Historical Context," p.18. Paper presented at the 1989 Annual Meetings of the Association for the Sociology of Religion, San Francisco, California.
6. See John W. Padburg, SJ, "The Contexts of Comings and Goings," in Laurie Felknor, ed., *The Crisis in Religious Vocations: An Inside View* (New York: Paulist Press, 1989), pp.26–27; Daniel Meenan, SJ, "On Dreaming Dreams, or the Making of a Revolution," in *Review for Religious*, vol.43 (1984) pp.547–557; Helen Rose Ebaugh, *Women in the Vanishing Cloister* (New Brunswick, NJ: Rutgers University Press, 1993), p.100; and Helena O'Donoghue, RSM, "Women's Congregations Twenty-Five Years after Vatican II," *Religious Life Review*, vol.30, no.3 (1993), pp.115–123, for citations of these arguments.

7. David Nygren, CM, and Miriam Ukeritis, CSJ, "The Future of Religious Orders in the United States: A Summary Report," *Origins*, vol.22, no.15 (1992), p.271, make this argument from their research.

8. Stephen Stein, *The Shaker Experience in America* (New Haven: Yale University Press, 1992), p.246.

9. John McKelvie Whitworth, *God's Blueprints: A Sociological Study of Utopian Sects* (London: Routledge, 1975), p.79.

10. See Patricia Wittberg, SC, *The Rise and Fall of Catholic Religious Orders* (Albany, NY: SUNY Press, 1994), pp.57–67 for a fuller listing of these advantages.

11. ibid., p.111.

12. Paul Andre Turcotte, CSV, "Le recrutement dans les congregations religieuses canadiennes" *Studies in Religion*, vol.9, no.4 (Fall, 1980), p.416, noted that the vocation literature of one men's order began in the late 1960's to emphasize the opportunities for self-denial afforded by religious life—not a satisfactory substitute for the opportunities for professional and personal growth it had once uniquely afforded.

13. Teresa White, FCJ, "Our Readers' This and That: Fostering Vocations," *Religious Life Review*, vol.33 (1994), p.365. See also Donna Markham, OP, "The Decline of Vocations," in Felknor, op. cit., p.183, and "The Decline of Vocations," in *New Catholic World*, vol.231 (January/February 1989), p.14.

14. Elizabeth Rapley, *The Devotes: Women and Church in Seventeenth Century France* (Montreal: McGill Queens University Press, 1990), p.187.

15. O'Brien, op. cit., p.577.

16. Elizabeth Ann Clifford, OLVM, *The Story of Victory Noll* (Fort Wayne, IN: Keefer Printing Co., 1981).

17. See Wittberg, op. cit., p.103.

18. *Newsweek*, August 16, 1993, pp.42–43. See also Mary Johnson, SNDdeN, "No Nunsense: Attitudes of the New Generation of Catholic Women Religious in New England" (Paper read at the November 1992 Annual Meeting of the Society for the Scientific Study of Religion, Washington, DC), Donna Markham, OP, "Psychological Factors Influencing the Decline and Persistence in Religious Vocations" (Unpublished paper, 1257 East Siena Heights Drive, Adrian MI 49221) pp.15–16, and Sarah Marie Sherman, RSM, "Fewer Vocations: Crisis or Challenge?" pp.15–18 in Felknor, op. cit., all of whom report a similar parental reluctance.

19. O'Donoghue, op. cit., p.119.

20. Points made by Ewens, op. cit., p.59.

21. O'Malley, op. cit., p.54.

22. Lester K. Little, *Religious Poverty and the Profit Economy in Medieval Europe* (Ithaca: Cornell University Press, 1978), pp.173–176.

23. See C.H. Lawrence, *Medieval Monasticism* (London: Longman, 1989), p.11, and Thomas P. Rausch, *Radical Christian Communities* (Collegeville, MN: The Liturgical Press, 1990), pp. 36–38, 70, for the influence of these works.

24. Margaret Brennan, IHM, "'A White Light Still and Moving': Religious Life at the Crossroads of the Future," in Cassian J. Yuhaus, CP, ed., *Religious Life: The Challenge for Tomorrow* (New York: Paulist Press, 1994), p.94, makes this assertion about Thomas Merton.

25. See, for example, Nathan O. Hatch, *The Democratization of American Christianity* (New Haven: Yale University Press, 1989) pp.56–57. See also Roger Finke and Rodney Stark, *The Churching of America, 1776–1990* (New Brunswick, NJ: Rutgers University Press, 1992), chapter 3.

26. Ewens, op. cit., p.60.

27. David Meyers, "Faith and Action: A Seamless Tapestry," *Christianity Today*, vol.24, no.20 (November 21, 1980), p.16.

28. David J. Nygren, CM, and Miriam D. Ukeritis, CSJ, *The Future of Religious Life in the U.S.* (Westport, CT: Praeger, 1993), pp.183–184. See also p.159.

29. Interview notes, May 25, 1994.

30. See Wittberg, op. cit., pp.102–103 for more examples.

31. See Basil Pennington, "The Cistercians," in Bernard McGinn and John Myendorff, eds., *Christian Spirituality I: Origins to the Middle Ages* (New York: Crossroads, 1985), p.210, for this incident.

32. See, for example, "Sisters in Sagebrush Country" about the new Disciples of the Lord Jesus Christ community, and "A Special Kind of Love," about the new T.O.R. Franciscan Sisters in Steubenville. The former article appeared in the November 1989 issue of *New Covenant*, a magazine devoted to the charismatic renewal. The latter article appeared in *Franciscan Way*, the alumni magazine published by the Franciscan University of Steubenville, in the fall of 1990.

33. Albert DiIanni, SM, *Religious Life as Adventure* (New York: Alba House, 1994), pp.149–151.

34. ibid., pp.150–151.

35. S. Marie Augusta Neal, SNDdeN, "A Report on the National Profile of the Third Sisters' Survey" (Boston: Emmanuel College, 1991), p.3.

36. O'Brien, op. cit., p.219.

37. See Caitriona Clear, *Nuns in Nineteenth Century Ireland* (Dublin: Gill and MacMillan, Ltd., 1987), and Janet A. Nolan, *Ourselves Alone: Women's Immigration from Ireland, 1885–1920* (Lexington, KY:

University Presses of Kentucky, 1989), for summaries of the status of women in nineteenth-century Ireland.

38. Interview notes, May 24, 1994.

39. Gerald A. Arbuckle, SM, provides the characteristics in this and the previous sentence in his *Out of Chaos: Refounding Religious Congregations* (New York: Paulist, 1988), pp.34–38, 96–101.

40. Nygren and Ukeritis, *The Future of Religious Life,* op. cit., pp.67–71.

41. Arbuckle, op. cit., pp.101–103, Nygren and Ukeritis, op. cit., pp.73–76.

42. Max Weber, "The Sociology of Charismatic Authority," in H. H. Gerth and C. Wright Mills, trans. and eds., *From Max Weber: Essays in Sociology* (New York: Oxford University Press, 1958), pp.245–248.

43. Nygren and Ukeritis, op. cit., pp.59–66. See Weber, op. cit., p.247, 299.

44. Weber, op. cit., p.250.

45. For example, the thirteenth-century Servites were founded by seven hermits. Many nineteenth-century women's congregations were founded by bishops for ministerial purposes and did not have a charismatic personality among their first sisters. As Ilana Friedrich Silber, in *Virtuosity, Charisma, and Social Order* (New York: Cambridge University Press, 1995), p.189, has pointed out, most religious virtuosi are *not* charismatic leaders. Most virtuosi devote themselves to seeking spiritual perfection within an established tradition, not to creatively devising a new one.

46. Simon Tugwell, "The Spirituality of the Dominicans," in Jill Raitt, ed., *Christian Spirituality II: High Middle Ages and Reformation* (New York: Crossroad, 1987), p.23. See also Benedict Ashley, *The Dominicans* (Collegeville, MN: The Liturgical Press, 1990), pp.2, 17.

47. Keith J. Egan, "The Spirituality of the Carmelites," in Jill Raitt, ed., op. cit., pp.50–51, 58–59.

48. Arbuckle, op. cit., pp.113–124.

49. ibid., p.125.

50. See, for example, Ebaugh, op. cit., pp.78–93.

51. Joseph Fichter, SJ, *A Sociologist Looks at Religion* (Wilmington, DE: Michael Glazier, 1988), p.80.

52. Ebaugh, op. cit., p.41.

53. Interview Notes, May, 1993.

54. C.C. Martindale, SJ, *The Saints: A Concise Biographical Dictionary* (New York: Hawthorn Books, 1960), p.53, has an anecdote of how, at the Synod of Bourges, St. Anthony pointed at the presiding archbishop and proceeded with an eloquent denunciation of the sins of "you over there with the miter on your head."

55. See *Religion Watch*, vol.5, no.3 (January, 1990), p.7 for the increase in religious vocations in El Salvador. See Barbara Strassberg, "Polish Catholics in Transition," in Thomas Gannon, ed., *World Catholicism in Transition* (New York: Macmillan, 1988), p.192. See Kenneth L. Woodward and Andrew Nagorski, "The Troubled Altar of Freedom," *Newsweek* (June 17, 1991), p.43, for how this situation has changed in post-Communist Poland.

56. See Judith D. Taylor, "From Proselytizing to Social Reform: Three Generations of French Female Teaching Congregations, 1600–1720" (Ph.D. Dissertation, History Department, Arizona State University, 1980), p.112, for an example.

57. Elio Gambari, SM, "Preparatory Association of a Religious Institute," S. Maria Michele Armato, OP, and Rev. Thomas Blessin, SJ, translators (available through Sister Maria Michele Armato, Piscataway, NJ, 1993), #98.

58. Martin Farrell, OSD, Interview for the *National Catholic Register*, October 11, 1992. Quotation taken from the typescript of the interview.

59. Doris Gottemoeller, RSM, "Befriending the Wind," *Review for Religious*, vol.53, no.6 (Nov/Dec. 1994), pp.812–813.

60. See A. O. Hirschman, *Exit, Voice and Loyalty: Responses to Decline in Firms, Organizations and States* (Cambridge, MA: Harvard University Press, 1974), for a discussion of how authorities may prefer that obsteperous members exit the system rather than stay and exercise their voice.

61. Quoted in Patrick O'Connor, SVD, "An Australian Saint—Mary McKillop."

62. John M. Lozano, CMF, *Foundresses, Founders, and their Religious Families*, (Chicago: Claretian Center for Resources in Spirituality: 1983), p.70.

10. JOURNEY DISRUPTIONS: LOST ROUTE RETRIEVAL AND VEHICLE MAINTENANCE

1. John R. Hall, *The Ways Out: Utopian Communal Groups in an Age of Babylon* (London: Routledge and Kegan Paul, 1978), p.27.

2. Hall, op. cit., p.29.

3. Rosabeth Moss Kanter, ed., *Communes: Creating and Managing the Collective Life* (New York: Harper and Row, 1973), p.21.

4. Both Bennett Berger, *The Survival of a Counterculture* (Berkeley: University of California Press, 1981), pp.130–150, and Benjamin

Zablocki, *Alienation and Charisma: A Study of Contemporary American Communes* (New York: Free Press, 1980), pp. 150–165, make this point.

5. See Ritamary Bradley, SFCC, "Religious Life in the Future: Historical Precedents for Emerging Paradigms," in Dolores Steinberg, OSC, ed., *The Future of Religious Life* (Collegeville, MN: The Liturgical Press, 1990), pp.82–83, for the fear that refounded communities may become cults. See my own "'Real Religious Communities': A Study in Authentication in New Roman Catholic Religious Orders" in Lewis Carter, ed., *The Problem of Authenticity in the Study of Religion*, Religion and the Social Order Series Vol. VI (Greenwich, CT: JAI Press, 1996) for the difficulties some new religious communities have had with church officials.

6. Berger, op. cit., pp.131–159; Zablocki, op. cit., pp.150–165.

7. See, for example, Yacov Oved, *Two Hundred Years of American Communes* (New Brunswick: Transaction, 1988), p.469.

8. Kanter, op. cit., p.494.

9. According to Zablocki, op. cit., pp.150–165, "authority questions" were responsible for 25% of all the communal failures in the nineteenth and twentieth centuries. See also Seymour R. Kersten, *Utopian Episodes: Daily Life in Experimental Colonies Dedicated to Changing the World* (New York: Syracuse University Press, 1993), pp.71–77.

10. See Kersten, op. cit., pp.71–77, 282–285, for the quotations in this and the next sentence.

11. Rosabeth Moss Kanter, *Commitment and Community* (Cambridge: Harvard University Press, 1982), p.129.

12. Kersten, op. cit., p.267.

13. Kersten, op. cit., pp. 275–278. Oved, op. cit., pp.468–469, makes a similar point.

14. Kersten, op. cit., p.279.

15. Roger Allain, *The Community That Failed* (San Francisco: Carrier Pigeon Press, 1992), p.193.

16. Kersten, op. cit., p.6. See also Hall, op. cit., p.34.

17. See Berger, op. cit., p.15.

18. See Max Weber, "Charismatic Authority," in H.H. Gerth and C.W. Mills, translators, *From Max Weber* (New York: Oxford University Press, 1958), pp.245–248.

19. Weber, op. cit., p.245.

20. Benton Johnson, "On Founders and Followers: Some Factors in the Development of New Religious Movements," *Sociological Analysis*, vol.53, supplement (1992), p.7. See Weber, op. cit., p.248.

21. Stephen J. Stein, *The Shaker Experience in America* (New Haven: Yale University Press, 1992), p.66, and Aryei Fishman, "Religion and Communal Life in an Evolutionary-Functional Perspective: The Orthodox Kibbutzim," *Comparative Studies in Society and History*, vol.29, no.4 (1987), p.767, both make this point.

22. Weber, op. cit., p.246.

23. Johnson, op. cit., p.6.

24. Johnson, op. cit., pp. 4–5.

25. B. Nelson, "The Future of Illusions," *Man in Contemporary Society* (New York: Columbia University Press, 1956), p.976.

26. Zablocki, op. cit., p.326.

27. Kersten, op. cit., p.274.

28. Weber, op. cit., pp. 253,262.

29. Johnson, op. cit., p.7. See also Zablocki, op. cit., p.291 and Kanter, *Commitment and Community*, op. cit., p.228.

30. Johnson, op. cit., pp.8–10.

31. Patricia Wittberg, SC, *Creating a Future for Religious Life* (New York: Paulist Press, 1991), pp.13–22.

32. See Patricia Wittberg, SC, *The Rise and Fall of Catholic Religious Orders* (Albany: SUNY Press, 1994), pp.198–201, for examples of these variations.

33. Stephen J. Stein, *The Shaker Experience in America* (New Haven: Yale University Press, 1992), p.113.

34. Wittberg, *Creating a Future*, op. cit., pp.22–24.

35. Wittberg, *The Rise and Fall*, op. cit., pp.203–204.

36. Quoted in Elizabeth Rapley, *The Devotes: Women and Church in Seventeenth Century France* (Montreal: McGill Queens University Press, 1990), p.185.

37. Ephrem Hollermann, OSB, *The Reshaping of a Tradition: American Benedictine Women, 1850–1881* (Ph.D. Dissertation, Marquette University, 1991), p.44. Ilana Friedrich Silber, in *Virtuosity, Charisma, and the Social Order* (New York: Cambridge University Press, 1995), pp.144–145, states that wealth was often a destructive force in medieval Christian monasticism, whereas in Theravada Buddhist monasticism, it was not the possession of wealth *per se* that was corrupting, but rather "failing discipline in the use of wealth." (p.114).

38. See David Knowles, *Bare Ruined Choirs: The Dissolution of English Monasticism* (New York: Cambridge University Press, 1976), p.308; and Peter McDonough, *Men Astutely Trained: A History of the Jesuits in the American Century* (New York: Free Press, 1992), pp.374–375, for examples from two different time periods.

39. Oved, op. cit., p.472. See also Silber, op. cit., p.41, for this dilemma in medieval Christian monasticism and Theravada Buddhism.
40. Barry Shenker, *Intentional Communities: Ideology and Alienation in Communal Societies* (London: Routledge and Kegan Paul, 1986), p.71, Bennett M. Berger, "Utopia and Its Environment," in Yosef Gorni, et al., eds., *Communal Life: An International Perspective* (New Brunswick: Transaction, 1987), p.414, and Oved, op. cit., p.470, all make this point.
41. Oved, op. cit., p.470.
42. Rapley, op. cit., p.33.
43. Jon Wagner, "Success in Intentional Communities: The Problem of Evaluation," *Communal Societies*, vol.5 (1985), pp.89–100.
44. The following four sections are based on Wagner's article. All quotations are from Wagner, unless otherwise indicated.
45. See John W. O'Malley, SJ, *The First Jesuits* (Cambridge: Harvard University Press, 1993), pp.21,227, and Lester Little, *Religious Poverty and the Profit Economy* (Ithaca: Cornell University Press, 1978) for examples of this with St. Francis and St. Ignatius.
46. Wagner cites Rosabeth M. Kanter, "Family Organization and Sex Roles in American Communes," in R.M. Kanter, ed., *Communes: Creating and Managing the Collective Life,* op. cit., and Patrick W. Conover, "An Analysis of Communes and Intentional Communities with Particular Attention to Sexual and General Relations," in *The Family Co-ordinator*, October 1975, pp.453–463, as examples.
47. Gerald A. Arbuckle, SM, "The Survival of Religious Life?" *Religious Life Review*, vol.32, no.3 (1993), p.134.
48. Edward A. Wynne, *Traditional Catholic Religious Orders: Living in Community* (New Brunswick: Transaction, 1988), pp.176–178.
49. Kersten, op. cit., p.265, makes this point. See also Silber, op. cit., pp.144–145.

CONCLUSIONS

1. Raymond Hostie, *La vie et mort des ordres religieux* (Paris: Desclée de Brouwer, 1972), p.316. Translation and italics mine.